D1544942

The Eagle & The Serpent

OTHER TRANSLATIONS FROM THE SPANISH

>>>>>>>>>>>>>>>>>>>><<<<<<<<<<<<<<<<<<<<

By Pio Baroja

THE STRUGGLE FOR LIFE
(A TRILOGY)
I THE QUEST   II RED DAWN
III WEEDS

><

THE TREE OF KNOWLEDGE

><

THE LORD OF LABRAZ

By V. B. Ibanez

THE CABIN

By Manuel Ugarte

THE DESTINY OF A CONTINENT

By Miguel De Unamuno

ESSAYS & SOLILOQUIES

><

MIST: A TRAGI-COMIC NOVEL

><

THE LIFE OF
DON QUIXOTE & SANCHO
(*Expounded with comment*)

>>>>>>>>>>>>>>>>>>>><<<<<<<<<<<<<<<<<<<<

MARTÍN LUÍS GUZMÁN

The Eagle & the Serpent

Translated from the Spanish by Harriet de Onís

New York · ALFRED·A·KNOPF · 1930

Withdrawn from

Copyright 1930 by Alfred A. Knopf, Inc.
All rights reserved—no part of this book may be reprinted
in any form without permission in writing from the publisher

Originally published as
EL AGUILA Y LA SERPIENTE
Copyright, 1928, by M. L. Guzmán
Madrid

Manufactured in the United States of America

Withdrawn from
Cleveland Inst. of Art Library

>>>>>>>>>>>>>>>>>>>>>><<<<<<<<<<<<<<<<<<<<

FOREWORD

In order that readers not familiar with the origin
and nature of the Mexican Revolution may better
understand the spirit of this book, we have thought
it advisable to give a brief résumé of the political
events that took place in Mexico from 1910 to 1915.

In 1910 Porfirio Díaz's dictatorship was still
supreme in Mexico—a liberal, progressive dictatorship. That same year, as the time for presidential
elections approached—a periodical farce by which
the letter of the Constitution was observed—the nation began to give evident signs that it wanted to
regain possession of its civic will, which had been
lost since 1880. In opposition to the invariable candi-
dacy of Díaz, which satisfied only the groups in
power, the nation put forward another, that of Francisco I. Madero. The dictator, however, paid no attention to these premonitory indications; he and his
supporters attempted to continue in power, whereupon Madero, at the head of a rising which was not
merely political, but revolutionary in character, over-
threw Porfirio Díaz and took over the presidency
after new elections held in 1911.

Madero was a reformer of gentle, apostolic char-

71-530

acter. He preached ideals of justice and a faith in the triumph of the right. As head of the government he attempted to divert the revolutionary tendencies he headed into legal channels. He also decided, in order to preserve the material well-being of the country, not to destroy the administrative machinery or the political instruments created by the dictatorship. He maintained the existing army; he respected the courts and the legislative bodies and made no changes in the personnel of the government departments. And in this way he lost the sympathy and support of his friends and delivered himself into the hands of his enemies, with results that were soon to prove fatal. A part of the army, headed by two ambitious generals, Bernardo Reyes and Felix Díaz, rose in February, 1913; another division, under the command of Victoriano Huerta, revolted a few days later, after solemnly swearing its loyalty. And then, all joining forces, Huerta had the revolutionary President assassinated a few hours after usurping his office.

The indignation and anger of the populace were so great that the day after Madero's death the real revolution broke out; the ideals of justice and agrarian reform the "martyr President" had advocated seemed too conservative; a vehement desire to regenerate everything asserted itself, an impulse to transform the whole social fabric of Mexico in its diverse aspects; and before the end of February the conflict had been kindled again. Venustiano Carranza, the

>>>>>>>>>>>>>>>>>>>>><<<<<<<<<<<<<<<<<<<<

governor of Coahuila, a civilian, was named First Chief of the revolutionary army; the political purposes of the new uprising were outlined in the Plan of Guadalupe, drawn up on March 27, 1913.

This new phase of the revolution was much more widespread than the first. From the beginning there were four principal centres of revolutionary action, three in the north: Sonora, Chihuahua, and Coahuila; and one in the south: Morelos. The military leaders in the various sections of the north were respectively, Alvaro Obregón, Francisco Villa, and Pablo González; the leader in the south was Emiliano Zapata.

The advance of the four revolutionary armies, which was very slow at first, finally became irresistible, especially after the big battles won by Villa and Felipe Angeles in Torreón and Zacatecas. In the northwest, through the states of Sonora, Sinaloa, Nayarit and Jalisco, Obregón marched from victory to victory, all the way from the American border to the heart of Mexico. After Villa had broken through the main division of Huerta's army, Pablo González could move forward from the states of the northeast—that is to say, Tamaulipas, Nuevo León, and San Luis. And as Zapata was becoming more and more of a menace from the south—his activities had spread through the states of Morelos, Mexico, and Puebla, surrounding the capital—Huerta fled from the country seventeen months after his crime. After wiping out a part of Porfirio Díaz's former army and discharging from the service those who surrendered, the revolutionary troops marched into the city of Mexico in August 1914.

But the revolution was already divided in its hour of triumph. Carranza, whose background and formation were those of the dictatorship, and who was devoid of ideals and eager only for power, from the first moment did all he could to bar the advancement of all those revolutionists whose independence or whose faith in the just character of the revolution might prove a stumbling-block to the new leaders in the race of their personal ambitions. He was supported in this by Obregón and by the groups of Sonora and Coahuila, and he even went so far as to put obstacles in the way of Villa's and Angeles's military operations. This lost him the support of many leaders and large sections of the country; and it brought about a wide breach, which was already evident in December 1913, and of a frankly hostile character by August 1914.

To put an end to these dissensions, which threatened to destroy the fruits of the revolution's military victories, the leaders of the different groups decided to call an assembly which should have sovereign authority, to be composed of generals and governors. This was the Convention. It met in October 1914, first in Mexico City and then in Aguascalientes, and voted to remove both Carranza and Villa from their

commands, as their quarrels were the principal cause
of strife, and to name General Eulalio Gutiérrez
president *pro tem.* of the Republic. The generals and
governors in favour of Villa submitted to the terms
laid down by the Convention; but as Carranza and
his adherents demanded, as a preliminary to their
obedience of orders, the fulfilment of certain conditions that could not be accepted, the new President
had to temporize with Villa while waiting for the Carranza faction to recognize his authority. Finally, dis-
owned by the one and at the mercy of the other, he
left the power in December 1914 and took refuge
with his soldiers.

By the beginning of 1915 the revolution had de-
generated into a veritable state of anarchy, into a
simple struggle between rivals for power. This went
on until 1916, when Obregón and Carranza, in great
part with the help of the United States, managed to
reduce Villa to a position in which he could do nothing, though without ever conquering him. As a guerrilla leader Villa was invincible. In May 1920 he was
still lording it in the stronghold of the sierras. His
energy and his daring were unrivalled. Even General
Pershing's famous expedition—the ten thousand men
that Wilson sent to Mexico, with Carranza and Obregón's approval, "to get Villa dead or alive"—had to
relinquish the undertaking.

Contents

The Eagle & The Serpent

Chapter I

My First Glimpse of Pancho Villa

To go from El Paso, Texas, to Ciudad Juárez in Chihuahua was, to quote Neftalí Amador, one of the greatest sacrifices, not to say humiliations, that human geography had imposed on the sons of Mexico on that part of the border. Yet that night, when we arrived from San Antonio, Pani and I went through this ordeal with a certain joy that was somehow bound up with the very sources of our nationality. We realized once for all that we had been born and would die a part of the soul of our country.

Ciudad Juárez is a sad sight; sad in itself, and still sadder when compared with the bright orderliness of that opposite river-bank, close but foreign. Yet if our faces burned with shame to look at it, nevertheless, or perhaps for that very reason, it made our hearts dance as we felt the roots of our being sink into something we had known, possessed, and loved for centuries, in all its brutishness, in all the filth of body and soul that pervades its streets. Not for nothing were we Mexicans. Even the sinister gleam of the occasional street-lights seemed to wrap us round in a pulsation of comforting warmth.

Hoarse, noisy Neftalí Amador acted as our guide. He walked with short and rapid steps. He talked without a pause, stringing together flat-toned words, words redolent of chewing-gum, which he ejaculated from between rigid jaws. On the street-corners the night light glanced off his pox-pitted face. Every time we had to cross the street, as our feet sank into the mud, he would repeat: "This is a pigsty. When the revolution wins we're going to clean it up. We'll make a new city, bigger and better than the one across the river."

Beams of light which were powerless to dispel the gloom filtered through the doors to the public mud. Street-cars clanged by. People and shapes resembling people crowded the streets. Occasionally above the mass of noise in Spanish—spoken with the soft accent of the north—phrases of cow-boy English exploded. The hellish music of the automatic pianos went on incessantly. Everything smelled of mud and whisky. Up and down the streets, rubbing shoulders with us, walked ugly prostitutes, ugly and unhappy if they were Mexican; ugly and brazen if they were Yankees; and all this intermingled with the racket and noise of the gambling-machines that came from

4

the saloons and taverns. We stopped for a few minutes before the doors of a large hall where a hundred or more people sat bent over the tables, their attention fixed on a number of placards covered with figures. Raucous voices called out numbers in English and Spanish.

"They play the lottery here," said Amador.

A few steps farther on we stopped at the entrance to a long hall at the rear of which, among the groups of men and women, could be seen the gleam of green tables with piles of red, blue and yellow chips. It seemed a big place.

"That's for poker, for the roulette-wheel, for monte, for shooting craps."

And after blurting out those words, one on top of the other, Amador paused for a few seconds and then went on, as if he were answering himself: "No doubt about it, it's a low-down business; but there's nothing like it when funds are low. When the time comes, we'll get rid of it. We'll drive it out. But not now. Anyway, in the mean time it's the Yankees who keep it going. They come with their money and leave it here for us to buy rifles and ammunition. They're helping along the good cause; though I realize that, as we buy our munitions from them, in the end they get back the money they left here for a little while. Still, we have the arms. But we don't have them either, for we destroy them. And, what's worse, we destroy each other with them."

5

>>>>>>>>>>>>>>>>>>>>>>>>><<<<<<<<<<<<<<<<<<<<<<<<<

With this speech, Amador came to the end of the most populous and least badly lighted street, but he began a new monologue for the next one. He flitted agilely from one to another of the various themes our walk afforded him. Pani and I hardly answered a word; we looked, or rather peered, from left to right trying to get a glimpse of the places he was pointing out.

The sidewalks had become still more primitive; they crept along beside walls whose soft colours made the darkness more friendly. The street was lined with low, flat buildings, whose windows and doors were set in at rude right angles. They might have been houses in Mesopotamia five thousand years ago or in Palestine three thousand years ago. There was the same relation between their solid mass and the banks of clouds in the dim sky as between the fence of a park and the overhanging tree-tops.

A little farther on, the walk disappeared completely from under our feet. The light became a mere furtive gleam from some window or door; silence began to rise over the barking of the dogs and the remote sadness of faint yet audible singing. Every now and then, for greater safety, I steadied myself against the wall that ran along beside me; I could feel the roughness of the uncovered, chipped adobes, and the gravel in the joinings.

"In 1911," went on Amador's voice, "during the attack of the Madero forces, one of the fiercest battles took place here. They say it was here that the revolutionists began to breach the walls to advance under cover of the houses. I don't care what anyone says, Tamborrell was a great fellow and a first-class fighting man."

A short pause, and then he added, turning to me: "He died like your father, a hero who had performed his duty, which is the saddest of all the forms of heroism, for it is filled with melancholy, not enthusiasm."

We went on awhile longer until we came to a place that in the blackness of the night gave the feeling of being near the river, towards the part where the bank and the lower end of the city came together.

Amador interrupted himself: "Here it is. Right round the corner."

Saying this, he stepped a couple of paces ahead of us, straightening up his shoulders with the air of one who is conducting a party. A short throaty cough replaced his talk.

And, sure enough, just round the corner we almost bumped into a group of the rebels on guard. They were lined up along both sides of the door of one of the first houses, some squatting against the wall, some standing up. From between the two halves of the door, which was ajar, a few faint gleams of light radiated out into the thick shadows, throwing the forms of the soldiers into a kind of distorted visibility. The brim of their enormous hats seemed to weigh them down, making them still more squat. Each one seemed to have across his breast ten or twenty cartridge-belts with hundreds and hundreds of shells. The movements of their legs in their tight trousers imitated the swell and fall of a wheezy accordion. Across their shoulders, between their hands, beside their feet, gleamed the rifle-barrels, and the rifle-butts made a dark, triangular blotch.

As soon as they heard our steps, they jumped to their feet, making a brilliant play of lights and shadows in the pale rays that filtered through the door. One of them, heavy with the weight of his rifle and cartridge-belts, shuffled forward to meet us. His dark face was framed by a huge hat, the brim of which, turned up in front and down in back, buckled against the thick folds of his blanket, which he wore in a roll over his shoulders.

"Say, where are you headed for?"

Amador went towards him, assuming a friendly, somewhat familiar air, and answered him in a voice that was meant to be low, but which was toneless: "We're friends. These two gentlemen, who are revolutionists, just got here from Mexico City, and want to see the General. I'm Neftalí Amador. One of them was a minister under President Madero—"

"Not minister," interrupted Pani, "under-secretary."

"That's it, under-secretary," and Amador rambled on with a thousand unnecessary explanations.

We had stopped in front of the door. The soldiers, quiet in their places, were listening to Amador's chatter with the rapt attention of those to whom a discussion is all Greek. They had about them that air of humble pride which characterizes our victorious revolutionists.

"Then it's Mr. Amador and two ministers . . . ?"

"That's right. The Under-secretary of Public Instruction in President Madero's Cabinet and the director general. . . ."

"Say, how do you expect me to say all that?"

"Well, then, just Mr. Amador and a minister of President Madero."

"One minister or two ministers?"

"It doesn't matter, one or two. . . ."

The door was opened wider to let the soldier in and then was shut completely. In a minute it opened again:

"Well, come in, if you're who you say you are."

We went in. The door opened into a low-ceilinged square room, with a damp, dirt floor. A kerosene lamp on top of a pile of saddles and boxes shed its dim light and smoke through the room, which was nothing but a shed.

Once across the threshold, Amador turned to the left, slipping between the door and the soldier. Pani followed him. I was the last. Four or five steps more and the three of us were in the corner opposite the lamp, the darkest of all.

There was Pancho Villa.

He was lying on a cot, covered to the waist with a blanket. He had raised himself up a little to receive us, one arm acting as a column of support between his body and the bed. His right arm hung by his side; it was unbelievably long. But Villa was not alone. At the head of his bed two other revolutionists were sitting on turned-up boxes, with their backs to the light. They seemed to have cut short an important conversation. Neither of them moved as we came in, or showed more than a vague curiosity, indicated by the way they turned their heads, half-hidden in their enormous hats, towards the door.

Amador's words of introduction were as flowery as they were long. Villa listened to him unblinkingly. His mouth was a little open and there were traces on his face of the mechanical smile that seemed to start at the edge of his teeth. At last Amador stopped short, and Villa, without answering him, ordered the soldier to bring up chairs. But apparently there were only two, for that was all the soldier brought. Pani and Amador sat down. At the general's invitation I had seated myself on the edge of the cot, about an inch from him. The warmth of the bed penetrated through my clothes to my flesh.

It was evident that Villa's intention had been to rest for only a little while; he had on his hat, his coat, and, to judge from some of his movements, his pistol and cartridge-belts. The rays of the lamp shone

straight into his face and brought out a gleam of
copper around the brilliance of the whites of his eyes
and the enamel of his teeth. His curly hair lay in a
tangled bushy mass between his hat and his broad,
curved forehead. As he talked the short ends of his
reddish moustache made moving shadows across his
mouth.

His attitude, his gestures, the movement of his
restless eyes, gave him a resemblance to a wild animal
in its lair; but an animal that defends itself rather
than one that attacks. He looked like an animal that
was beginning to feel a little confidence, but at the
same time was not sure that the other animals would
not leap upon him suddenly and devour him. In part
his attitude was in contrast with that of the other revolutionists. Who were they?—Urbina? Medina?
Herrera? Hipólito? To judge from their appearance they were perfectly calm, smoking, one leg
crossed over the other, and every now and then leaning forward with elbow on knee and chin on fist.

"Why didn't you put a bullet through that son of
a bitch of Victoriano Huerta?" Villa interrupted
Pani in the middle of his account of Madero's death.

Pani repressed a tendency to smile, for he grasped
the psychological import of the situation, and answered very seriously: "That wasn't easy."

Villa reflected for a moment.

"You're right, boy. It wasn't easy. But, believe me,
it will be."

And in this way, for over half an hour, a strange conversation went on. Two absolutely opposed categories of mind were revealed. Every question and every answer from one side or the other made it plain that here were two different, two irreconcilable worlds whose only point of contact was the chance fact that they had joined forces in the same struggle. We, poor visionaries—for then we were only that— had come armed only with the feeble experience of our books and our early ideals. And into what had we walked? Full-face, and without a word of warning, into the tragedy of good and evil, which knows no compromise. One or the other had to win or be defeated; there was no middle ground. We came fleeing from Victoriano Huerta, the traitor, the assassin, and this same vital impulse, with everything that was good and generous in it, flung us into the arms of Pancho Villa, who had more of a jaguar about him than a man. A jaguar tamed, for the moment, for our work, or for what we believed was our work; a jaguar whose back we stroked with trembling hand, fearful that at any moment a paw might strike out at us.

As we were crossing the river back into the United States, I could not get the figure of Villa as I had just seen him out of my mind. It obsessed me and kept me thinking of what Vasconcelos had said to us in San Antonio: "Now we'll win all right. We've got a man!"

A man! A man!

Chapter II

General Headquarters

IT was dark when Alberto J. Pani and I, once more in Mexico, reached Nogales. At the station, an ugly shed like those we had seen on our long trip through Arizona, except for its typical Mexican patina, there were friends and friends' friends waiting for us. They greeted us with affectionate warmth. They took our suit-cases out of our hands, smiled at us, hugged us, asked us a thousand questions. This was like wine to the spirit, both to theirs and to ours, for it was proof of a comforting bond of union. They represented our first real contact with the revolution, and they were evidence to us that the struggle, at least on the border, was a reality. We, who had just come from the city of Mexico, perhaps meant to them a new link in the endless chain of volunteers who renewed the ranks and the faith from day to day.

As a last touch of extreme luxury the mayor of the town had brought his Ford to conduct us to the hotel, which was hardly two steps away. But as the car was too small to hold all of us, we left it in a lot near the station and all went together on foot, a friendly, noisy group.

We crossed one street and walked a part of another to the hotel. The door opened into a hall which became a stairway in the rear: first a long entrance passage and then a long ascending passage, all dirty, shabby, miserable. A familiar figure appeared at the head of the stairs and stood there with outstretched arms all the time we were ascending. It was Isidro Fabela. When we reached the top, he greeted us with the greatest effusiveness, embracing us and giving way to transports of affection, accompanied by shouts of rejoicing that were almost terrifying. The doors of the rooms began to open and the different characters of the revolution made their appearance one by one. Out came Adolfo de la Huerta, Lucio Blanco, Ramón Puente, Salvador Martínez Alomía, Miguel Alessio Robles and many others whose identity I cannot recall now. We knew some of them, but many were strangers to us.

Rafael Zubaran, the leader of the group that had been waiting for us at the station, made the necessary introductions. He presented us to General Lucio Blanco and Adolfo de la Huerta with particular interest. Blanco's noble air and handsome features made the most agreeable impression on me. We felt drawn to each other at once. I hardly noticed De la Huerta, beyond the fleeting impression of his marked

>>>>>>>>>>>>>>>>>>>>>>>><<<<<<<<<<<<<<<<<<<<<<

resemblance to a Yaqui Indian and his richly sonorous voice.

Where to put us up was a serious problem. Escobosa, the owner of the hotel, swore that there was not
room for two more pins, let alone two more people.
But finally the difficulty was straightened out; a corner was found for me in the room that was occupied
by Adolfo de la Huerta and somebody else; and they
put Pani in with Martínez Alomía and I don't recall
whom else. There we brushed off some of the dust,
gave ourselves a cat-wash, and made ourselves half-
way presentable.

"And now to G.H.Q.," said Fabela, as soon as we
were ready. "The Chief knows that you're here and
wants to meet you."

The Chief! General Headquarters! I felt a thrill
of emotion as I heard those words for the first time,
spoken in that familiar, off-hand fashion. When I
think today of my formal initiation as a revolutionist
my heart still swells as it did while we walked from
the dirty Hotel Escobosa to the offices of General
Headquarters.

These were located two blocks from the Customs
Building, in a low corner-house facing both ways, the
hall of which opened on to two perpendicular wings
of rooms, and at the back on to a dismal court,
lighted by the last gleams of day. Two sentinels, on
duty at the door, presented arms as we passed. Eight

or ten more soldiers who were seated on benches in
the hall got up and stood at attention. The habili-
ments of these soldiers were not so picturesque as
those of Villa's men whom we had seen a few days
before at Ciudad Juárez but they had a more martial
air—in so far as a martial air is possible in Mexico's
improvised armies—and a more austerely revolutionary appearance. At least that was the impression
they made on me at the moment.

After a half-hour's wait in a small ante-room, we
entered the office of the Chief. There was a certain
solemnity about our entrance. Not less than fifteen
people escorted us in, among them several of the
most important figures in the revolutionary movement. Rafael Zubaran, Secretary of State and a
personal friend of Pani's introduced us. My good
friend Fabela went into a panegyric of praise of me
with that kindly eloquence so characteristic of him.
Carranza received us with a friendly and patriarchal
air. He had risen from his arm-chair and come forward to meet us, and then he remained standing in
the centre of the room, surrounded by the group of
us. I do not recall what he said to Pani, but I know it
was very flattering. He held my hand in his for
several seconds and regarded me fixedly from his
great height. His glasses, over which he looked at
me a little sidewise, shed on my face not only the
softness of his expression, somewhat bovine, but the
reflection of the electric lights.

>>>>>>>>>>>>>>>>>>>>><<<<<<<<<<<<<<<<<<<

I was somewhat prejudiced against Don Venustiano by what Vasconcelos had told me about him
while we were in San Antonio. His appearance, besides, wakened in me the memory of the typical figures of the Porfirio Díaz régime; in contrast to the
democratic frankness of Madero I seemed to notice
in him something very reminiscent of Don Porfirio
as I had last seen and heard him. Nevertheless my
first glimpse of Don Venustiano did not dampen my
budding revolutionary ardours. In that interview he
impressed me as a plain, calm, intelligent, upright,
and capable man. His habit of combing his beard
with his left hand, which he would put under the
snowy cascade, palm outward and fingers curved,
throwing back his head a little with each movement,
seemed to indicate tranquil habits of thought which
made unthinkable—so I thought at the time—all
violence and cruelty. "This may not be," thought I,
"the man of genius that Mexico needs, nor the hero,
nor the great, self-sacrificing statesman, but at least
he does not play his title false: he knows how to be
the First Chief."

It was the custom in Nogales at that time for the
more prominent revolutionists to eat every day or
nearly every day with Carranza. Pani and I were
immediately invited to join them, not by reason of
our importance, of course, but out of courtesy
towards two new-comers in the city.

"We'll all have dinner in a moment," Don Venus-

tiano said to us. "If you care to join us, I won't make
you wait long. I just have to answer two or three
urgent telegrams."

We all went into an adjoining room except Carranza, who went over to his desk, and a tall, pale, ex-
cessively thin, exquisitely mannered young man who
went over to the desk with him and gathered up some
papers. Afterwards I learned that the young man
was Gustavo Espinosa Mireles, and that he was Carranza's private secretary.

We began to talk in the next room, first all together, then in groups, then in couples. Fabela took
me over in a corner and began to ask me questions
about our friends, the members of the Ateneo who
were still in Mexico City. "How's Carlos González
Peña? How's Antonio Caso? And Julio Torri? And
Pedro?"

In one of the frequent interlocutory readjust-
ments I managed to slip away to the courtyard. At
close view it looked even more dismal than before,
when I had caught a glimpse of it from the tunnel of
the hall. All around it, level with the ground, ran a
narrow corridor covered by the four overhanging
eaves of the roof, which were supported by tall,
bare, dry posts. To one of the posts there was fastened a dim and feeble electric bulb, which opened
its melancholy fan of light over one area, and shed a
cone of darkness over the other. In the illuminated
section all was stark and bare; in the darkness the

shadows thickened into huge piles in the corners. Without being able to say why, there was something infinitely depressing about that court; in contact with its atmosphere the very sound of the voices that filtered through the walls from the waiting-room, mingled with the talk of the soldiers in the hall, seemed to become blighted as though by frost.

I walked through the sections of the corridor that came within the fan of light. Then I prolonged my stroll into that part that lay hidden in the shadow. Then I discovered that I was not alone in the court. The shadow of a man leaned motionless against the shadow of a post. Curiosity drew me closer; the shadow did not move. I passed by again, closer this time, and looked at it more insistently, though out of the corner of my eye. The shadow was that of a tall, slender man. A ray of light fell on the brim of his hat and bit a spot of grey out of the silhouette. His left arm was folded across his breast, and his chin rested on his fist; his other forearm acted as a cross-support for the first. From the position of his head it was evident that the man was absorbed in the contemplation of the sky; the light of the stars fell on his face with a dim glow.

That figure, lost in its meditation, was not wholly unfamiliar to me. I walked back from the end of the corridor and stopped directly before the motionless shadow. Little by little the man came out of his reverie, lowered the hand on which his head was resting,

straightened up, and asked in a mild, soft-toned
voice, that was in strange contrast to the energy of
his movements: "Good evening. Who is it?"

"An old acquaintance, General. Or am I mistaken?
Am I not talking to General Felipe Angeles?"

It was Angeles. What was he doing there alone
and melancholy, his head lost in the stars, he, the
man of action and great initiative? What was he doing there, incarnating the heart-rending sadness that
emanated from the court of General Headquarters,
instead of devoting himself with all enthusiasm to
the military affairs of the revolution, for which he
possessed a thousand times more ability than the
generals who were improvised for this work? I was
so taken aback at finding Angeles there in that way
that I avoided talking to him about what mattered
to me most of all: the successful organization of the
constitutional forces; and in the short time we stood
there, I let him select the topics of conversation.
Naturally, he at once spoke of my father, whose
student he had been at Chapultepec. He recalled him
with pleasure, affection, and admiration.

"Your father," he said, "not only had the spirit,
but he had the voice to go with it, in which his spirit
made itself felt and obeyed. It was the voice of a
leader such as I have never heard in another; there
was something mysterious about its sonority. When
the military school was in formation in a whole
square of the Paseo de la Reforma, his orders, even

when given in a low voice, could be heard from one end of the column to the other."

Perhaps it was because there was something that touched me intimately in Angeles's reminiscences, but the fact is that his words seemed in keeping with the penetrating sadness of that courtyard. Occasionally he would emphasize a phrase with a sober gesture of his small hands, dark in the shadows, or the hint of a smile, which never quite shaped itself.

The noise of arms and hurried steps interrupted our conversation. The guard was preparing to do honours to the Chief.

"Don Venustiano is coming out," said Angeles. "We'll have dinner now."

When we came back to the waiting-room Carranza was there. He wore a broad-brimmed hat, and he towered above all the others. The light burnished his beard, and ran down the single row of buttons on his coat in a stream of gilded drops.

He went out and the others followed after him. Angeles and I formed a part of the group, I with the timidity of a new-comer, he with his habitual timidity. In a little while we were out on the street. The cornet of the guard played a march of honour.

Neither Pani nor I talked much at the dinner, which was excellent from the point of view of the food, and which brought together a most interesting group of people. We both preferred to see, hear and

taste. Of course, I (it is to be hoped that some day
Pani will write his memoirs) did not miss certain
details that might be significant for a budding revolutionist. I noticed, for example, that Rafael Zubaran
sat on Don Venustiano's immediate right, as was
fitting and proper. Zubaran was Secretary of State
in the Revolutionary cabinet. I noticed that Angeles,
who had recently been named Secretary of War, did
not take the first seat on the left, but that this was
reserved for Colonel Jacinto Treviño, Carranza's
chief of staff. I noticed that Adolfo de la Huerta, in
spite of his relatively high official rank, deliberately
took his place among the less important diners. And
I also noticed that Don Venustiano did not for one
moment let the direction of the conversation get out
of his own hands. His talk, which bristled with historical allusions—most of them referring to the
Mexican Reform period—was listened to with profound respect even when he fell into the most obvious
mistakes, some of which would have made even a
first-year law-student smile.

Chapter III

The First Chief's Table

DINING with Carranza and his immediate aides
finally became, during the time that we were in
Nogales, the most important act of the day for me.
Aside from this duty, which I performed zealously
both noon and night, I had no other steady occupation,
and round it revolved my interest and my viewpoint.
It was like having an official post *sui generis,* almost
palatial, one might say, in spite of the fact that it was
on the border of the wilderness.

De la Huerta and I used to wake up very early.
This required no great effort on our part, for the
Hotel Escobosa possessed, among its scant virtues,
the doubtful one of becoming flooded with the bright-
est light of day at the very hour in which sleep,
wearied of itself, becomes doubly sweet. Our awakening was followed by a long chat from bed to bed.
Sometimes we followed up the conversation where
it had broken off the night before. Sometimes we
began on a new topic. Sometimes we amused ourselves

commenting on some of the extraordinary things I had said in my sleep; De la Huerta had soon discovered that I talked better asleep than awake. Finally we jumped out of bed, dressed quickly, and went down to struggle with the bad breakfast Escobosa offered his lodgers, and then each went his own way. De la Huerta, first secretary of the Department of Interior, went to meet Rafael Zubaran. Having nothing to do until lunch-time, I wandered idly about the streets, looking for someone to talk with, or set resolutely out towards the foot-hills, to climb them by way of amusement.

At first my status as a mere gatherer at the board of Don Venustiano seemed insufferable to me; a long morning of waiting for lunch; the long wait of the afternoon for dinner. I had not the resource of Luis Cabrera and Lucio Blanco, who used to arrange noisy billiard matches in the bar beside the boundary line. Nor could I make verses like Salvador Martínez Alomía, before he was selected to prepare the biographical portrait of Carranza. In his hours of leisure Zubaran found solace in the guitar, for which he possessed a positive gift; Angeles, in the severe disciplinary program he had laid out for both body and soul: so many hours riding, so many hours walking, so many jumps, so many hours of study, so many hours of meditation; Isidro Fabela and Miguel Alessio in the secret polishing of phrases and weighing of paragraphs to see which should finally carry

off the palm as the revolution's best orator; Pani
in his training as an engineer, which made it possible
for him to systematize everything, even emptiness.
But I, a fervent believer at the time in the active
revolutionary virtues, had nothing to fall back on.
Luckily I soon discovered that in Nogales, Sonora,
there was a book-store, though not a very good one.
The novels of Dumas seemed to be its specialty, and
I undertook to bridge some of the gaps that had been
left in my reading when I was thirteen. Later on
I found out that in Nogales, Arizona, there was
actually a public library, and that even the works
of Plotinus could be read there. My temporary immer-
sions in the Alexandrian mysticism and its spiritual
purity, independent of mere knowledge, date from
this period, as well as my passing acquaintance with
Porphyry and Iamblichus.

At lunch- or dinner-time I would appear at G.H.
Q. Not before this, so as not to cause any uneasiness,
for nothing worried the First Chief's immediate en-
tourage quite so much as the presence of new revolutionists without any clearly defined job. A panic came
over them at the thought of finding themselves done
out of their positions, which seemed to them full of
importance and promise. This does not take from the
fact that they were excellent fellows, all of them,
from Jacinto Treviño, whose peace of mind collapsed
in the presence of Angeles, to the young aviator

Alberto Salinas, who would have been capable, decent chap though he was, of blocking the way of Guynemer himself. I fully understand Treviño's attitude towards Angeles. Which of the revolutionary generals was not jealous of Angeles? Their name was legion who were furiously opposed to him—with envy as their only motive—and who publicly maligned him.

To go to the refectory the group of us used to set out in close formation, with Don Venustiano at the head, and walk to the Customs House. On these occasions, as on the night of our arrival, cornets and drums would play a march of honour. Apparently it was a matter of great interest to tell the world that the Commander-in-Chief of the revolutionary cause and his right-hand men were leaving their desks to lunch or dine. Thus the humble inhabitants of Nogales might know this and rejoice.

One time we were sitting around the table after dinner, fifteen or twenty of us, Carranza, Zubaran, Angeles, Pesqueira, Fabela, Pani, De la Huerta, Treviño, Espinosa Mireles. . . . We were all feeling good. That morning the military band had marched through the town twice playing the reveille to celebrate the two latest victories of our troops, at Chihuahua and Tepic. With this motive, Carranza began to pontificate, as usual, and finally set up, as an indisputable fact, the superiority of an improvised and enthusiastic army over a scientifically organized

one. A statement of this sort must perforce smack
of heresy to any trained soldier, and it did so that
night. Angeles waited until Carranza had finished
and then, gently in the phrasing, but most energeti-
cally in his arguments, rose to the defence of the art
of warfare as something that can be learned and
taught and that can be better exercised the better one
has studied it. But Carranza, despotic in his conversations as in everything else, interrupted his Secretary of War brusquely with this bald statement, closing the matter:

"In life, General," he said, "especially in leading
and governing men, the only thing that is necessary or
useful is goodwill."

Angeles took a sip from his coffee-cup and did not
say another syllable. All the rest of us kept quiet, and
the final words of the First Chief floated in the silence
that hung over us. "Is it going to end like this?" I
wondered. "It isn't possible. Somebody will surely
put things in their proper place."

But, unfortunately, over a minute elapsed before
anyone made a move to speak. Don Venustiano
savoured in silence the pleasure of dictating even over
our ideas. Perhaps he enjoyed the spectacle of our
servility and cowardice. I do not know whether
I did right or not. A feeling of shame overwhelmed
me. I remembered that I had thrown in my lot with
the revolution, and to do this I had been obliged to
sacrifice all my previous life; and I felt myself on the

horns of a dilemma. Either my rebellion against Victoriano Huerta was senseless or I was in duty bound to protest here, too, even if only by word.

The silence about the table continued even more dense than before. Was that going to stop me? Decidedly not. I flung myself head first into the small adventure that would immediately classify me forever among the dissenters and malcontents of the revolutionary field.

"Isn't it queer?" I said, without hedging, looking straight into the depths of the First Chief's benignant eyes; "I think just the opposite. I absolutely reject the theory that goodwill can replace ability and efficiency. The saying, 'Hell is paved with good intentions' seems to me a very wise one, because those whose chief characteristic is goodwill are always taking on tasks that are beyond their strength, and that is their weakness. It may be because I haven't been out of school long, but I am an ardent believer in books and training and I detest improvisations and makeshifts, except when they cannot be avoided. I believe that from a political standpoint technique is a vital necessity for Mexico, at least in three fundamental aspects, finance, public education, and war."

My outburst produced stupefaction rather than surprise. Don Venustiano looked at me with a benevolent air, so benevolent that I at once understood that he would never forgive my audacity. With the exception of Zubaran, who flashed me a glance of friendly understanding, Angeles, who looked at me approvingly, and Pani, who showed his solidarity with me in enigmatic smiles, nobody raised his eyes from the table-cloth. And only Adolfo de la Huerta, trying to turn the whole thing off as a kind of joke, came to my support, or rather to my assistance. He did everything he could to efface the bad impression my presumptuousness had left on Carranza's mind. This was a brave and honourable act on his part, born of his conciliatory spirit, for he did it at the risk of falling into disfavour himself.

Chapter IV

The Early Days of a Leader

SEVERAL days later we went on to Hermosillo. Nothing there interested me so much as knowing Alvaro Obregón. Would he be the great man that Pani was already heralding as our outstanding political figure of the future? Or would he be—as Vasconcelos, blinded by Villa's dazzling triumphs, thought him—one of the many whose ambitions clouded the revolution's horizon? I knew that neither of these opinions was worth anything as a reliable judgment; first, because Pani, perhaps instinctively, seemed to base his conclusions on qualities favourable to his own views and interests rather than on a sense of real human values; and secondly, for the opposite reason, that Vasconcelos, always on the alert to discover extraordinary ability, often jumped at conclusions which he was later the first to rectify. All this, together with the news of new military victories to the south of Sonora, only heightened my curiosity.

Adolfo de la Huerta, faithful proselyte and efficient propagandist, had neglected no opportunity to
kindle in me, while we were in Nogales, the flame of
the Obregonism then in vogue, overshadowed by
and submissive to the Carranza boom.

"You can't help admiring Obregón," was the sub-
stance of what he said, "not only as a soldier, but as
a thinking man, with original ideas, and as a leader,
of sincere revolutionary convictions. Besides, he is a
man of great natural ability. You should read his
manifestoes."

As nobody in Nogales happened to have these
manifestoes, De la Huerta made up for the lack of
them by reciting again and again—as though I were
to learn it by heart—the message that he himself
had carried to Carranza on behalf of Obregón on
the occasion of the meeting at Piedras Negras. Obregón had requested the first Chief to publish a decree
depriving all military leaders of the right to hold
office, "for," he said "all Mexico's troubles come
from the unrestrained ambitions of the army."

I must confess that De la Huerta's admiration for
Obregón impressed me at times and even half won
me over on the occasions when the canny wisdom of
the famous messages was put into evidence. De la
Huerta at this period felt strongly the responsibilities
of the revolutionary work; and as he was a model of
austerity and free from all taint of self-seeking
interest, he was able to transmit to others, in his

31

moments of restrained eloquence, his own emotions. His beautiful voice trembled as—though perhaps not in these exact words—he made comments of this sort:

"Obregón knows that his chief work is with the army, and yet he wants to prevent the officers of today from becoming the executives of tomorrow. Obregón knows that he will stand out among our greatest soldiers, and yet he makes no bones about saying that Mexico's worst troubles come from her military caste."

Really, Obregón's attitude was extraordinary; extraordinary when he sent his message to Carranza—days after the capture of Cananea—and still more extraordinary when De la Huerta was emphasizing to me his patriotic altruism after the battles of Naco, Santa Rosa, Santa María. Who, lacking political and human guile—or deaf to them—would not have waxed enthusiastic? It seemed to me that I was being witness to an unheard-of event: the formation of a revolutionary leader capable of voiding from the very start the privileges of his leadership. It was like seeing a lion draw his own teeth and pull out his own claws.

In Hermosillo the diligence of someone—I can't recall who—finally secured for me one of the manifestoes so highly praised by De la Huerta and I read it. It was the one Obregón had addressed to the town of Sonora the day the revolutionary forces first marched through the Sonoran capital. It began: "The hour has arrived. . . . Already we feel the convulsions of our beloved land which agonizes in the clutches of the matricide." And then, in the well-known tone of our political proclamations, it painted with terrible metaphors Victoriano Huerta's crime and invited the populace to take up arms.

My first impression was that this document did not do justice to its author's mental capacity, or, if it did, from the point of view of literature and ideas, that capacity was not worth much consideration. For, aside from the civic indignation—obvious in all of us who were then in arms against the author of Madero's death—and aside from the germ of an idea: that a rebellion was necessary to establish a state of law; and a noble ideal: not to execute prisoners, the manifesto was nothing but a string of words and literary figures, striking only by reasons of their high-flown aggressiveness. It was apparent that Obregón had tried to produce, on the spur of the moment, a document with literary pretensions and, lacking talent, or the experience that takes its place, had fallen into the grotesque and ridiculous.

In the first three lines of the manifestoes Victoriano Huerta was "the matricide who after plunging a dagger into the heart of his country continues to brandish it as though to destroy all her vitals." In the four following lines Huerta and his henchmen

33

were metamorphosed into "a pack that with blood-stained jowls howls in every key and threatens to dig up the remains of Cuauhtémoc, Hidalgo, and Juárez." Later on, the pack is converted into octopuses, "with which we must struggle for the bloody scraps of our Constitution" and "from which we must tear with one blow, but with patriotic dignity, all their tentacles."

But the worst of the manifesto—or the best from the view of comic effect—was not in the play of similes and metaphors. It came particularly from a certain melodramatic tone, at once childish and pedantic. It was apparent in the opening words: "The hour has arrived"; and it resounded heavily in the final apostrophe: "Cursed be ye"; and it found its perfect expression in this hair-raising phrase: "History recoils in horror at the thought that she must give a place in her pages to this avalanche of monstrosities" (the monstrosities of Huerta).

All my goodwill was helpless in the face of this literature and the spirit it revealed. After the image of "History recoiling in horror" it was impossible to go on with the rest of the proclamation, even if it had deserved it. There came to my mind that delicious old ballad in which, describing a night of storm on the sea, the poet, among other verses I cannot recall, sang these:

"The fish gave loud groans because of the bad
weather."

>>>>>>>>>>>>>>>>>>>> <<<<<<<<<<<<<<<<<<<<

But the ballad, despite imaginative errors that a naturalist would have deplored, had a quaint charm which in the manifesto of March 1913 was not only lacking, but would have been out of place.

Eduardo Hay admired Obregón, too, and enjoyed describing the battles of Santa María and Santa Rosa. But it was easy to reach an understanding with him. Colonel Hay would take out his pencil and with a deep breath and pedantic air would begin:

"The battle of Santa María was carried out, precisely, geometrically, admirably. See, the water was here. . . . "

And it was plain to anyone listening with interest that Hay was right, though his grasp of the battles had more descriptive geometry in it than strategy. Obregón was a good general, as the facts showed; at least, compared with the opposing generals, Medina Barrón or Pedro Ojeda.

As Hay went on tracing lines and dots on his sketch, the military personality of the Sonoran leader began to appear as in profile. It was evident that he was possessed of untiring activity, a serene temperament, a prodigious memory—a memory that broadened his range of attention and co-ordinated information and facts; one saw at once that his intelligence was many-sided, though astuteness was its signal quality, and that he was gifted with a certain

psychological insight into the will and intentions of
others, similar to that of a good poker-player. Obregón's tactical art more than anything else consisted
in cunningly drawing the enemy on, in making him
attack and wear himself down, and then defeating
or wiping him out when his own material and moral
support was such as to eliminate any possibility of
defeat. Probably Obregón never did essay any of
those brilliant sallies that were already making Villa
famous; he lacked the audacity and the gift for it;
he lacked that faith in the irresistible impulse of the
moment which reveals almost incredible possibilities
and suddenly makes them feasible. Perhaps he never
learned to manœuvre either, in the sense in which this
is really understood in the art of war, as Felipe
Angeles understood it. But he had his own way of
fighting, based on very practical and definite combinations, and this he understood and managed to perfection. Obregón knew how to accumulate resources
and wait; he knew how to select the site where the
enemy would hold all the unfavourable positions and
he knew how to give the *coup de grâce* to armies
that were destroying themselves. He always took
the offensive, but with defensive methods. At Santa
Rosa and Santa María, Obregón—counting on the
incompetence of their generals—made the Federals defeat themselves. To be sure, this in itself was
evidence of undeniable military ability.

At last one night, by the light of a corner lamp-post, I met Obregón. He had reached Hermosillo that afternoon to advise with the First Chief about operations at Sinaloa. Culiacán had just fallen into the hands of the Constitutional forces. The troops of Iturbe, Carrasco, and Buelna formed a solid line to Tepic.

We were walking down the street, an idle group of friends, De la Huerta, Martínez Alomía, Pani, Zubaran, myself and several other civilians, when suddenly, a short distance off, we saw Obregón. We all hurried to meet him and gathered around him, under the rays of the street-light, to congratulate him on his recent triumph. He was returning victorious once more; he radiated the satisfaction success gives.

Those of us who already knew him embraced him; the rest, on being introduced, shook hands with timid warmth. And then, while some talked with him, the others—or I, at least—observed him with the interest his growing fame warranted. De la Huerta, on purpose, asked him important questions in a light tone, fearful, no doubt, of violating the secrecy of the great revolutionary problems. But Obregón answered jokingly and as though his only desire at the moment was to talk just to be talking. He mentioned his wound, making fun of himself because the bullets did not seem to take him seriously enough: "Yes, I was wounded, but the wound couldn't have been more ridiculous: a Mauser ball ricocheted against a stone and struck me in the thigh."

Out from his eyes, whose golden glints made them reminiscent of a cat's, a continual smile spread over the rest of his face. He had a way peculiarly his own of looking sidewise, as though the smile of his eyes and that of the corners of his mouth were going to converge in a lateral point situated in the same plane as his face. There was nothing military about his appearance. His white uniform with its copper buttons looked out of place on him. His cap, white, too, and with an eagle embroidered in gold above the black visor, was unbecoming, both because of its size and the way he wore it. It was too small and slanted down from the top of his head to his forehead. The appearance of his clothes made it plain that he affected untidiness, and that he affected it as though it were one of his campaign virtues. Since the fighting at Culiacán he had had more than enough time for his orderlies to polish his shoes and puttees and for a barber to shave him. But the dust on his feet and the stubble on his face were the same that had witnessed the triumph at Culiacán.

The famous wound—ridiculous only because it was mentioned—gave Obregón occasion to talk about himself enough for me to begin to know him in spite of the jovial tone of his words. From this first moment he seemed to me a person who was convinced of his immense importance, but who pretended not to take himself seriously. And this pretence lay at the bottom of every one of his acts. Obregón did not live in the world of matter-of-fact sincerity, but on the boards; he was not a man of action, but an actor. His ideas, his beliefs, his feelings were intended, like those of the theatrical world, for the public. They lacked all roots and inner conviction. In the literal meaning of the word, he was a comedian.

ONE morning in Hermosillo it was briskly decided that Miguel Alessio Robles possessed unusual qualifications for the post of Secretary of State of Sinaloa, and that my gifts as chief clerk were no less exceptional. So we were accordingly given our passports, supplied with money and letters explaining the object of our trip, and ordered to take immediate leave for the capital of the state that was to enjoy the benefits of our unquestionable but hitherto untried aptitudes for the difficult art of government.

Our trip from Hermosillo to Maytorena was made under almost normal conditions. It was a bright day, a day such as one finds only in Mexico, which makes the distant mountains seem only a step away, and turns the air to pure transparency. The train rushed along in the sunlight without any untoward incident. Every now and then we plunged over the abyss of a trestle, but the passengers' nerves soon grew accus-

Chapter V

From Hermosillo to Culiacán

ONE morning in Hermosillo it was briskly decided that Miguel Alessio Robles possessed unusual qualifications for the post of Secretary of State of Sinaloa, and that my gifts as chief clerk were no less exceptional. So we were accordingly given our passports, supplied with money and letters explaining the object of our trip, and ordered to take immediate leave for the capital of the state that was to enjoy the benefits of our unquestionable but hitherto untried aptitudes for the difficult art of government.

Our trip from Hermosillo to Maytorena was made under almost normal conditions. It was a bright day, a day such as one finds only in Mexico, which makes the distant mountains seem only a step away, and turns the air to pure transparency. The train rushed along in the sunlight without any untoward incident. Every now and then we plunged over the abyss of a trestle, but the passengers' nerves soon grew accustomed to the thrill this occasioned. From time to time the Yaqui soldiers riding on top of the cars yielded to the irresistible temptation of shooting at the peaceful animals grazing in the fields. In that clear transparent air they made fascinating targets, and we saw cows, horses, and mules falling along the track. At times Eduardo Hay, who was going to Culiacán to take his post as General Iturbe's chief of staff and, who, as ranking officer, was in command of the train, grew furious at these acts of barbarity. Whereupon the train would be halted, a couple of officers would go up to the top of the train and issue stern orders to the troops, and for a little while we would proceed quietly on our way.

That night I travelled for the first time over the emergency road that had been cut through the underbrush to join Maytorena to Cruz de Piedra. Victoriano Huerta's troops, which had fallen back to Guaymas, held Empalme also, which was the point of intersection of the railroad from the north and the one going south. As a result the communications of the revolutionists from Hermosillo to Sinaloa suffered a hiatus here. The country around Sinaloa was flat and open and the occasional thickets and clumps of shrubs offered no protection. And, as this area lay open to the fire of the Federals, it seemed more prudent to traverse it at night, and not too early. The majority went on foot; the others in

buggies or wagons which they hired at one extremity
or the other—Maytorena and Cruz de Piedra—
like a ferry-boat on the banks of a river.

Alessio, Hay, and I picked out the best of the
vehicles at our disposal and we left Maytorena at
ten that night. I knew there was no danger or importance to the trip, and yet to me it was filled with
charm and excitement. I seemed to find in it some
subtle meaning, something that revealed I hardly
know what intimate essence of Mexico, in the movement of those men through the darkness, rifle on
shoulder, and hip as though grown to the shape of
the revolver, sure of their way, indifferent to their
fate. An atmosphere of mystery, and the men with
faces and souls just as mysterious!

In the distance we could see the gleam of the
Federal camp-fires, which formed a distant semicircle on our right. Sometimes the fireflies of the
soldiers' cigarettes carved out of the darkness with
their illumination the wavering lines of dark faces,
the gleam of buckles and rifle-barrels, the shiny wood
of gun-stocks, the criss-crossing of cartridge-belts
over the folds of dirty shirts. The creaking roll of
carts flowed around us like the breaking of the sea.
Out of the darkness came the sad, hungry, incessant
baying of the dogs.

In the back of our carriage Hay's orderly drowsed,
huddled among the luggage and bundles. We sat in

>>>>>>>>>>>>>>>>>>>>><<<<<<<<<<<<<<<<<<<<<<<

the driver's seat, talking, and at our feet the coachman hummed softly.

Cruz de Piedra loomed up before us in rough,
geometrical masses, among which an occasional
lantern winked or moved.

"Now," said Hay, "the important thing is to get
some sleep so we can start out again early tomorrow
morning."

And taking our suit-cases, we started to look for
a place to rest our bones. The best thing in such circumstances is a box car. The first ones we looked
over were no good. They had no doors and smelled
bad. Finally we found one that seemed tolerable. We
climbed in. Hay's orderly lighted his lantern and
began to make up his officer's bed: a fine soft pillow,
the cleanest of sheets, and a soft warm blanket.
Alessio and I, who had neither blankets, sheets, pil-
lows, nor orderly, piled our suit-cases up in the corner and, resting our heads on them, went off to
sleep.

The traveller has a choice of two methods for
securing breakfast in Cruz de Piedras: one the every-
day manner, the other the unusual. The first consists
in merely buying at one of the stands that sell supplies
to the soldiers a pitcher of coffee and some *tortillas,*
the big, round flat ones made of white flour that one

folds over and over in layers, and that taste as though one were trying to chew thin, fragrant paper. The out-of-the-ordinary method was more complicated: it consisted in getting one of the important personages round the camp to invite one to eat with him, which meant that one would get better rations than in the strictly commercial breakfasts.

With the meticulous knowledge of a person who takes his campaign life in all seriousness, Colonel Hay expounded to Miguel Alessio Robles and me the advantages and drawbacks of each of the above-outlined methods and finally decided in favour of the second.

"I can assure you," he said, "that if we go to call on Colonel Sosa, whom I have known ever since the battle of Santa María, he will invite us to eat with him and treat us like princes. The visit will not surprise him either, because we really should show him this courtesy as officer in charge here, and besides he'll understand perfectly well what is our real reason."

Of course, Hay was right. Colonel Sosa outdid himself entertaining us. We found him in a most unusual kitchen, improvised of boards, pieces of tin, and boughs of trees. In one corner was an open fire. From a can the foaming, fragrant coffee bubbled out on the blaze. A shiny, sizzling frying-pan poured forth smoke and delicious smells. In one corner, almost over the hearth, chunks of beef and pork hung by cords from the roof-trees. And in the other corner dangled festoons of dried beef and red and green peppers.

Introductions were brief, for Colonel Sosa, who was no fool, understood to perfection his duties as a host. After expressing his great pleasure in meeting Alessio and me, he ordered more meat to be put in the frying-pan, more coffee in the coffee-pot, and more chile and tomato in the sauce. He drew up to the boards he used as a table the three chairs he owned, improvised a fourth out of a box, and invited us to be seated.

It was a delightful moment; we had found, not only food, but warmth and a cordial welcome. Naturally, to Miguel Alessio and to me Colonel Sosa seemed the most delightful person for miles around. Besides, my attention was caught by a detail that perhaps another might not have noticed: that morning Colonel Sosa was wearing two coats, one civilian and the other military, the first a greyish blue, with greenish buttons, and the other black, with brass buttons and scarlet pipings.

Breakfast over, Hay went to make arrangements about the train that was to take us to Culiacán. Miguel Alessio wanted to get a look at Guaymas, even though from a distance, to see the Federals' heavy artillery, and he set off for one of the hills

45

near by. I strolled round the encampment, talking
with the soldiers and observing the excellent organization that General Alvarado had worked out. . . .

Hours later the train began its long, tiresome
interminable journey, within sight of the majestic
blue hills of the Sierra, down whose jagged sides
flowed the sinuous lines of mountain streams and
mysterious paths.

The stations at which the train stopped from time
to time were desolate towns, enveloped—even the
most important of them, such as Navajoa—in a
stifling atmosphere of ignorance and rudeness, whose
lack of any spark of beauty or refinement flung itself
at one on first sight. They were made up of clusters
of yellowish adobe shacks—flat, square, and bare
—squatting complacently in a sea of dust, which
in the rainy season became without doubt a sea of
mud. Through the one street of the town occasional
buggies and wagons rolled up clouds of dust or,
dustier than the very earth, stood where their horses
or mules were tied to a stake driven into the ground.
It was a Mexican Far West, newer than that of
the United States and with less promise of industry,
less machinery, less energy; with a greater aboriginal
influence, which was revealed in the use of mud as
building-material, but as barbarous as the other, more
so perhaps, its brutality unrestrained by a tradition
of civilization, and ignorant of all the amenities

46

invented by human culture. The civilizing influence
of the Jesuit fathers had had no time to flourish in
those regions; currents of authentic savage life still
floated in the tragic, miserable atmosphere, in which
every feeble better impulse was crushed out by the
uncontrolled passions of men who responded to none
but the zoological stimuli. I felt no surcease of this
depressing atmosphere until the train entered the
gentle regions of Sinaloa. Compared with southern
Sonora, even the poorest farms of Sinaloa seem outposts of civilization.

Chapter VI

First Impressions of Sinaloa

EDUARDO HAY entered at once on his duties as Iturbe's chief of staff. But Miguel Alessio and I had given up our idea of getting appointed to some official post and had become once more the masters of our time and our actions.

To amuse ourselves we wandered about, getting acquainted with Culiacán, which offered the double interest of a city we had never seen and a city recently evacuated by Huerta's troops. There was something unpretentious and agreeable in that little city, a brightness that invited one to stroll about it; a fullness of life in mid December, which, after the dry, dusty days in Hermosillo, revived a person, sharpened the wits, cleared the mind, and aroused a desire to establish contacts with all things. During the day everything took on a rare splendour in Culiacán. The waters of the Tamazula had the same blue hue as the sky, broken only by the dark splotches of stones and backed by the sand of the river-bed. On the outskirts of the city, rubbing elbows with the walls of the last houses, grew a rich vegetation: lush gardens, thick cane-brakes, meadows that were always green, dotted here and there with flowers. And the sky, whose brilliance almost blinded one at times, shed over those fields and the streets that the groups of houses marked out through them rays of light that gilded everything they touched. In this splendour nothing seemed ugly or dull. The very mud gave off a radiance that seemed to ennoble it.

So great was the brilliance and vitality of the natural elements there that it was hard to realize the effects of man's recent struggle in the city. We had to pass the plundered stores with their broken-in doors and empty shelves again and again before we took in their full significance. The abandoned houses, which the mob had despoiled of all their furnishings, merely brought to mind the confusion of a passing moment of disorder, a momentary wrinkle in the social fabric, nothing of civil war in its wildest riotousness. Small groups of the city's inhabitants wandered about the streets engaged in the difficult task of earning a living in a place where there was hardly anything to eat. Yet, notwithstanding these trying circumstances, they appeared happy, self-assured, optimistic. To get a new shirt or pair of socks one had to wait for Schwab, the famous Jewish trader of that day, who used to make trips to Nogales, Arizona, and come back with job lots of clothes whose style

>>>>>>>>>>>>>>>>>>>>>><<<<<<<<<<<<<<<<<<<<

and prices were incredible, and in which we looked
even more incredible. There were suits of underwear
of colours and designs so weird as to hint of some
supernatural origin; shirts that opened down the
back; green suits with rhomboidal stripes, which
made us seem first cousins to the snake family;
other suits were such strange combinations of different elements that they seemed the product of some
powerful mysterious imagination, and in them we
acquired a grotesque personality: some were half
baseball-player and half cowboy, or a combination
of mountain-climber and summer-resort visitor. But
this counted for nothing in the rhythm of the surrounding forces of nature, just as it did not seem
to matter that there was not always bread in the
city, or meat, or coffee, or other supplies. December
that year was like spring. The vital forces thrived
and flourished and seemed to live and multiply on
their own strength.

Some weeks later Laveaga, who was to become
senator, but at that time was engaged in the noble
duties of the business man, appeared on the scene like
a god of mythology, in the midst of that brilliant and
sensual existence. For a long time Culiacán had not
tasted beer. Laveaga heard about it and, shrewd
revolutionary merchant that he was, ran a car-load of
it past the Federal troops in Guaymas to Culiacán.
The city received him in triumph and paid the bitter

>>>>>>>>>>>>>>>>>>>>>>><<<<<<<<<<<<<<<<<<<<<<<

beverage's weight in gold; and had the natives of Culiacán possessed the imagination of other ages, a legend and a myth would have grown out of the rejoicing, which lasted several days.

Withdrawn from

97.3·81
G99

Chapter VII

A Night in Culiacán

DURING this time the name of General Juan Carrasco, the Sinaloan guerrilla leader, was on everybody's lips. Aside from his military exploits, there was not a soul in Culiacán who was not talking about the persistent enthusiasm with which he celebrated the revolutionist's latest triumphs, especially the capture of the state capital by our forces. One morning I saw him driving through the main streets, bearing out perfectly what was said of him. He was in an open carriage, his gun over his shoulder, and his breast crossed with cartridge-belts. He was accompanied by several masculine officers and a notorious feminine one, the famous "Carrasco's blonde." Behind the carriage, in good Sinaloan fashion, a band of four or five musicians did their best to keep pace with the horses, without interrupting their playing. And the oddest thing about it was that the musicians, in spite of the double strain on them, seemed less fatigued than the General and his train. The contrast puzzled me, and I stopped to get a better look at the spectacle and its actors.

Of these the dominant figure was unquestionably Carrasco; with his tall, shapely body, his small head, his bronzed face with its angular features, he easily held the centre of the stage. The "blonde," it was quite evident, was doing her best to play her part and attract attention, but Carrasco put her in the shade. Without his realizing it, perhaps, and in spite of his dog-tiredness, the glances of the public were all for him. Everybody turned round to look at that face, which the dark line of the greasy chin-strap divided in two, shaded by the drooping brim of his hat, which he wore with a jaunty grace.

"This is the third day," observed a voice at my side, "that my General Carrasco has spent this way."

"Three?" I asked, turning round, eager to learn more.

"Three days and three nights," was the answer. "And if I am making a mistake, it's on the side of less, not more. You see how the General looks now? Well, there's still five or six days ahead of him. But when you want to see him is at night."

"Why at night?"

"Because then the soldiers join him."

That very night, a little after ten, I decided to see for myself what my unknown informer had praised so highly. I left Alessio Robles preparing the speech he was to deliver the next day at Garmendia's grave, and started out to see the celebration of Carrasco and his men.

At that hour it was very rare then to see anybody on the streets in Culiacán. Only around the market-place did one see a few inveterate night-hawks out for the classic dish of chicken, to be eaten by the smoky light of candles and lanterns. Culiacán was the deserted town of the days following the siege, houses abandoned, stores twice sacked, by the Federals in flight and by us when we entered. And the desolation, which was frightful during the day, but partly hidden under the cloak of the rich and exuberant natural scenery, even in mid-winter, seemed at night to rise out of the very shadows, invisible, yet real; impalpable and yet oppressive. After walking several blocks at night, one lost all the agreeable impressions received during the day, and it seemed as though one were wandering through the inside of a body whose soul had been torn away. As though it came from the depths of the dead being, one could hear the beating of one's own heart, which seemed the only guide, the only contact with the world of the living.

In the midst of the most complete silence in the open country or in the mountains, one can always hear or feel at night the palpitation of life. In a city in ruins the shadows seem the next thing to the flickering-out of the last breath into nothingness. Even the occasional flashes of life are brusquely stripped of their reality, and lose their content. The half-starved dog that rushes by passes like the spectre of a dog; the distant voice reaches our ear with its human quality transmuted into an echo. The figure that moves through the lighted space under the remote street-lamp is the ghost of a body, partaking of the insubstantiality of a flat surface, without a third dimension.

I wandered about the dark and solitary streets for over an hour. The farther I walked from the centre of the town, the darker became the shadows and the more opaque the silence. Finally I got lost and had to feel my way along. Then a momentary far-away flash of light gave me my bearings and I started towards home, trusting to my sense of direction. My long walk began to seem foolish and futile. Most probably the celebration of Carrasco and his troops was the invention of my unknown informant of the morning.

Just as I was thinking this, I perceived, through the veil of darkness, a faint sound of voices. It came from the direction in which I was going. I kept on. A few steps more and I heard several pistol-shots, which rose above the sound of the voices, nearer now, but still confused, a sort of buzzing. I stopped. It was impossible to make out a thing. I could feel the darkness against my face. To judge from their muffled sound, the shots had been fired in a house. They had followed one another in rapid and uniform succession. "From the same pistol," I said to myself, "and fired by the same hand." I waited quietly.

The sound of the voices kept on. In a minute another series of shots, rapid and regular like the first, rose again above the other noises. These shots were of a different calibre. The voices, like a rising tide, grew louder and formed themselves into a sharp, guffawing cry, which, after several short, rapid, guttural notes, spread into a strangled "Ay," and wound up with a hoarse, obscene exclamation. Then I understood: it was Carrasco and his followers.

The cry localized for my ears, if not for my eyes, the point from which the shots had come. The house was on the same side of the street as that on which I was walking, about two or three hundred feet ahead. I hesitated as to what I should do. Should I go ahead? Should I turn back? I finally decided to cross over to the other sidewalk, and as I did so, I discovered that the street turned into a mud-puddle, or, to be more exact, a river of slime, into which I sank above my ankles. I managed to go ahead little by little, almost dizzy with the darkness, until I touched the wall on the opposite side. There seemed to be no sidewalk on this side. The blackness of the sea of mud melted into the barely discernible greyness of the walls of the houses. It seemed absurd to keep on walking under these conditions, but, as one could see nothing, it was impossible to look for a better path. So I went ahead.

As I came nearer the place where I had heard the

shots and the scream, the voices, no less confused and
blurred, grew louder. "There must be a lot of them,"
I was thinking when I stumbled against what seemed
to be the legs of somebody leaning against the wall,
and I fell forward in the mud. But as I threw out my
arms in falling, my hands, as by a miracle, caught
hold of the clothing of another body, and I hung on
to it. My invisible saviour seemed to understand what
had happened to me, for I felt a strong hand under
my arm, which helped me to my feet and released me
for a moment, only to come up around my shoulder,
squeezing my neck with unexpected affection. The
most disagreeable human odour, mingled with the
reek of *mezcal,* accompanied the embrace. With a
vigorous jerk I tried to free myself from that body,
which was hanging on to mine, but the arm tightened
its hold. At that moment a ray of light filtered
through the door across the way. Whoever was holding on to me said: "Well, now, if you're not trying to
get away from me!"

The light from the door fell slanting across us.
I wanted to see who had hold of me, and I looked up.
My captor was a ragged soldier. His palm-leaf hat
rested half-way down on his nose, and the broad, flop-
ping brim touched the neck of the bottle he held in
his other hand, the bottom of which rested in the
angle formed by the two cartridge-belts crossing his
dirty shirt. The narrow parallelogram of light that
the half-open door poured out on the street revealed

many more such hats. It was impossible to guess at the number. It might as easily have been two hundred as four hundred or a thousand. And at the same time I saw this, I saw several men come out through the lighted door, among them one tall, unmistakable silhouette: Carrasco. The door closed.

The darkness blinded me now more than before, but, thanks to the awakening of some new sense, I became more aware of the multitude. Within its limits, which I could not see, but divined, there existed the soul of a collective unity. The mass began to move like one body, swaying, weaving about, stumbling, all in the heart of a thick, dull noise. For the same low, vague murmur of the voices kept on as before. Whatever collisions took place while moving were deadened by the mattress of mud. It was evident that the mass was guided now by a single will. A sort of current seemed to flow from body to body. First it reached out like a wave towards the part where I and the brute who held me more and more tightly were standing. Then the wave ebbed. Next I felt that a slow forward movement had begun; it was so slight that it seemed more the intention of moving than a movement.

As we moved along, I noticed that little by little, behind and beside the group my captain and I formed, emerged other groups, which rubbed and pushed against us. There were couples like us, or groups of three or four or six men, their arms around each other. Desperately I tried to get loose again, but my partner, with a rapidity and strength far beyond mine, held me tight around the neck. It was impossible for me to struggle, for he was at the stage of inebriety in which the muscles are of an invincible agility, and, besides, he was tall and strong. My efforts made him laugh, a low, self-satisfied little laugh, but without the least hint of malice in it. Apparently I amused him. Little by little he raised to my face, in proof of his friendly intentions, no doubt, the hand in which he held the bottle. I felt the cold, sticky mouth of the bottle against my lips, and for several seconds the *mezcal* trickled down my chest. Then he raised the bottle to his own mouth and drank down great gulps of the liquor.

The human mass of which we formed a part was moving towards the end of the street. Several tall silhouettes as of men on horseback formed the pivot round which the rest of us milled. The tallest of these must have been Carrasco. Every now and then there floated down from them shouts that had an intonation of command, but to me they sounded confused and inarticulate. One of the queerest things was that in the midst of that sea of human beings I had not been able to make out a single intelligible word except those first ones my captor spoke. The only sound made by that whole mass was nothing but whispers, murmurs: the murmur of snatches of songs, the whisper of words. Once in a while a strident cry would rise above the rest; then the buzzing of the hive would resume its sinister dominance. Sometimes, too, a rapid series of pistol-shots would envolop us in a reddish intermittent glow, which died away with the last report. Both the shouts and the shots seemed like a sort of climax to vague desires, and they were heard when the formless murmurs, with a harmony of their own, achieved, in their mumbling, a vague resemblance to song.

Strange intoxication of the mass, as sad and noiseless as the shadows which folded it around! Herd drunkenness, like that of ants, happy in their reek and contact. It was the bestiality of the *mezcal* filling the most rudimentary need of self-liberation. Floundering about in the mud, lost in the shades of night and conscience, all those men seemed to have renounced their quality of human beings on coming together. They seemed the soul of a huge reptile with hundreds of heads, thousands of feet, which crawled, drunk and sluggish, along the walls of a cavernous, dark street in a deserted city.

As my companion and I turned a corner, I managed to get away from him. How long was I held in that nauseating embrace—one hour, two, three? When I jerked myself free, I seemed to rid myself of a greater oppression, both physical and moral, than if all the blackness of the night, converted into some horrid monster, had been resting on my shoulders.

Chapter VIII

The Piety of General Iturbe

GENERAL ITURBE, who was in command of the revolutionary forces in Sinaloa, used to invite us to accompany him when he drove out in his carriage. Culiacán lay before us (or, at least, so it seemed, to judge from the happy, satisfied air with which Iturbe surveyed it) like the crowning reward of an arduous effort. Of course, the final triumph of the revolution was far off—the struggle had barely begun—but at the same time some secret sentiment or presentiment gave us the sensation that, driving through the recently conquered city as we did, we were somehow enjoying to the full and setting the seal of victory on one stage of the contest.

The comfortable carriage, drawn by an excellent pair, rolled smoothly over the soft dirt of the main streets. After we had exhausted the heart of the city, we went bumping along—bumps which the excellent springs of our conveyance turned into swinging— over the mud and the puddles of the outlying sections. In this way we visited the most out-of-the-way places and took in even the most insignificant details of everything we saw. The city was small for the pace at which we drove and we had to go back and forth through the same streets to make our amusement hold out.

Iturbe, either from a habit of his own or following the customs of Sinaloa, never gave the driver any general instructions when we started out. As we went along, he would instruct him as to the road he should take. Every minute he would say: "Right," "Left," "Back," "Over the bridge," "Towards the chapel." And if he was in the midst of a conversation, he would interrupt himself to give the driver his order and then go right on with what he had been saying. It was a rare ability, which impressed me as a valuable exercise to train the attention to follow two different trains of simultaneous thought with equal efficiency. At first it just amused me; then, little by little, I began to try it myself, taking an active part in the conversation and at the same time analysing the logic behind Iturbe's itinerary.

The monotony of these drives was made agreeable more than by anything else by a sort of effervescence, as of champagne, in the air, which induced us to see everything with intelligent and understanding eyes. There were, however, two exceptions which seemed to me of great interest in themselves: one, the crossing of the bridge over the Tamazula River; and the other, the invariable halt at the foot of the hill on whose crest gleamed the whitewashed walls of a little chapel.

The long bridge over the shallow blue waters of the river seemed to possess the hidden power to open horizons to the contemplative soul. It was rough, ugly, with nothing artistic to it, but there was something new and fresh about it, or at least about in the landscape around it. It took longer to get there than to feel that one had been translated to a different sphere, a kind of nook meant for the spirit, a temple. Slowly our carriage rolled along between the two red iron arcades whose sinuous parallel lines advanced, as in a series of leaps, from one side to the other. We generally drove over it at nightfall, just at the hour in which the individual characteristics of the different things, so soon to be swallowed up in the shadows, become more accentuated. The hoofbeats of the horses struck a sonorous resonance from the wooden floor which rested on the metal ties of the arches, and the hollow reverberations of the boards awakened answering metallic harmonies, which blended into a rare music. That music made me lift up my eyes to the hills, towards the horizon, and gave me a sense of contact between the immediate and the remote. I could see the sun turning ruddy; the bridge, like a pivot between earth and sky—a sky whose steely brilliance was turning to red—seemed to

>>>>>>>>>>>>>>>>>>>>>>><<<<<<<<<<<<<<<<<<<<<<<

divide the universe into two contrasting perspectives. Below, on the earth, these two perspectives were so small and modest that their existence seemed reduced to a mere aspiration, a humble acceptance of those above. On the one hand, the dwellings of the city grouped about the white towers of its largest church—low, poor, discouraged little houses—and on the other, the outposts of the invading countryside, with its luxuriant, almost rank vegetation, overgrown with underbrush, with pushing cane-brakes, and here and there a thick, sturdy tree.

The interest provoked in us by the hill that the chapel topped was of a very different order. Here I could not but meditate on the spiritual connotation of the revolution. Using my daily contact with the men with whom I was associated as a basis for my judgments, I tried to forecast what the consequences of this struggle in which we were threshing about would be for the soul of the Mexican people. What I used to see at the foot of the hill, in the light of the spirit that dominated in most of the partisans of the revolution, might be considered exceptional, almost unique.

We used to get out of the carriage in the midst of piles of masons' materials, stones, bricks, sand, mortar. Iturbe would go over to talk with the foreman; he would inspect what had been done during the day and find out what were his plans for the next day. When he came back to us, he would explain in detail how the work was coming along. The first time we went there he began in this fashion:

"One day—a long while back—when I was still hiding in the mountains, I promised, as soon as I took Culiacán, to build a stairway from the foot of the hill to the door of the chapel. And now, as you see, I am keeping my promise."

As he said this, Iturbe had his eyes fixed on the little shrine on the hill-top, not on us, and he pronounced the last words with a somewhat forced firmness, as though by his tone he wished to make the point, on which he admitted no argument, clear. But in spite of his effort he faltered a little over the words, and it was apparent that he was trying to seem natural. Reading between the lines, it was evident that Iturbe was afraid of being misunderstood or misjudged on account of his piety. But though this fear affected his words, it did not affect his acts. Iturbe might blush at the thought of his comrades in arms or in political ideals seeing him build a stairway in obedience to a religious impulse, as a simple act of faith in a divine power; but, despite his embarrassment, he built it.

This detail gives an idea of the kind of man General Iturbe was. And, except in the eyes of a few fools, it paints him a most flattering light. For very few revolutionists of the day dared to confess openly their religious beliefs, even if they had any. The atmosphere and the state of affairs put a premium on the lack of faith. It was, one might almost say, an official duty to deny God. Don Venustiano, who on the one hand tried to be like Don Porfirio, at the same time wanted to be like Juárez. This explains his fondness for playing the virtuous citizen in the border cities— an innocent mimicry of what was a necessity for Juárez—as well as other more serious imitations, such as the revival of the law of January 25, 1862, in the name of which unspeakable assassinations were committed, in spite of the fact that Carranza was not a bloodthirsty person. With regard to his religious policy, the First Chief's determination to win himself a certain pedestal in the halls of history set the pace. Those of us who, really or outwardly, followed him flaunted a Jacobinism, a reform spirit of the newest vintage, and all-embracing content. But it was different with Iturbe and a few others. In matters pertaining to his soul he, who was at the time a Catholic and later on became a spiritualist, obeyed only his own impulses and refused to be swept along with the rest. He did this in a manner that won for him all respect, in this as well as in the military field. In the latter he had completely convinced Obregón that he deserved his rank of general in the Constitutionalist army. Iturbe knew how to command, make his plans, carry them out, and win, as he had proved again and again during the attack on the very city where we were. Nobody could overlook the fact that the capture of Culiacán had been characterized by true military heroism: the serenity of Gustavo Garmendia, the gallant stubbornness of Diéguez, and, standing out over them all, the undeniable leadership, the brave leadership, of Iturbe. After the battle Obregón's praises were almost exclusively for the young general of Sinaloa.

What took place in the civil field was very similar, at least as far as his personal attitude was concerned. In contrast to the mass of servile revolutionists, which was steadily growing larger and more confused, Iturbe, without realizing it, stood out as an example of independence. His loyalty to his religious faith revealed him as a man who would tolerate no compromise in matters concerning his convictions and his emotions.

I have visited Culiacán in later years, and the streets and the landscape have not always been able to evoke in me the impressions and emotions of the days I spent there as a rebel. But one thing always revived in me, as fresh as the first afternoon: my feelings at the sight of the construction of the stairway by which, later on, the faithful should climb to the shrine of Guadalupe. Before that hill I always felt the same thrill of profound admiration for the general of the revolution who possessed the hardihood of soul to fulfill publicly his religious vow. Those were other days; the waters of the revolu-

tion's stream still showed much of their pristine
clarity; as yet, ambition, greed, treachery, and cowardice had not completely muddied them. Even at
the risk of losing with the world, Iturbe fulfilled his
vow to God, and to do so employed the official resources that were his to command. His act stands
out by contrast with what happened months later in
Chihuahua, when a Catholic bishop was appointed
by the Constitutionalist forces, amidst applause and
shouts of laughter, and months after this, in Monterrey, where the Saint's images were ordered to be
shot.

Chapter IX

Murder in the Dark

GENERAL ITURBE offered me, through Colonel Eduardo Hay, a military post in his brigade organization which held out not a few attractions. I was to be lieutenant-colonel and assistant chief of staff, and I should have no one over me except Colonel Hay himself. Nevertheless, I did not accept the offer, in spite of my friendship for Hay, and the admiration and affection I was beginning to feel for Iturbe. The motives for my refusal were simple enough: I could not bring myself to trade my precious independence of word and action for the stiff discipline of the soldier, and one of the reasons for not doing so was that I saw no reason for making such a sacrifice. I had no political or military ambitions; and, besides, the important leaders of the revolution were far from being, in my opinion, unselfish and idealistic enough for me to want to bind myself to them, even indirectly, with chains that are always dangerous and not always easy to break.

"Anyway," I told Hay, "I think the revolution has too many officers. Why aren't civil matters given more attention? But I do want you to understand and make it clear to General Iturbe that there is nothing personal in my refusal. On the contrary, on account of you people, I'm sorry not to accept the offer. After Iturbe's brilliant action in the capture of Culiacán, I should consider it an honour to serve under him."

General Iturbe accepted my excuses kindly and did not insist on my becoming a soldier. But at the same time it seemed that he did not want to relinquish the idea of winning me over in some way, and he suggested that, without giving up my civilian status, I should help him in the enormous tasks he had laid out for himself. This new offer seemed splendid to me, and I accepted it without a moment's hesitation, with positive enthusiasm.

Hay and I understood each other with few words and we decided to get busy at once. But the task was an overwhelming one. Where should we begin? In the Quartermaster's Department? In the Military Hospital? The reorganizing of the hospital seemed the most urgent thing, so we decided to begin with that; though in those first days such an extraordinary incident took place that it distracted our mind from our work considerably. Some of the details of the strange affair are not quite clear in my memory any more, but I can still recall enough, drawing on the

>>>>>>>>>>>>>>>>>>>>><<<<<<<<<<<<<<<<<<<<

legend that sprang up about it overnight, to outline
its main features.

One morning they brought into the Military Hospital of Culiacán a man who was dying, with three
bullet-wounds in his body. He had been found in
the street at daybreak, close to a corner, face down
on the sidewalk and unconscious. When they went
to pick him up, his hands and face were stuck to the
sidewalk with dried blood. The first investigations
threw no light on the affair, or so little that it remained practically in the dark. The people who
lived in the houses near the spot where the wounded
man was found said that about midnight they had
heard revolver-shots closer than usual, and that the
next day they had heard that a man had been found in
the street almost shot to death. That was all.

Colonel Hay and I made all sorts of conjectures
about the matter. As Iturbe's chief of staff he was
determined to have perfect order in Culiacán, and
he went to the most painstaking lengths to clear up
the mystery. But the mystery only grew deeper. For
the next morning, in a different part of the city, and
near a corner, too, a similar find to that of the
preceding day was made. Only this time it was not
a dying but a dead man. The result of new investigations: shots late at night, followed by silence and
at daybreak the body lying in a pool of blood. It
was impossible to advance a theory of murder as the
result of a quarrel or hold-up in connection with

either of the victims. The first, who died in the
Military Hospital a few hours after he was brought
in, without regaining consciousness, and the dead
man found the next day were both of poorest appearance, with nothing on them except the clothes they
were wearing; there was no indication that they were
in the habit of carrying weapons, nor did they seem
the sort to be mixed up in adventures or brawls.
And this was borne out by the testimony of their
relatives and their general reputation.

But, strange as all this already was, it wasn't the
end. More was to occur that would make the mystery
still more puzzling. On the morning of the third day
as it was getting light, in a different part of the city
and close to a corner, another man was found shot
to death, and the circumstances were as mystifying
as those of the preceding days.

Our surprise turned to bewilderment in the face
of this new crime. Iturbe, who was as a rule cool
and self-possessed, flew into a rage; Hay redoubled
his police efforts, and Culiacán enjoyed the weird
sensation of feeling itself under the sway of some
unknown fiend, who revealed himself only in the
darkness, under cover of which he killed his chosen,
and who selected a man for every night.

The third crime added a slight detail to the few
we had discovered in connection with the first two.
One of the persons we questioned said he thought
he had heard, a few seconds before the shots were

fired, a buggy pass by very quickly, but he did not hear it clearly enough, for the street was unpaved, to know exactly what kind of vehicle it was.

"This is a diabolical piece of work," said Hay. "Fifteen or twenty people will have to die in the same way before we can get to the bottom of this infernal plot, in which Heaven knows what scoundrels are amusing themselves."

But, fortunately, he was wrong. Not fifteen or twenty victims were needed; two more were enough. For the next night, in view of what might happen, Hay planned certain measures that could not fail to bear fruit of some sort. Patrol squads were stationed in the different sections of the city with orders to rush immediately to the spots where they heard shots.

The patrols worked for a long time without any results. The reports that were heard from time to time were like most of those that continually broke the silence of the night in the revolutionary cities, meaningless and distant explosions, fantastic, unreal, like the far-off baying of a dog; dull explosions followed by a faint dry cracking noise as though the bullets had gone through a door or perforated a ceiling. But after a number of profitless chases the most diligent of the squads discovered, close to the corner, a man who had just been shot in the chest and in the abdomen and who was dying. Between the gasps of his death-agony he pronounced a few intelli-

>>>>>>>>>>>>>>>>>>>>>>><<<<<<<<<<<<<<<<<<<<<<<

gible phrases about the terrible wounds he had received. It seemed—he told the leader of the patrol—that two men, or perhaps just one, had fired on him without a word of warning from a buggy that drove by at a furious pace.

The mention of the buggy together with what we knew about the crime on the preceding night gave us a definite clue. The night before, a vehicle had been heard to go by. Today a buggy was mentioned. So it became clear that the author—or authors—of these four consecutive homicides had committed the crimes from one of those low two-wheeled buggies in great vogue in Culiacán, which were popularly nicknamed "spiders."

That night nothing further could be discovered. Nor could Hay's efforts at investigation the next day bring out anything new, in spite of the fact that all livery-stable proprietors were questioned, and many private owners of vehicles of this type. But our lack of success did not discourage us. We were more determined than ever to solve the mystery, and as we were sure that the nocturnal crime would repeat itself, like a natural phenomenon, General Iturbe urged that no effort be spared, and Colonel Hay laid his secret plans to capture the guilty party or parties.

Even Hay's best friends complained of his passion for detail; he was one for whom the trees hid the forest. But on this occasion he proved the value of

>>>>>>>>>>>>>>>>>>>>>>>><<<<<<<<<<<<<<<<<<<<<<<

his obsession, at least for certain things. By working from detail to detail Hay had managed to build up a series of deductions about the movements of the "death spider" that enabled him to predict with remarkable accuracy in what part of the city the next shooting would take place. But this knowledge alone was not enough, for the problem consisted not only in avoiding crimes like those that had already been committed, but in catching the criminal, or criminals. And for this the most important thing was not to frighten off the prey. In other words, the plan had to be laid without any fuss, if possible throwing off suspicion on a false scent so as to cover up the real preparations.

Hay did it that way. He ostensibly gave orders to station soldiers in two or three places far from the spot he had secretly fixed on. And here, hidden in the shadows and unawares to all, he hid his best men close to certain corners. And to avoid any slip Hay took charge of operations himself. This zealousness was not without its dangers; rather, it attracted them. For in his role of director of these nocturnal manœuvres he was obliged repeatedly to pass the spots he had selected as the probable scene of the new crime, and each time he did so, he became a possible target for the unknown assassin.

Everything was carried out as had been planned and ordered. Until a little after ten, occasional "spiders" drove through the streets where Hay and

>>>>>>>>>>>>>>>>>>>>>><<<<<<<<<<<<<<<<<<<<<<

his men were hidden. These were peaceful, inoffensive vehicles engaged in taking home some belated traveller or the drivers themselves, worn out at the end of the day. But from that time on, no "spider" was seen; or, to be more exact, glimpsed or heard in the darkness of the night. The silence of the streets was interrupted only two or three times by the hollow step of pedestrians, who scurried along hugging the houses for protection and hurried as fast as they could or broke into a frank run as they turned the corners.

In this fashion it struck eleven, twelve; and nothing happened until well on towards one, when suddenly the empty silence of the night, faintly underscored by the ever-present distant pistol-shots, was broken by the sound of a "spider" drawn by a horse galloping at full speed. Ten minutes later a similar sound was heard two or three streets farther away and in a few minutes in a cross-street not far off. The horse hitched to the "spider" wore no bells or anything that particularly distinguished it, but from the broken gallop it was soon plain that it was the same that was driving through the different streets.

Suddenly, after a new gallop, the noise of the buggy stopped. The spider seemed to have pulled up short, though it was not easy to say exactly where, for the only two street-lamps burning in all that section barely lighted the houses on two corners far from each other. Aside from these two spots the darkness was dense and impenetrable.

Several minutes went by like this. But at the very moment in which a human figure could be seen in the distance rapidly crossing one of the illuminated spaces, the "spider" was heard again. It seemed to have started off suddenly, and in a few seconds its low, yellow shape was seen crossing rapidly under the light of the same lamp that had just revealed the pedestrian. Immediately afterwards three shots rang out; a scream pierced the night, and the spider, which had slowed up, galloped off again like mad.

It could not go far in the direction it had chosen, however, for in the cross-street through which it had to pass, the flash of four rifle shots revealed a group of soldiers. The spider turned round quickly to avoid the soldiers who were coming towards it. It reached the corner lighted by the street-lamp and tried to escape down the street that ran perpendicular to the first. But in a moment this street, too, glowed with the discharge of rifles, which revealed another picket of soldiers. The "spider" whirled round and galloped off in the opposite direction. This time it reached the corner at the same time as the first detachment of soldiers that had cut off its escape. There was a point-blank encounter. Two shots were fired from the spider. One soldier fell wounded, and another was trampled down by the horse, and the spider managed to escape again, though not so tempestuously as before. But another squad came running to meet it from the end of the street, firing as it came. Above the noise a voice rang out: "Shoot the horse!"

It was Hay. More shots were fired. Finally the buggy stopped, and from all quarters the soldiers ran forward to surround it.

"I surrender," came a voice from inside the buggy.

And when the soldiers were near, they saw a man with a smoking pistol still in one hand, and the lines in the other, who offered them no resistance.

The prisoner was brought up to the light—where the body of his latest victim still lay—and some of the soldiers recognized him immediately. He was an officer who was notorious for his bad conduct and disreputable escapades, though nobody suspected that these included the horrible sport of shooting down defenceless and harmless people at night.

Chapter X

A Revolutionary's Journey

WHEN the day came that I was to leave Culiacán, my friends came for me about ten in the morning, and the group of them accompanied me to the
station.

The train was already in when we got there. It
was a typically revolutionary conveyance, dusty, out-
landish, made up of coaches and box cars of the
most varied kinds and in a state of very evident
decay, which gave it much of its picturesqueness.

My farewells at the station were prolonged, for,
as always, the train proved true to its nature and
took over an hour to start moving. Finally the
whistle blew and I jumped on to the steps of one
of the cars. The movement of the train was so slow
that for several minutes my friends could continue
our conversation, walking along beside the train at
its own pace. The uniformed group they made,
topped with their light hats, moved aloof and compact through the swarming crowd gathered along

the track. Finally the train accelerated its pace; the tall figures of Alessio and Robinson and the others who surrounded them were slowly left behind. The station buildings grew more squat; the panorama of Culiacán began to revolve round its own centre and to diminish and shrink away as though irresistible ropes were pulling at it from the background of the horizon. A rising in the land came between us and the town, then a descending curve made the earth rise towards the sky like the surface of the ocean when the boat rolls, and finally that landscape faded into another, became another.

The crowd of passengers was so great that it took me some time to find the boy who was travelling with me in the role of orderly. I came upon him barricaded behind the bundle of his belongings and my suit-cases and ready to hold with military valour the two seats he had taken by assault. As I approached, he was defending himself skilfully against the attack of two officers who were determined to secure possession of those two valuable places—valuable because the trip might as easily last twenty days as two. His adversaries were a captain and a very resolute major. But my orderly, who was both brave and resourceful, made use of the insignia of their rank, with which they sought to impress him, to strengthen his own position. To their offensive of three bars and a star he answered with a defensive, which, though false, was irresistible: three stars and an eagle. To keep a good seat in the train he had conferred on me the rank of his liking: he talked of nothing but the privileges of his "colonel" and at every possible juncture introduced the name of General Iturbe. My arrival calmed down the aggressiveness of the officers, who accepted me as their superior in rank, and we displayed the utmost courtesy towards one another, they saluting me as colonel, and I inviting them to share as best they could the space which, thanks to the warlike attributes of my orderly, they looked upon as mine.

In spite of the dispute it had occasioned, the space in question was far from being the last word in comfort. One of the window-panes was out; the curtain, which was torn down the middle, hung dejectedly by one corner from a roller without springs; and the seat itself, with its back torn all the way across and its cushions destroyed to the very bottom, invited one to assume a standing rather than a sitting posture. But we had only to let our glances travel over the rest of the car to make our places seem delightful, for if two or three window-panes, an occasional curtain, and—to judge by the satisfied expression of their occupants—several seats were intact, everything else was enough to frighten

>>>>>>>>>>>>>>>>>>>>>><<<<<<<<<<<<<<<<<<<<

one. In the majority of places, not the glass, but the window itself was missing; in many the tear in the curtain was a prolongation of the tear in the roof; and in many not a trace of a seat remained.

This state of things was eloquently reflected in the passengers. To the destruction—or great deterioration—of the material instruments and mechanisms had followed a corresponding descent and deterioration in the spiritual make-up of those who still employed the damaged instruments. At every point life on the train showed clearly a return to the primitive. The structured complexities of civilization were only partially effective. The distinction between freight and passenger cars had disappeared; coaches and box cars were used interchangeably for the same purposes. As a result the difference between people and bundles had disappeared; in certain places men, women, and children were piled up like bundles; in other places suit-cases and trunks were riding in the seats. But, even more, all the distinctions that link one's ideas of bodily decorum to such things as chairs, tables, and beds were gone. The passengers seemed nowhere so much at ease as in the freight cars, where they stretched out or sat up on the floor as they pleased. And there, as in the aisles and on the platforms of the coaches, a new pleasure, long forgotten, was rediscovered: that of eating on the floor, amidst all the dirt and rubbish.

At first a few passengers, not infected as yet by

the rising tide of barbarism, attempted to stem the
disorderliness a little; but they soon desisted. The
downward tendency was like a snowslide; only vio-
lent measures could have held it back.

About the middle of the afternoon the train's
stops became more and more frequent, and the movement of the train—when it did move—went from
slow to imperceptible. These inexplicable stops were
maddening. The passengers would swarm out of
the cars and spread out in the fields on both sides
of the road. The more impatient or the more inquisitive would go over to the engine to inspect it
or to talk with the engineer or fireman, and then
come back to inform us as to the result of their
investigations. The train did not run because the
engine could not get up steam, and the engine could
not get up steam because the water ran out of the
boiler into the fire. The struggle, therefore, between
steam and distance had been changed into a struggle
between fire and water. And meanwhile we remained
motionless.

There were moments in which the fire gained
ground over the water. On such occasions the whistle
would blow and the train would begin to jerk forward with the feeble, discouraged impulse of its
worn-out machinery. But its motion was so slow
that the passengers did not even bother getting
back into the train. They either walked along beside

>>>>>>>>>>>>>>>>>>>>>>>>><<<<<<<<<<<<<<<<<<<<<<<<

it or remained seated on the embankment, with the fatalistic assurance that the train would soon stop again.

It became evident that at this pace it would take us four or five days to reach San Blas, the only place where the engine could be repaired. This seemed too much, so the train crew and the passengers held a conference. "If we had some wood to mix with the coal," said the fireman, "we might get somewhere, for mixing the two together you get a hotter fire." To which the passengers replied that if there was no wood on hand, we would supply it. And no sooner said than done. An army of destruction scattered over the fields and set to work. It gathered up dry branches, boards, fence-posts, and the cross-supports of telegraph-poles and in less than half an hour had piled up in the coal-car several tons of firewood, with the aid of which the trip was accelerated somewhat.

The supply of wood was replenished several times that afternoon and that evening; the same operation was repeated the next morning and afternoon, and, thanks to this, the second evening we were rewarded by the sight of San Blas and a round-house. Soon afterwards I reached Nogales safely and went on to New York, where I had some affairs to attend to. Upon my return to Nogales, I asked permission to serve with Obregón, but Carranza arbitrarily ordered me to Ciudad Juárez, where at that time I had no wish to go.

Chapter XI

Pancho Villa's Escape

MY first weeks in Ciudad Juárez were a sort of baptism by immersion in the world that revolved round General Villa. Besides the General himself, I came to know his brother Hipólito, Carlitos Jáuregui (the youngest of his partisans, and the one in whom he reposed his greatest confidence). Juan N. Medina (until shortly before, his chief of staff). Lázaro de la Garza (his financial agent), and many other of his immediate subordinates and satellites. All of them—each in his separate way—drew me nearer and nearer to the Chief of the Division of the North and enveloped me in that atmosphere which his mere presence created.

One night when Carlitos Jáuregui and I were waiting for Villa in Juárez, he told me how he had come to be associated with him. For greater comfort we had climbed up on a pile of boxes and bundles near the tracks in the lower level of the station. It was a soft, warm night in May. Jáuregui had been leaning against the boxes and had slid down until he was stretched out, face upward towards the sky.

He kept his eyes fixed on the stars as he talked. I was leaning against some bales, and I listened without interrupting him, at the same time that I amused myself watching the orbits described by the little red lights that moved in the pitch-blackness of the night on the platform across the way. They were the cigarettes of the soldiers and officers waiting for the military train.

"When Villa was a prisoner in Santiago Tlaltelolco," began Jáuregui, "I was working as clerk in one of the military courts. I have never been in such straits as I was then. I was making about forty or fifty pesos a month, and the life I lived on this was so miserable that my despair must have shown in my face, in strange contrast to my youth. In order to make a little more I used to go to the court-house in the afternoons, after office hours, and do extra copying for the lawyers or the prisoners. My desk was near the iron grating that shut off the prisoners. So from where I sat I could see a part of the prison corridor, which was generally deserted at this time of day.

"One afternoon, as I happened to look up absentmindedly from my desk towards the corridor, I saw Villa standing behind the grating. He had come up so quietly that I had not heard his steps. As usual, he had on his hat, and his sarape around his shoulders.

" 'Good afternoon, friend,' he said, pleasantly and affectionately. He didn't look quite the same as the mornings he had appeared before the judge or had been called to testify. He seemed less suspicious and crafty, and franker. What was the same in him was the touch of tenderness of his eyes when he looked at me. This look, which I shall never forget, I noticed from the first time the judge had ordered me to enter the declarations Villa was making in the record. 'I wonder if you'll do me the favour of copying a letter for me?'

"We talked for quite a while; he gave me the paper he wanted me to copy, and agreed to come for it the next day at the same time.

"The next day, after I gave him his letter, he looked me in the eye for a long time, accentuating still more the affectionate note of his smile and his expression.

" 'Say, buddy, what's the matter that you look so sad?'

" 'Nothing, General'—I don't know why I called Villa 'General' from the first time I saw him—'I'm always like this.'

" 'Well, if you're always like that, it means that there's always something the matter. Come on, tell me about it. Maybe I can help you out.'

"His tone, half rough, half affectionate and paternal, won me over. Carried away by the friendship he showed me, I described my miserable, half-starved existence to him. He listened to me with the closest attention, and when I had finished, he put his hand in his trousers-pocket.

" 'Friend,' he said, 'it's not right for you to go on suffering this way. I'm going to see to it that things change. As a start I want you to take this.'

"And he held out, through the bars of the grating, a bill that was folded so many times that it looked like a little note-book.

"At first I emphatically refused this money which I had not asked for. But Villa soon convinced me with the following argument:

" 'Take it, my boy. Take it and don't be foolish. I can do you a favour today. Who knows whether tomorrow things won't be the other way round. And you may be sure that if there's something you can do for me some day, I won't wait for you to offer it to me. I'll ask you for it myself.'

"That night, out in the street, I almost fainted under the first street-light. For, as I unfolded the bill he had given me, I could scarcely believe my eyes. It was a hundred-peso bill. I had never had one in my hands before. Against the red background there was a beautiful Mexican eagle with wide, outspread wings.

"The next day, though I didn't have anything to do there, I went to the court-house after office hours.

I felt a secret urge to talk with Villa, to express my gratitude and show him that I was happy. But, for reasons that I understood when I came to know him better, he did not appear at the grating that day. I was greatly put out by this, for I had nobody with whom I could share my feelings. Villa had warned me not to say a word, even at home, about the money, and I was determined to keep my promise. Finally we saw each other two days afterwards.

" 'How are things going, friend?' he asked me as soon as he came up. 'I think you look better than you did.'

" 'I'm fine, General, and I'm certainly very grateful to you for the favour you insisted on doing me.'

"And we talked on like that. This time our conversation was longer and livelier. I certainly felt a deep gratitude to that rough man who had been so good to me, and I tried to make him feel my appreciation. When we said good-bye, he stretched out his arms through the bars to shake hands with me. I took his hand without suspecting anything, but as I noticed, when our fingers came together, that Villa was trying to slip something into mine, I tried to pull my hand back. But he clasped it still tighter and said:

" 'This here is for you, too. When a fellow has been poor for a long time, a little money doesn't go very far. I'll bet you haven't got a cent left from the other day.'

" 'Yes, I have, General. I've got nearly all of it.'

" 'Well, if you have, you haven't done right. What you've been needing for a long time is some fun and a good time, and a good time runs into money, even when you don't have to buy it. Besides, isn't it queer! I was just thinking about a favour I was going to ask you for. A much bigger favour than these little ones I have been doing for you, and I'm sure you won't refuse me.'

" 'What favour, General?' I asked him; and I was willing to lay down life for that man, the first kind-hearted person I had ever met.

" 'I can't tell you today, my boy. Have a good time today and enjoy yourself. Tomorrow will be my turn.'

"I did not amuse myself that night. On the contrary, I suffered more than I ever had before. I couldn't close my eyes for a minute. Could I do what Villa wanted of me? The thought that he might ask something wrong never entered my mind. The only thing that worried me was the thought that he might ask something beyond my strength and my ability. I was afraid I couldn't return the favour, and I felt very badly about it.

"Our next interview was brief. Villa began by saying, in a very persuasive tone, that if I was brave, I could do him a great favour, but that if I was a coward, it was better not to talk about the matter.

" 'I'm not afraid of anything, General,' I hastened to assure him.

" 'Not even of doing something bad, son?'

" 'Well . . .' I stammered.

" 'Of course you are, because you are a good lad. I only asked to see what you would say, for you may be sure I am not going to ask anything wrong of you.'

" 'I know that you are a good man, General.'

" 'Now that's just what I was going to talk to you about. You have been writing up the evidence in my trial; do you think it's right for the government to keep me a prisoner?'

" 'No, General, I don't.'

" 'Don't you think it's all a frame-up?'

" 'Yes, I do, General.'

" 'Then don't you think I ought to take things in my own hands, since the judges won't release me?"

" 'Yes, I do.'

" 'And don't you think it would be right for you to help me out of this hole?'

" 'Yes.'

" 'Well, sir, then you're going to help me. But remember: that's if you are brave. If you're afraid, it's no use.'

" 'I'm not afraid, General. I'll do whatever you tell me.'

"Villa's doubts about my bravery put me on my

mettle, and my only thought was to attempt whatever he suggested, no matter what it might be.

" 'That's the kind of talk I like to hear,' he went on. 'We're all set. Now, first, take this package and lock it away in your desk where nobody can see it.'

"As he said this, he took from under his sarape a little package, which he held out through the grating. I took it and put it in the drawer of my desk, under some papers. Villa went on:

" 'In this package there is an iron saw, a handle, and a lump of black wax. Tomorrow when you come here, you fix up the saw—' as he said this he lowered his voice, and his tone became more impressive and confidential—'then you lock the door and begin to saw the bars of the grating. There's a little bottle of oil in the package to put on the saw so it won't get hot or squeak. Cut here first—' he pointed out one of the cross-bars—'and then here. After you have them sawed through, fasten the ends together with the wax, so nobody can tell they've been cut. Then day after tomorrow cut these other two bars here. Pay attention, buddy: here and here. When you finish, fasten them together with wax, like these others. Then in two more afternoons you saw these four places; but not quite all the way through, so the bars won't fall down. The last afternoon I'll come to see you, and if you've finished sawing the eight bars, I'll tell you what else you have to do. Well,

so long! I'm going because I've been here talking
a good while now. Oh, yes, be sure to gather up the
filings from the floor. What you can't scrape up
with your fingers, gather up with the wax. And now
we'll find out if you really don't know what fear
is.'

"As Villa was giving me these instructions, I
could feel cold chills going over me, and I felt numb,
though whether from fear or emotion I couldn't
tell. The words of the *guerrillero,* which had such
an effect on me that I have never forgotten them,
whirled about in my mind grotesquely mixed with
the figures of the eagle with its wide outspread wings
that I had seen that first time on the hundred-peso
bill by the street-light.

"As he had said, Villa did not come back to see
me again for four days. During this time I followed
his instructions to the letter. My only trouble was
that at first the saw-teeth often broke. When Villa
sauntered up to the grating at dusk the fourth day,
he asked me in his usual easy manner:

" 'Well, partner, how is everything going?'

" 'O. K., General. I've done everything as you told
me,' I answered, deeply moved and lowering my voice
till he could hardly hear me.

" 'That's fine,' he said passing his fingers as though
idly over the places where the bars were cut. Then
he went on: 'Tomorrow I'll come round at the usual
time. You saw through the places where the bars

are still fast. But don't cut them all the way through. And only cut three. Leave the other one the way it is now, so the grating will stay in place. Then I'll come.'

"The next day Villa came a little while after I had finished sawing three of the spindles that were still holding the bars in place. He asked me if I had finished, and I told him I had. Then with one hand he pulled towards him the square of the grating that had been cut, which yielded without much effort, as it was barely held in place at one corner. Villa quickly handed me through the opening a bundle of clothing which he carried in his other hand, hidden under his sarape. Then he glanced up and down the corridor, jumped lightly through the hole, pushed the piece of grating down into its place again, and in a corner of the office quickly changed his clothes. He put on a different hat, pulling it down low. In place of the sarape he put on a cape and wrapped it around him, so as to conceal the lower part of his face.

"When he had finished, he said: 'Now let's get away from here quick, buddy. You walk ahead and I'll follow you. Don't be afraid of anything, and no matter what happens, don't stop.'

"I was so frightened that I don't know how I managed to put one foot before the other. Fortunately the corridors and the stairs were almost dark. As we were coming out into the hall that led to the door, I saw, a few steps away, a guard on duty who was coming towards us. My heart almost stopped beating, and, not knowing what to do, I stood still. But Villa walked right ahead; he passed me at the same time as the official and greeted him with perfect ease:

" 'Good afternoon, chief,' he said in a hoarse, steady voice.

"When I saw that the guard walked ahead and paid no attention to us, I pulled myself together and followed a little behind Villa.

" 'Some friend!' said Villa as soon as we could talk. 'Didn't I tell you not to stop and not to be afraid no matter what happened?'

"We worked our way through the side-streets until we came to the centre of the city, and as we made our way there, Villa convinced me that I ought to escape with him.

" 'You don't want anything to happen to you, do you?' he asked.

" 'Well, naturally, General.'

" 'Then you come with me. Otherwise tomorrow you'll be in jail. With me there's no danger of them catching you. Don't worry about your mother and your brothers and sisters. We'll let them know in time, and we'll send them anything they need.'

"In the market-place we took an automobile. Villa told the chauffeur to take us to Tacubaya. There we got out and went up to a house as though we were going in. Then we came back to the car.

" 'The fellow we are looking for left for Toluca this morning. It's very important for us to see him. Can you drive us there? We'll pay you well, provided you don't ask too much.'

"The chauffeur agreed to make the trip, after Villa had driven a hard bargain about the price. And when we got to Toluca, Villa said to him as he paid him:

" 'Here's your money. But I'm going to give you ten pesos besides, so that you will come back for us day after tomorrow. We'll wait for you right here. If you don't come, it will be your loss, my boy. We'll pay you better on the trip home than we did coming here.'

" 'But are we going back to Mexico City, General?' I asked Villa as soon as we were alone.

" 'No, buddy. We're going to take the train now to Manzanillo. There we'll sail for Mazatlán, and from there we'll go by train to the United States. I gave that money to the chauffeur, telling him to come back, so that if the police get hold of him and question him, they won't suspect that it was us in his car. That's why I bargained with him about the price.' "

Some months afterwards, when the Constitution-alist revolution broke out, Villa said to Carlitos

Jáuregui: "When I take Juárez City, buddy, I'm going to make you a present of the lottery houses in return for what you did for me." And the day after the brilliant manœuvres that gave the Division of the North the frontier city to have and to hold, Jáuregui received the monopoly of the famous *quinos*. These were the most innocent of the gambling-establishments in Juárez City. The least innocent were the poker games, the roulette-wheels, and the crap games. This prerogative Villa had given to his brother Hipólito.

Chapter XII

The Carnival of the Bullets

MY interest in Villa and his activities often made me ask myself, while I was in Juárez City, what exploits would best paint the Division of the North: those supposed to be strictly historical or those which were rated as legendary; those which were related exactly as they had been seen, or those in which a touch of poetic fancy brought out their essence more clearly. These second always seemed to me truer, more worthy of being considered history.

For instance, where could one find a better painting of Rodolfo Fierro—and Fierro and Villa's movement were two facing mirrors that reflected each other endlessly—than in the account of how he carried out the terrible orders of his chief after one of the battles, revealing an imagination as cruel as it was fertile in death devices. This vision of him left in the soul the sensation of a reality so overwhelming that the memory of it lives forever.

That battle, which was successful in every way, had left not less than five hundred prisoners in Villa's hands. Villa ordered them to be divided into two groups: the Orozco volunteers, whom he called "Reds," in one, and the Federals in the other. And as he felt himself strong enough to take extreme measures, he decided to make an example of the prisoners in the first group and to act more generously with the second. The "Reds" were to be executed before dark; the Federals were to be given their choice of joining the revolutionary troops or returning home, after promising not to take up arms again against the Constitutionalist cause.

Fierro, as might have been expected, was put in charge of the execution, and he displayed in it that efficiency which was already winning him great favour with Villa, his "chief," as he called him.

It was growing late in the afternoon. The revolutionary forces, off duty, were slowly gathering in the little village that had been the objective of their offensive. The cold, penetrating wind of the Chihuahuan plains began to blow up, and the groups of cavalry and infantry sought protection against the groups of buildings. But Fierro—whom nothing and nobody ever held back—was not to be put out by a cool breeze that at most meant frost that night. He cantered along on his horse, whose dark coat was still covered with the dust of battle. The wind was blowing in his face, but he neither buried his chin in his

breast nor raised the folds of his blanket around his
face. He carried his head high, his chest thrown
out, his feet firm in the stirrups, and his legs grace-
fully flexed under the campaign equipment that hung
from the saddle-straps. The barren plain and an
occasional soldier that passed at a distance were his
only spectators. But he, perhaps without even thinking about it, reined his horse to make him show his
gaits as though he were on parade. Fierro was happy;
the satisfaction of victory filled his being; and to him
victory was complete only when it meant the utter
rout of the enemy; and in this frame of mind even
the buffeting of the wind, and riding after fifteen
hours in the saddle, were agreeable. The rays of
the pale setting sun seemed to caress him as they
fell.

He reached the stable-yard where the condemned
Red prisoners were shut up like a herd of cattle, and
he reined in a moment to look at them over the fence-
rails. They were well-built men of the type of Chihuahua, tall, compact, with strong necks and well
set-up shoulders on vigorous, flexible backs. As Fierro
looked over the little captive army and sized up its
military value and prowess, a strange pulsation ran
through him, a twitching that went from his heart
or from his forehead out to the index-finger of his
right hand. Involuntarily the palm of this hand
reached out to the butt of his pistol.

"Here's a battle for you," he thought.

The cavalrymen, bored with their task of guarding the prisoners, paid no attention to him. The only thing that mattered to them was the annoyance of mounting this tiresome guard, all the worse after the excitement of the battle. They had to have their rifles ready on their knees, and when an occasional soldier left the group, they aimed at him with an air that left no room for doubt as to their intentions, and, if necessary, fired. A wave would run over the formless surface of the mass of the prisoners, who huddled together to avoid the shot. The bullet either went wide or shot one of them down.

Fierro rode up to the gate of the stable-yard. He called to a soldier, who let down the bars, and went in. Without taking off his sarape he dismounted. His legs were numb with cold and weariness, and he stretched them. He settled his two pistols in their holsters. Next he began to look slowly over the pens, observing their lay-out and how they were divided up. He took several steps over to one of the fences, where he tied his horse to a fence board. He slipped something out of one of the pockets of his saddle into his coat-pocket and crossed the yard, at a short distance from the prisoners.

There were three pens that opened into one another, with gates and a narrow passage-way between. From the one where the prisoners were kept, Fierro went into the middle enclosure, slipping through the bars of the gate. He went straight over

>>>>>>>>>>>>>>>>>>>>>>><<<<<<<<<<<<<<<<<<<<

to the next one. There he stopped. His tall, handsome
figure seemed to give off a strange radiance, something superior, awe-inspiring, and yet not out of keeping with the desolation of the barn-yard. His sarape
had slipped down until it barely hung from his
shoulders; the tassels of the corners dragged on the
ground. His grey, broad-brimmed hat turned rose-
coloured where the slanting rays of the setting sun
fell on it. Through the fences the prisoners could see
him at a distance, his back turned towards them.
His legs formed a pair of herculean, glistening com-
passes: it was the gleam of his leather puttees in the
light of the afternoon.

About a hundred yards away, outside the pens,
was the officer of the troop in charge of the prisoners.
Fierro made signs to him to come closer, and the
officer rode over to the fence beside Fierro. The two
began to talk. In the course of the conversation Fierro pointed out different spots in the enclosure in
which he was standing and in the one next to it. Then
he described with gestures of his hand a series of
operations, which the officer repeated, as though to
understand them better. Fierro repeated two or three
times what seemed to be a very important operation,
and the officer, now sure about his orders, galloped
off towards the prisoners.

Fierro turned back towards the centre of the
stable-yard, studying once more the lay-out of the
fence, and the other details. That pen was the largest

of the three, and the first in order, the nearest to the
town. On two sides gates opened into the fields; the
bars of these, though more worn-out than those of
the farther pens, were of better wood. In the other
side there was a gate that opened into the adjoining
pen, and on the far side the fence was not of boards,
but was an adobe wall, not less than six feet high. The
wall was about a hundred and thirty feet long, and
about forty feet of it formed the back of a shed or
stalls, the roof of which sloped down from the wall
and rested on the one side on the end posts of the
lateral fence, which had been left longer, and on the
other on a wall, also of adobes, which came out perpendicular from the wall and extended some twenty-
five feet into the barn-yard. In this way, between the
shed and the fence of the adjoining lot, there was a
space closed on two sides by solid walls. In that
corner the wind that afternoon was piling up rubbish
and clanging an iron bucket against the well-head
with an arbitrary rhythm. From the well-head there
rose up two rough forked posts, crossed by a third,
from which a pulley and chain hung, which also
rattled in the wind. On the tip-top of one of the forks
sat a large whitish bird, hardly distinguishable from
the twisted points of the dry pole.

Fierro was standing about fifty steps from the well.
He rested his eye for a moment on the motionless
bird, and as though its presence fitted in perfectly with
his thoughts, without a change of attitude or expres-

sion, he slowly pulled out his pistol. The long, polished barrel of the gun turned into a glowing finger in the light of the sun. Slowly it rose until it pointed in the direction of the bird. A shot rang out—dry and diminutive in the immensity of the afternoon—and the bird dropped to the ground. Fierro returned his pistol to its holster.

At that moment a soldier jumped over the fence into the yard. It was Fierro's orderly. It had been such a high jump that it took him several instants to get to his feet. When he did, he walked over to where his master was standing.

Without turning his head Fierro answered:

"What about them? If they don't come soon, we aren't going to have time."

"I think they're coming."

"Then you hurry up and get over there. Let's see, what pistol have you got?"

"The one you gave me, chief. The Smith and Wesson."

"Hand it over here and take these boxes of bullets. How many bullets have you got?"

"I gathered up about fifteen dozen today, chief. Some of the others found lots of them, but I didn't."

"Fifteen dozen? I told you the other day that if you kept on selling ammunition to buy booze, I'd put a bullet through you."

"No, chief."

">>>>>>>>>>>>>>>>>>>><<<<<<<<<<<<<<<<<<<<<"

"What do you mean: 'No, chief'?"

"I do get drunk, chief, but I don't sell the ammunition."

"Well, you watch out, for you know me. And now you move lively so this stunt will be a success. I fire and you load the pistols. And mind what I tell you: if on your account a single one of the Reds gets away, I'll put you to sleep with them."

"Oh, chief!"

"You heard what I said."

The orderly spread his blanket out on the ground and emptied on to it the boxes of cartridges that Fierro had just given him. Then he began to take out one by one the bullets in his cartridge-belt. He was in such a hurry that it took him longer than it should have. He was so nervous that his fingers seemed all thumbs.

"What a chief!" he kept thinking to himself.

In the mean time behind the fence of the adjoining barn-lot soldiers of the guard began to appear. They were on horseback, and their shoulders showed above the top fence-rail. There were many others along the two other fences.

Fierro and his orderly were the only ones inside the barn-yard; Fierro stood with a pistol in his hand, and his sarape fallen at his feet. His orderly squatted beside him lining up the bullets in rows on his blanket.

The commander of the troop rode up through the gate that opened into the next lot, and said:

"I've got the first ten ready. Shall I let them out for you?"

"Yes," answered Fierro, "but first explain things to them. As soon as they come through the gate, I'll begin to shoot. Those that reach the wall and get over it are free. If any of them doesn't want to come through, you put a bullet into him."

The officer went back the same way, and Fierro, pistol in hand, stood attentive, his eyes riveted on the narrow space through which the soldiers had to come out. He stood close enough to the dividing fence so that, as he fired, the bullets would not hit the Reds that were still on the other side. He wanted to keep his promise faithfully. But he was not so close that the prisoners could not see, the minute they came through the gate, the pistol that was levelled at them twenty paces off. Behind Fierro the setting sun turned the sky into a fiery ball. The wind kept blowing.

In the barn-yard where the prisoners were herded, the voices grew louder, but the howling of the wind made the shouts sound like herders rounding up cattle. It was a hard task to make the three hundred condemned men pass from the last to the middle lot. At the thought of the torture that waited for them, the whole group writhed with the convulsions of a person in the grip of hysteria. The soldiers of the guard shouted, and every minute the reports of the rifles seemed to emphasize the screams as with a whip-crack.

Out of the first prisoners that reached the middle courtyard a group of soldiers separated ten. There were at least twenty-five soldiers. They spurred their horses on to the prisoners to make them move; they rested the muzzles of their rifles against their bodies.

"Traitors! Dirty bastards! Let's see you run and jump. Get a move on, you traitor!"

And in this way they made them advance to the gate where Fierro and his orderly were waiting. Here the resistance of the Reds grew stronger; but the horses' hoofs and the gun-barrels persuaded them to choose the other danger, the danger of Fierro, which was not an inch away, but twenty paces.

As soon as they appeared within his range of vision, Fierro greeted them with a strange phrase, at once cruel and affectionate, half ironical and half encouraging.

"Come on, boys; I'm only going to shoot, and I'm a bad shot."

The prisoners jumped like goats. The first one tried to throw himself on Fierro, but he had not made three bounds before he fell, riddled by bullets from the soldiers stationed along the fence. The others ran as fast as they could towards the wall—a mad race that must have seemed to them like a dream. One tried to take refuge behind the well-head: he

was the target for Fierro's first bullet. The others
fell as they ran, one by one; in less than ten seconds
Fierro had fired eight times, and the last of the group
dropped just as his fingers were touching the adobes
that by the strange whim of the moment separated
the zone of life from the zone of death. Some of the
bodies showed signs of life; the soldiers finished them
off from their horses.

And then came another group of ten, and then
another, and another, and another. The three pistols
of Fierro—his two and that of his orderly—alter-
nated with precise rhythm in the homicidal hand.
There were six shots from each one, six shots fired
without stopping to aim and without pause, and then
the gun dropped on to the orderly's blanket, where he
removed the exploded caps, and reloaded it. Then,
without changing his position, he held out the pistol
to Fierro, who took it as he let the other fall.
Through the orderly's fingers passed the bullets that
seconds later would leave the prisoners stretched
lifeless, but he did not raise his eyes to see those that
fell. His whole soul seemed concentrated on the pistol
in his hand, and on the bullets, with their silver and
burnished reflections, spread out on the ground before him. Just two sensations filled his whole being:
the cold weight of the bullets that he was putting
into the openings of the barrel, and the warm smooth-
ness of the gun. Over his head one after another

rang out the shots of his "chief," entertaining himself with his sharpshooting.

The panic-stricken flight of the prisoners towards the wall of salvation—a fugue of death in which the two themes of the passion to kill and the infinite desire to live were blended—lasted almost two hours.

Not for one minute did Fierro lose his precision of aim or his poise. He was firing at moving human targets, targets that jumped and slipped in pools of blood and amidst corpses stretched out in unbelievable positions, but he fired without other emotion than that of hitting or missing. He calculated the deflection caused by the wind, and corrected it with each shot.

Some of the prisoners, crazed by terror, fell to their knees as they came through the gate. There the bullet laid them low. Others danced about grotesquely behind the shelter of the well-head until the bullet cured them of their frenzy or they dropped wounded into the well. But nearly all rushed towards the adobe wall and tried to climb it over the warm, damp, steaming heaps of piled-up bodies. Some managed to dig their nails into the earth coping, but their hands, so avid of life, soon fell lifeless.

There came a moment in which the mass execution became a noisy tumult, punctuated by the dry snap of the pistol-shots, muted by the voice of the wind. On one side of the fence the shouts of those who fled from death only to die; on the other, those who resisted the pressure of the horsemen and tried to break through the wall that pushed them on towards that terrible gate. And to the shouts of one group and the other were added the voices of the soldiers stationed along the fences. The noise of the shooting, the marksmanship of Fierro, and the cries and frantic gestures of the condemned men had worked them up to a pitch of great excitment. The somersaults of the bodies as they fell in the death-agony elicited loud exclamations of amusement from them, and they shouted, gesticulated, and gave peals of laughter as they fired into the mounds of bodies in which they saw the slightest evidence of life.

In the last squad of victims there were twelve instead of ten. The twelve piled out of the death pen, falling over one another, each trying to protect himself with the others, in his anxiety to win in the horrible race. To go forward they had to jump over the piled-up corpses, but not for this reason did the bullet err in its aim. With sinister precision it hit them one by one and left them on the way to the wall, arms and legs outstretched, embracing the mass of their motionless companions. But one of them, the only one left alive, managed to reach the coping and swing himself over. The firing stopped and the troop of soldiers crowded into the corner of the adjoining barn-lot to see the fugitive.

>>>>>>>>>>>>>>>>>>>>>><<<<<<<<<<<<<<<<<<<<<<

It was beginning to get dark. It took the soldiers a little while to focus their vision in the twilight. At first they could see nothing. Finally, far off, in the vastness of the darkling plain they managed to make out a moving spot. As it ran, the body bent so far over that it almost seemed to crawl along on the ground.

A soldier took aim. "It's hard to see," he said as he fired.

The report died away in the evening wind. The moving spot fled on.

Fierro had not moved from his place. His arm was exhausted, and he let it hang limp against his side for a long time. Then he became aware of a pain in his forefinger and raised his hand to his face; he could see that the finger was somewhat swollen. He rubbed it gently between the fingers and the palm of his hand and for a good space of time kept up this gentle massage. Finally he stooped over and picked up his sarape, which he had taken off at the beginning of the executions. He threw it over his shoulders and walked over to the shelter of the stalls. But after a few steps he turned to his orderly:

"When you're finished, bring up the horses."

And he went on his way.

The orderly was gathering up the exploded caps. In the next pen the soldiers of the guard had dis-

>>>>>>>>>>>>>>>>>>>>><<<<<<<<<<<<<<<<<<<<<

mounted and were talking or singing softly. The
orderly heard them in silence and without raising his
head. Finally he got slowly to his feet. He gathered
up the blanket by the four corners and threw it over
his shoulder. The empty caps rattled in it with a dull
tintinnabulation.

It was dark. A few stars glimmered, and on the
other side of the fence the cigarettes shone red. The
orderly walked heavily and slowly and, half feeling
his way, went to the last of the pens and in a little
while returned leading his own and his master's
horses by the bridle; across one of his shoulders
swung the haversack.

He made his way over to the stalls. Fierro was
sitting on a rock, smoking. The wind whistled through
the cracks in the boards.

"Unsaddle the horse and make up my bed,"
ordered Fierro. "I'm so tired I can't stand up."

"Here in this pen, chief? Here . . . ?"

"Sure. Why not?"

The orderly did as he was ordered. He unsaddled
the horse and spread the blankets on the straw,
making a kind of pillow out of the haversack and the
saddle. Fierro stretched out and in a few minutes was
asleep.

The orderly lighted his lantern and bedded the
horses for the night. Then he blew out the light,
wrapped himself in his blanket, and lay down at the
feet of his master. But in a minute he was up again

and knelt down and crossed himself. Then he stretched out on the straw again.

Six or seven hours went by. The wind had died down. The silence of the night was bathed in moonlight. Occasionally a horse snuffled. The radiance of the moon gleamed on the dented surface of the bucket that hung by the well and made clear shadows of all the objects in the yard except the mounds of corpses. These rose up, enormous in the stillness of the night, like fantastic hills, strange and confused in outline.

The blue silver of the night descended on the corpses in rays of purest light. But little by little that light turned into a voice, a voice that had the irreality of the night. It grew distinct; it was a voice that was barely audible, faint and tortured, but clear like the shadows cast by the moon. From the centre of one of the mounds of corpses the voice seemed to whisper:

"Oh! Oh!"

The heaped-up bodies, stiff and cold for hours, lay motionless in the barn-yard. The moonlight sank into them as into an inert mass. But the voice sounded again:

"Oh . . . Oh . . . Oh . . ."

And this last groan reached to the spot where Fierro's orderly lay sleeping and brought him out of sleep to the consciousness of hearing. The first thing that came to his mind was the memory of the execution of the three hundred prisoners; the mere thought of it kept him motionless in the straw, his eyes half open and his whole soul fixed on the lamentation of that voice:

"Oh . . . please . . ."

Fierro tossed on his bed.

"Please . . . water . . ."

Fierro awoke and listened attentively.

"Please . . . water . . ."

Fierro stretched out his foot until he touched his orderly.

"Hey, you. Don't you hear? One of those dead men is asking for water."

"Yes, chief."

"You get up and put a bullet through the snivelling son of a bitch. Let's see if he'll let me get some sleep then."

"A bullet through who, chief?"

"The one that's asking for water, you fool. Don't you understand?"

"Water, please," the voice kept on.

The orderly took his pistol from under the saddle and started out of the shed in search of the voice. He shivered with fear and cold. He felt sick to his soul.

He looked round in the light of the moon. Every body he touched was stiff. He hesitated without knowing what to do. Finally he fired in the direction from which the voice came. The voice kept on. The orderly fired again. The voice died away.

The moon floated through the limitless space of its blue light. Under the shelter of the shed Fierro slept.

Chapter XIII

Villa or Carranza?

THE long months of my stay in Chihuahua brought about my gradual—gradual and voluntary—separation from the faction that had formed round Carranza and his unconditional adherents. The other faction—a rebellion within a rebellion—restless and impatient of restraint, represented an aspect of the revolution with which I felt more in sympathy. This second group had already drawn together men like Maytorena, Cabral, Angeles, Escudero, Díaz Lombardo, Vasconcelos, Puente, Malváez—all those, in a word, who wanted to preserve the democratic and impersonal character of the revolution, so that in the course of two or three years it should not have become the mere instrument of another oligarchy, perhaps more ignorant and selfish than that of Porfirio Diaz. To be sure, I didn't see how we were going to realize our ideals; it seemed to me enormously difficult, improbable—as improbable for a small group, however heroic its determination to fight

to the last ditch against personal ambition and cor-
ruption, as it would have been easy if it had represented the unanimous undertaking of a well-directed,
unified revolution. But I had seen beyond evidence of
doubt in Sonora that under Carranza's leadership the
revolution was headed for the most unbridled and unrestrained absolutism, and this was enough to turn
me in any other direction in the hope of salvation.

The mere fact that all the group opposed to Carranza rallied round Villa as its military leader might
have been taken, if not as a presage of our eventual
defeat, as evidence of the internal conflict that
thwarted the revolution in its noblest objects; because it was impossible to think of Villa as the
standard-bearer of an elevated, reconstructive movement; and even as a mere brute force he had such
serious limitations that dealing with him was like
handling dynamite. But, in spite of this, the fact remained that the only military elements on which we
could count for the support of our ideas were those
commanded by him. The other important winner of
battles, Obregón—Angeles, without any troops of
his own, so to speak, had thrown in his lot with Villa
—was following the lead of the new absolutism. So,
for us, the future of the Constitutionalist movement
was bound up in the following question: would it be
possible to control Villa—Villa, who was too irresponsible and instinctive even to know how to be
ambitious? Would he put his force at the service of

>>>>>>>>>>>>>>>>>>>>>><<<<<<<<<<<<<<<<<<<<<<

principles that either did not exist for him or were incomprehensible to him?

This was the dilemma: either Villa would submit to the fundamental principles of the revolution, and, if so, he and the revolution would triumph; or Villa would follow nothing but his own blind impulses, and he and the revolution would go down to defeat. And it was round this dilemma that the tempest of the revolution was to revolve in the hour of triumph.

Chapter XIV

A Night in Coatzacoalcos

WHEN Victoriano Huerta's fall was merely a matter of a short time, Villa ordered Colonel Carlos Domínguez and me to be in Mexico City during the entrance of the Constitutionalist forces and to act as his representatives to the First Chief. The breaking-off of relations between Villa and Carranza gave the commission rather a perilous nature. But, notwithstanding, Domínguez and I accepted—as we had already before accepted other things even more dangerous—and we set out from El Paso, Texas, for the capital by way of Cayo Hueso and Havana.

Ten days after we reached Cuba, we sailed for Vera Cruz in the *Maria Cristina*. There were several ticklish points about that trip, and one of them was the danger that we might be caught when the boat stopped at Puerto Méjico, which was still in the hands of Huerta's troops. But as it did not seem prudent to wait longer, for fear we might not be in

>>>>>>>>>>>>>>>>>>>>><<<<<<<<<<<<<<<<<<<<<

the capital in time to carry out General Villa's orders, we decided to proceed on our way.

It was painful to break off our stay in Havana, so unexpected, so welcome, so agreeable had it been after the political agitations of the preceding months. Menocal, a brother of the President of Cuba, and Arturo Grande, an architect friend of Domínguez's, made of our stay in their lovely country an endless procession of pleasant hours. Even after we had left, in the ship, on the sea, I caressed the memory of those perfect days.

In spite of our fears nothing serious happened in Puerto Méjico, although we could not resist the temptation of going ashore on our native soil the night we landed.

To carry out this small adventure in patriotic enthusiasm—or sudden home-sickness—Domínguez decided that we ought to disguise ourselves. How? As Spanish sailors. This was not difficult, thanks to the help of two officers with whom we had struck up an acquaintance on board, and who lent us part of their outfit. I do not recall with what naval rank I invested myself as I got into a handsome uniform trimmed with anchors and gold braid, but I had been metamorphosed into a figure that seemed to me fantastic as I stepped on to Mexican territory.

It was late as we strolled down the wharf, affecting a sailor's roll in our walk, and made our way into the town. The streets were deserted and dark. The feeble animation that existed near the wharf died away, like a flame that gutters out, in the faint flickers of a few thin scattered groups of people that sat and chatted beside their door-steps.

Finally, in a little park we saw some booths that had managed to hold a few small clusters of men and women under the spell of their melancholy lights. We sauntered over towards them. There was a lottery stand, tastefully decorated with rows of pitchers, glasses, dishes, and other ornaments of pottery and glassware. There were two or three simple roulette-wheels, three tables for cards and dice, a stand where rings were tossed on boards scattered over with coins, and a miserable eating-place on wheels.

Domínguez and I stopped in front of the ring stand with the authentic curiosity of strangers. Ten or fifteen queer-looking fellows were throwing away their money, ballyhooed on by the proprietor of the stand and his wife. She seemed to be unusually clever at turning mere spectators into performers, because she was the one that extracted most of the copper coins from everyone's pocket. One of the players stood out among the rest. He was young and had on a yellow shirt, white trousers, black leggings, no coat, collar, or tie, and a pistol on his hip, and a belt full of cartridges. He was playing with a furious determination to win, but he was so clumsy that every time he tossed, the rings bounced off the red cloth where the coins were scattered as though they had been made of rubber.

The game, though extremely difficult, seemed at first glance very easy. Two minutes after we came up, Domínguez and I had a supply of rings in our hands. Domínguez was eager to win something and he made his throws very carefully; he tried to work out a technique, using first one method and then another. To me it seemed that it was next to impossible to throw the ring over a coin, and I threw just for the fun of it. And it happened by the merest chance that one of my shots fell over a ten-centavo piece. My skill caused such surprise among the bystanders that they stopped playing for a few seconds. The woman of the booth came over to me and, smiling, handed me the money I had won; and while all this was going on, the fellow in the yellow shirt kept watching first me and then Domínguez and then said something in a low voice to a friend who was standing near.

A few minutes later, playing in the same nonchalant fashion, I won again. But this time the ring fell over a twenty-centavo piece instead of a ten. It caused a sensation. The woman came over again to pay me, but this time she wasn't smiling, and she was clearly put out. And the fellow with the pistol, looking at me again, this time insolently, said to his friend in a voice loud enough for us to hear: "You might have known they would be *gachupines*. . . ." [1]

It wasn't hard to see what he meant. Partly because of the Spanish uniforms we were wearing and partly because we had won while the others lost, it was plain that we weren't very popular with the crowd. So we decided it would be better policy to move away from the ring stand, and we went over to a near-by dicing-table.

There was nobody near the place except the old woman in charge of it, who was half asleep beside the kerosene lamp.

"I'm very lucky at this," said Domínguez as he picked up the shaker and the cubes.

The old woman came to life when she saw us and became almost cheerful as Domínguez asked her: "How much a throw, señora . . . ?"

"Whatever you like, sir," she said, "but two reales is the limit."

Domínguez then gave himself over to losing. And he did it so conscientiously that the old lady began to cheer him on with loud cries, evidently intended to attract other clients to her booth:

"This time you're going to win. Just roll a seven, and the money's yours."

And her shouts attracted several of the players from the ring stand, among them the one in the yellow shirt, with the revolver.

[1] A disrespectful, insulting name applied to Spaniards in Mexico.

Domínguez went on playing and losing. The fellow in the yellow shirt stood by, watching while Domínguez rolled the dice several times. He seemed to become convinced of Domínguez's bad luck and, thinking it would be easy enough to win merely by playing against him, buried his hand in his pocket. But it so happened—strange whims of chance—that he had no more than started betting his reales and pesetas when Domínguez's luck began to change. It seemed as though he could roll any number he wanted.

The man took the first three losses without blinking, hiding his real feelings behind a sarcastic little smile that made his dark oily skin seem still shinier. But as Domínguez went on steadily winning, he began to look lowering. At the end he began to play in such a hopelessly absurd manner that every time Domínguez tossed, the old woman simply gave him part of the money the other had bet, and kept part for herself.

There came a moment in which the other couldn't stand the situation any longer, and he called from his end of the table to the other, where a friend of his was standing: "What a good thing it will be when we win the revolution and settle the hash of all the *gachupines! . . .*"

As he said this, Domínguez very calmly set the shaker down on the table, gathered up his money, and, looking straight at the fellow with the revolver for the first time, took him by the arm and made a gesture as though inviting him to step over to the other side of the square: 'Excuse me, but I'd like to have a word with you."

"Wherever you like," said the other, walking along with him.

Everybody then—the fellow with the revolver, his friends, Domínguez, and I, started towards the darkest spot of the square. And there Domínguez, turning to face the man, said to him in the following terms, as befitted the occasion:

"Look here," he said; "in the first place, we're not *gachupines,* even though we look like it in these clothes. We're Mexicans and I want you to know that we belong to the forces of General Francisco Villa. In the second place, the son of a bitch hasn't been born yet than can insult us and get away with it. So right now you're going to take back all your insolence or we'll settle the matter right here, with fists or pistols, whichever you like."

When the fellow in the yellow shirt heard the name of the Chief of the Division of the North, he was struck speechless. But he wasn't altogether a coward or a fool, for he answered Domínguez's attack, which had been extremely harsh, in a firm though conciliatory tone:

"All right, if you're not *gachupines,* I take back what I said. But if you are, everything I said goes, and we'll see about the consequences."

"Well, you heard me say that we weren't," answered Domínguez, calming down a little.

"Yes, but how do I know it?" insisted the other, who was trying to cover up his retreat. "Because if it's true you are with General Villa, it wouldn't be loyal to the cause to fight with you. But if it isn't true, my honour has to be avenged."

Here I interrupted: "Do you want to see our documents? Come with me to the ship and I'll show them to you. You can convince yourself that . . ."

"Papers? What do we need papers for? Anybody can see a mile off that you're telling the honest truth. I didn't mean any offence, and I want you to consider me a friend and fellow-worker. I'm in the revolution myself. I'm General Pérez. I came to this port incognito to carry out a commission of my own. . . . This is Colonel Caloca, my chief of staff, and this is Captain Moreno, my adjutant and a man in whom I repose the greatest confidence."

Once peace was established, General Pérez, who was delighted to have made the acquaintance of two of Villa's representatives, invited us to have something to eat with him at the lunch-counter on wheels. The five of us sat down around a dirty table, like old friends, and we ate and drank everything the woman brought us. After the third bottle of beer General Pérez began relating his campaigns and something of his biography. Every now and then the sight of our Spanish merchant-marine uniforms seemed to make him uneasy. But finally, at about the sixth or seventh bottle of beer, the General became completely reconciled to the situation, thanks to one of those strange miracles of the language. He began to call both of us "Chief" every time he spoke to us. And in this way he brought his subconscious mind into a complacent mood with regard to a state of affairs that consciously it would not tolerate so long as he treated us as equals. But by establishing us as superiors the instinct of submission in General Pérez, standard-bearer of liberty, became stronger than his instinct of hate.

Chapter XV

Revolutionary Justice

TWO days after my arrival in Mexico City I met General Cosío Robelo in the Café Colón. He had just come from Teoloyucán, where Carranza still was, and he had just been appointed Chief of Police. We congratulated each other, though without knowing or saying clearly what about, and we felt it fitting to crown the expression of our rejoicing as triumphant revolutionists with great muscular demonstrations: my poor bones cracked in the General's bear-like arms, and my breast was almost crushed against his, which was like that of a gorilla.

A great friend was Cosío Robelo, and a man of discernment. At that time his conversation was still abundant. He had not yet reached that other stage— so characteristic of him and so wise—in which he has more and more abandoned words as an adequate vehicle of expression and has limited himself to the eloquence of the smile.

On this occasion he entered more determinedly

than usual into the realm of loquaciousness and
finally took me aside to propose that I should help
him to organize the metropolitan police force.

"I have special reasons for asking you to do this,"
he said. "Some day you'll know why."

I a detective, a policeman! The proposal was so
strange that if it had not been part of the whirlwind
of the revolution, I should have laughed at it. But
Cosío Robelo was so determined that I not only had
to accept, at least for the time being—hoping that
later on he would get over the notion—but I agreed,
for there was nothing else to do about it, to go
with him to headquarters immediately so that my
duties as reorganizer of the police force of the Republic's capital might be entered upon without delay.
And indeed I entered upon them. Cosío Robelo had
another desk put directly across from his and he at
once turned it over to me, giving the operation almost
the air of an official act. Then embracing me again, he
said : "This is your place. This way we'll be near each
other and we can work together on everything."

The truth is, there was something about the whole
affair that couldn't be explained by the mere fact that
Cosío Robelo and I had happened to meet in the
Café Colón. Everybody knew that I didn't know the
first thing about police service, and there was no reason why I should. There was something hidden, something that I couldn't figure out. And this doubt, which
took hold of me at once, bothered me for several

days; it would still puzzle me if several weeks later Cosío Robelo himself, loyal friend that he was, had not cleared things up for me.

But in spite of my uneasiness I began my duties as a reorganizer, or, rather, what I imagined these duties to be. Months before, in Sinaloa, the haphazards of the revolution had made a reformer of hospitals out of me; now the same blind and invisible force hurled me almost to the other extreme. Before, my duty had been one of mercy; now it was one of vengeance; before, consolation; now punishment. But I didn't want to make mistakes that I could avoid, if possible, so I began looking round for the classic authorities, in order to instruct myself on the subject. I discovered that there is a very copious bibliography on police questions, and I read the first two or three books I got hold of: *Justice and Police,* by Maitland, and *Mysteries of Police and Crime,* by Griffiths.

When the Constitutionalist troops entered Mexico City, Obregón issued a terrible proclamation against all disturbers of the public order. All thefts, assaults, or other acts of delinquency, the proclamation ran, would be punishable by death, without any legal procedure beyond establishing the identity of the criminal. The order also provided the same punishment for the military authorities who permitted such crimes or allowed them to go unpunished. And Cosío Robelo had orders to carry out this martial law without considerations of any sort. The orders were the kind usual in such circumstances, based not so much on actual needs as on the psychological effect they produced.

Now, one afternoon the police caught two poor devils in the act of robbing a small general store. They were taken red-handed, and that same night they were brought to the Sixth Precinct station and given what was known as a summary trial, which was nothing more or less than a simple method of legalizing and justifying plain murder. The simplicity of the proceeding was marvellous: any sergeant, any court-clerk, could apply it without the slightest difficulty. The policeman or policemen would set forth the nature of the crime committed by the prisoner, who in his turn gave his side of the case. It amounted to two or three declarations and a preliminary questioning before the officer in charge. When this had been done, the findings were laid before the Chief of Police, who, under penalty of suffering himself the punishment provided for the others, was obliged to order an immediate execution.

That night in less than two hours the documents of the case had been drawn up, and ten minutes later they were in the hands of the Chief of Police. Cosío Robelo read them, but did not want to decide anything right away. I remember his words perfectly as he laid the slender sheaf of papers on the table. The clock was just striking the hour. "Ten o'clock. It's too

>>>>>>>>>>>>>>>>>>>>>>><<<<<<<<<<<<<<<<<<<<<<

late to order them shot. We'll wait till tomorrow
to decide the matter."

But the next day there was no pretext for postpon-
ing the case. As soon as we reached the office, there
lay the papers in the middle of the table, demanding
examination and a decision.

Cosío Robelo went through them again. Then he
said to me:

"There's no question about the facts."

I kept quiet. Cosío Robelo began to stare at me. I
noticed that his complexion was even ruddier than
usual, and the very whites of his eyes were bloodshot.
The struggle between his head and his heart was making itself manifest.

"And there's no doubt either," he went on, "about
what was ordered by the Military Council."

I didn't say a word.

Several minutes went by like this. Then Cosío
Robelo, who had been pacing the room, stopped, and
asked me with the air of a person looking for help:

"What would you advise me to do?"

"I don't advise anything."

"Oh, come!"

"Remember that I'm a civilian."

"That doesn't make any difference in this case."

"Yes, it does," I replied. "Your duty is to behave in
accordance with the military code, which you have
accepted as the standard of your conduct, whereas

mine is to behave in accordance with my status as a civilian."

"Well, as a civilian, what would you do?"

"I wouldn't assume or share the responsibility of any execution."

"And as a soldier?"

"That's why I'm not a soldier."

"That means that you would shoot them?"

"I would obey orders or I would resign. The military career separates the range of human actions into two parts that cannot always be reconciled, and there are occasions on which a choice is required, even within strict military legality. Then it's a question of being a good man or a good soldier. Now, to decide this is a point of conscience—one could almost say, of religion."

As might have been expected, my words neither calmed nor fortified Cosío Robelo. On the contrary, they made him more uneasy and perplexed than before. But after struggling with himself for two hours —the struggle of the small but pressing duty against the larger, but more remote—he did what anyone else would have done in his place: he signed the order to apply martial law in the case.

But his decision did not make him any easier. After he had issued the order, he grew more nervous, more excited, and more unsatisfied with the sense of his responsibility. At that moment he was a good man who had been hemmed in between the sword and the wall and had chosen the wall, but for whom the wall had become as sharp and piercing as the sword.

A few moments after he had issued the order, he called in the Assistant Chief and ordered him to be present in person at the executions to see that everything was carried out in accordance with all the legal prescriptions for such cases. And a little while after the Assistant Chief had left, he said to me:

"I'd appreciate it very much if you would go and see how *that* is coming along, and if you find the slightest irregularity, come and notify me at once."

I set out.

Chapter XVI

In the Sixth Precinct Station

ON the way I kept thinking about what Cosío Robelo had said and wondering what he understood by irregularities in an execution that had been ordered without due process of law or guarantees of any kind for the accused. And the more I thought about it, the greater became my doubts. Because, once the supreme irregularity of ordering a group of men to stand another man before a wall with his hands tied behind his back and kill him is admitted, none of the other details seem important. Perhaps the rules of a proper shooting demand that the homicidal fusilade be fired by expert marksmen; in this way the cruelty of death is attenuated. Possibly the criminal is not supposed to be dragged to the spot of execution; this keeps the executioner from being too conspicuous. No doubt it is provided that if the condemned person offers resistance, he is not to be riddled with bullets, or thrust through with bayonets, or have his skull smashed in with gun-stocks. But in the last analysis what difference did these hypocritical and incidental details make beside the undeniable fact than an execution had been ordered without legal or moral considerations?

As the distance was short, I didn't get far along with my ideas. All the police stations in Mexico are sinister-looking places, but, above all, that of the Sixth Precinct. At the doors there was a crowd of curious spectators composed of the public and the police, and these two elements—at swords' points when it comes to respecting the law—were joined in a single morbid interest: hearing and seeing what was going on inside.

I went in. The filthy routine of that prison antechamber was in a state of suspense. There was a kind of cold, unfeeling expectation. There was something out of the ordinary in the air, which transformed the daily prison atmosphere, making it perhaps worse than usual.

As I crossed the courtyard, the eyes of the employees and prisoners who were watching from the doors of the different sections followed me. Then they turned back to the hall that communicated with the adjoining courtyard. There were four or five policemen waiting there, standing in single file and armed with Mausers. Their belts and puttees of yellow leather were in vivid contrast with the blue of the uniforms. They were standing with their backs

to the first courtyard and facing the second. Their
rifles were new or had seen little use, and between
every two ankles appeared the rear angle of a gun-
stock. Near the policemen and the official in charge
stood the Assistant Chief of Police, the captain of
the precinct, the clerks, a doctor, and two men of the
lower classes. It was evident at first glance that these
two were the leading characters in the execution. The
taller of the two was barefooted.

I did not join the group. I stood watching them
some six or seven feet off, through the grille that
separated the corridor from the office next to it. The
tall, barefooted prisoner was talking. The other
nodded his approval of what his companion was
saying.

"But how can I be resigned, Chief? Does that seem
like justice to you?"

He was addressing himself to the Assistant Chief
of Police, whose face I could not see, as it was hidden
under the brim of his wide hat. He must have seemed
unmoved, to judge by the rising emphasis that the
condemned man put into each new phrase. But if his
face was impassive, his hands revealed his nervousness. They were clasped behind his back, and his
fingers kept continually twisting and working.

Meanwhile the condemned man went on: "I'm not
saying anything against the orders, Chief, or what you
say about when the troops enter large cities. But,
honest to God, it isn't justice to shoot a man for such

a little thing. Just think of it—shooting! This gentleman here who knows all about it"—pointing to one of the clerks (dirty unkempt, with a greasy skull-cap pulled down almost to his eyes)—"can tell you, sir, that things are not done like that."

The clerk cut in: "I'm not saying anything; don't talk about what you don't know."

"About what I don't know, my Chief, and they're going to kill us? Well, then, let them fetch a lawyer and he'll tell them, because it's written in his books."

Here the Assistant Chief of Police interrupted: "I told you before that this was no time for lawyers."

"Then when is the time, Chief?"

"During the trial."

"But there hasn't been any trial. You know that."

"Yes, there was. That was the trial last night."

"I swear to you it wasn't, and if they say so, it isn't true. Trials, God help me, are very different. There are judges and witnesses and lawyers and people, and they last a long time. The papers tell about it and even print the pictures, especially if you're sentenced to death. They don't send a person to the grave like this."

The other prisoner had begun to cry, listening to his companion. His appearance was one of complete submissiveness, and he was inferior in intelligence and ability to the other, in spite of the fact that he wore shoes and was better dressed. Something in his attitude denoted astonishment at the tenacity with which his companion defended the lives of both of them, but at the same time he seemed resigned to the inevitable. This showed even in the slow trickle of his tears. Each time the Assistant Chief or the captain of the precinct indicated that there was nothing to do but yield, he looked up inquiringly at his companion and seemed ready to walk over to the wall and wait for the bullets. But afterwards, seeing that the other continued unshaken, he settled down again during the respite. The gentleness of the Assistant Chief was largely responsible for the delay. He was so determined that the rules for an execution should not be violated that he hardly made use of his authority. He talked in a persuasive, almost kindly tone. Moreover, his eloquence, like the captain's, was as nothing compared with that of the prisoner, whose arguments received hardly any reply. The truth was that at heart nobody believed that there was any need, much less justification, for shooting those two unhappy wretches. Only the dirty clerk kept repeating over and over with a hateful smile:

"Nothing can be done about it. Nothing can be done about it."

The prisoners kept turning towards him; the one in tears, in silent contemplation; the other to say, as in parentheses: "No, sir. Why can nothing be done? You know it can better than anybody else, for you wrote out the declarations."

And immediately the prisoner resumed his defence before the Assistant Chief and the captain.

"If it is true that General Obregón has ordered us to be shot—and it isn't that I doubt your word, Chief; it's that I can't believe it—at least let the General hear us. And I know that if he hears us, he won't have us shot even if I tell him the honest truth, Chief, just as I've told it. Because I don't want to deny that we did go into the place to see what we could pick up, but we didn't have any bad intentions; I mean, we didn't intend to kill or hurt anybody, and we didn't have anything to do it with. It's just being so poor that makes a fellow think about robbing, but that was all. . . . No knife or any kind of weapon. . . . The police testified to it, and it's all down in the papers. Now, Chief, how can you believe that if General Obregón knows all this, he is going to have us shot? That's all I want you to do, please—there's plenty of time afterwards to kill us—only that, to take us where General Obregón is and have him hear us. . . ."

The Assistant Chief began to show signs of pity and impatience, the latter for the very reason that he could not say anything that would carry weight against the eloquent, desperate obstinacy with which the court-martial prisoner pleaded his case. Suddenly he broke out, in a harsher tone than he had used before:

"Well, brother, it seems to me we've had enough arguing. Will you obey or won't you?"

"But, Chief (please God you never find yourself in a fix like this!), how can I obey when they're going to shoot me? Just put yourself in my shoes, have a little pity. Besides, I've got a little girl, Chief, a little girl four years old. What's going to become of her if they kill me? Why must she suffer for what I've done, and, besides, it doesn't deserve a punishment like this. I was only going to rob—yes, I admit I was going to rob—but do you think it's justice to punish me as if I were a murderer, and one of the very worst? If you could only see my little girl you'd realize that I don't deserve this. She's not like me; I'm bringing her up and educating her right. She goes to school already. The things I was going to steal were for her. Why, yesterday at this time I was with her, all my troubles forgotten, never doubting that I'd live to see her a woman; and now they want to kill me just because I had a wicked temptation and the Devil took advantage of me. No, Chief, don't shoot me, for your sweet mother's sake. The Holy Virgin will reward you some day, even if I can't. . . ."

"That will do," shouted the Assistant Chief. "I have to obey orders. If you won't go to the wall of your own accord, we'll have to take you there. Officer!"

"At your orders, Colonel."

The prisoner: "No, Chief, don't get angry. Not by force. It isn't necessary. I defended myself because

I think it's justice. But I'm not afraid, and I don't want them to say I am. When the time comes, I know how to die like anybody else. But I want to ask one favour: let them bring my little girl so I can tell her good-bye, and if it isn't too much trouble, I'd like to have a priest come. If they have to shoot me, I'd like to die with an easy conscience."

The Assistant Chief looked at his watch. Then he said something in a low voice to the captain. Meanwhile the two condemned men talked to each other, or, rather, the taller one spoke a few words to the other, who answered with several nods of the head.

"See here," the Assistant Chief ordered a policeman, "have this man explain where his daughter lives and have them bring her at once. We can't do anything about the priest. And you," he went on, turning to the other prisoner, "is there anything you want? What can we do for you?"

"Nothing for me, Chief. If they're bound to shoot us, what difference does it make if we die with consolation or without it? I see that they're making an example of us. Some day their conscience will accuse them."

I took advantage of this respite to go out to find Cosío Robelo. I wanted to let him know that the execution was being carried out with all regard for the rules, but that, notwithstanding, it seemed to me an abominable, gruesome action. The preserving of order in the city did not justify such measures against

two poor devils who were no guiltier than half of the
Constitutionalist army. But at headquarters I found
that Cosío Robelo had left. And though I looked
everywhere for him, I couldn't get hold of him until
two hours after the sentence had been carried out.

That same afternoon I passed by the Sixth Precinct
station again. In front of one of the sheds used for the
fire-engines a group of people was gathered. I drew
near. There were the two corpses on public view. The
face of the taller one still seemed to have a trace of
the persuasive power with which he had tried to save
himself. His bare feet—young, strong feet—were
stained with trickles of dried blood. The other corpse
lay not so much on the dirty canvas of the stretcher
as in the bosom of his utter resignation.

Chapter XVII

Pancho Villa's Pistol

REVOLUTIONARY justice as meted out by the police was so repugnant to me that I immediately decided to dissociate myself from the organization in charge of its administration. Only one thing detained me: I was afraid of hurting Cosío Robelo's feelings, and since all laws and personal guarantees had been suspended, he could not be held—nor did I hold him —personally responsible for these summary executions. But I soon saw that my fears were ungrounded. At my first words the Chief of Police admitted that I was right, and he even hinted that he would gladly imitate me if his military obligations only permitted.

And Cosío Robelo took advantage of the occasion to reveal to me the real reason for his insisting on my joining the force. With stupefaction I heard him say: "You know why I insisted as I did? Because that was the only way I could keep from arresting you, as Carranza had ordered me to do when he appointed me Chief. Fortunately, things have changed now;

thanks to the efforts of Eduardo Hay, who seems to be very fond of you, the First Chief has countermanded the order."

Soon afterwards other events, bearing more on the future developments of the revolution than on its immediate problems, took me away from there. What especially interested me was to see how events were slowly drawing together different leaders of the forces in Sonora and Sinaloa into an anti-Carranza faction.

The situation in this respect was so far advanced that I had set my heart on having Villa and Lucio Blanco join forces and purposes, even without their knowing each other. The opposition of both to Carranza's autocracy, clear and open in Villa, tacit as yet in Blanco, but determined, would bring them together, without a doubt, for the action that would very shortly get under way. But a common objective, born of similar, or outwardly similar, motives, did not satisfy me. It seemed to me that a sentimental bond of some sort was necessary, even if it did not outlive the moment of its usefulness.

The thing was not easy in spite of the favourable circumstances that Villa and Blanco had never met. In the realm of sentiment, how could one establish a sincere point of contact between Lucio, all bravery, generosity, and idealism, and Villa, uncontrolled blind force that stopped at nothing, illuminated only

by the feeblest ray of moral light, which filtered into
his soul through some almost imperceptible crevice?
Blanco was so noble that he disdained even glory—
this was his weakness; so human that the horror of
killing practically paralysed his activity after the
first revolutionary impulse. Villa, on the contrary,
could see only one clear guiding principle through
the shadows that surrounded him: to accumulate
power at any price, to get rid of obstacles by any
means whatsoever. The only way to carry out my
desire would be by a well-staged surprise, and the
first move must come from Villa. It could not come
from Blanco, for he was too proud. And Villa was
an ex-deserter who trusted nobody.

Back in Chihuahua again, the opportunity presented itself. Domínguez and I had returned to inform Villa as to the result of our trip to Mexico City
when the Constitutionalist troops had marched into
the capital. And we were also carrying a letter from
Blanco to the Chief of the Division of the North
saying that he had talked with us and had completely
outlined to us his ideas about Carranza and his adherents.

As we were waiting to be received, Villa suddenly
appeared in the doorway to say something to his
secretary, Luis Aguirre Benavides, who had been
talking with us while we waited. It was early in Sep-
tember and the weather was warm. Villa came out

in his shirt-sleeves. He had on his hat, his usual custom when he was in his office or in the house. As he talked with Aguirre Benavides, his robust, khaki-clad figure stood out sharply against the white painted door. From under his hat a number of saffron-coloured curly locks of hair clustered around his forehead, matching the thick, untidy moustache. But nothing about the man drew one's attention like the enormous pistol that hung from his hip in a huge holster. The butt of it shone with the gleam of a thing that is in constant use, not with the effeminate polish of something meant for show. Around both sides of his waist ran a thick row of bullets, whose size made one think of torpedoes. They looked like a row of copper columns without capitals, cut in two by the dark strip that held them in place on the belt.

"This man wouldn't exist if his pistol didn't exist," I thought to myself. "It isn't merely an instrument of action with him; it's a fundamental part of his being, the axis of his work and his amusement, the constant expression of his most intimate self, his soul given outward expression. Between the fleshy curve of his index-finger and the rigid curve of the trigger there exists the relation that comes from the contact of one being with another. When he fires, it isn't the pistol that shoots, it's the man himself. Out of his very heart comes the ball as it leaves the sinister barrel. The man and the pistol are the same thing. Whoever counts on the one can count on the other. Out of his pistol have come and will come his friends and his enemies."

And then the idea I had been looking for came to me.

"To bring Villa and Blanco together," I said to Colonel Domínguez, "we ought to have Blanco receive, as a present, Villa's pistol. If Villa offers it, there'll be no mistaking his attitude. And Blanco, when he accepts it, will understand what this means. You leave it to me."

Villa's great problem in those days was the question of who should be appointed president *pro tem*. At first glance it seemed as though he was willing to support anybody as long as it wasn't Carranza. But on closer investigation it was evident that he was interested in having a man he could count on. His candidate then was General Angeles, and it was with him that our conversation dealt. A strange combination, that of an illiterate guerrilla leader and our master technician of the war! Villa, the irresponsible, found in Angeles, a man tormented by the sense of his obligations as a revolutionist, a complement he could understand. In this—as in many other things— he showed his superiority over the half-educated leaders of Sonora—with the exception of Maytorena —and Coahuila, who hated and maligned Angeles from the start simply because they weren't fit to tie his shoes when it came to questions of culture or military strategy. It was natural that Sonora should have engendered the school that won its battles by bribing traitors among the enemy; and Angeles would have let himself be torn limb from limb before going to a framed-up victory. Angeles had been an honour cadet at Chapultepec and had assimilated a tradition of honour there that is worth more than all our revolutions put together. His attitude was radically opposed to the corruptness of Carranza's party and to that part of the Sonora group that for the time being was booming Carranza while waiting for a chance to betray him and assassinate him. But Villa did not see this diametrical opposition between Angeles and the Carranza group, or pretended not to see it.

"Angeles," I said, "is a splendid man, who deserves a lot, but as a coalition candidate he won't do."

At this Villa got excited. He broke off the mysterious form of secret conclave that our conversation had taken—he sitting very close to us, his elbows on his knees, and his face in his hands—and stood up. Still talking, he moved over to the door, and we after him. And the three of us went out into the reception room without having really finished our parley. A number of his subordinates and close friends were in the room, and they came over and began talking to him as soon as they saw him. Was he angry? I had a feeling that our plans had gone on the rocks that last minute because I had been too sincere. Yet I hated to admit defeat and decided to make a final test of the situation.

"Now, the matter of Lucio Blanco," I said to Villa, without any preliminaries, point-blank, "could be completely fixed up by a friendly gesture on your part. For instance, if you would send him your pistol with your compliments."

Villa looked at me, looked at Domínguez, and answered after a moment's pause, as he unfastened his belt:

"That's not such a bad idea."

Then, while all looked on in silence, he handed me his pistol, with cartridge-belt and everything. A shiver ran through me as I felt it in my hands, still warm, and I passed it on to Domínguez *in continenti.* It seemed to me that it burned me just to touch it.

And meanwhile Villa added: "Just tell General Blanco to be careful with it, as it's a very fluky pistol."

But before he had finished the phrase, he went pale. With a quick movement he felt both his hips and whirled round, looking at us all. And as though moved by instinct, he backed up against the wall.

"Say," he said excitedly, "somebody give me a pistol, I'm unarmed."

And he was so wrought up as he pronounced these words that I thought he was going to jump on Domínguez and take away the pistol he had given him a few minutes before. Without knowing it I had just done something nobody had ever tried with Pancho Villa. I had disarmed him. Disarmed him!

He realized the imprudence he had committed and

reacted immediately with all the brutality that comes from long years of living like a hunted animal, pursued by the mounted police. How long since Villa had found himself in a situation of this sort, defenceless in a group of armed men, several of whom had different ideas and interests from his? He, who never drew his pistol without having settled the matter in question before he returned it to its holster, had fallen by surprise into the thoughtless mistake of handing over his arms to a man he hardly knew, the very one who only two minutes before had aroused his anger by disagreeing with him.

As they heard Villa's alarmed request, several of those present held out their pistols to him. Luis Aguirre Benavides said, offering him his:

"I'd give you this one, General, but it's very small and besides it's an automatic, and you don't know that kind very well."

"Bah, what kind don't I know well?" said Villa, taking it.

It was a little thirty-two. Villa gripped it with a smile—it seemed that his annoyance at finding himself without arms had disappeared—and broke it, letting the bullets fall out one by one. As they dropped to the floor, Aguirre Benavides gathered them up and then handed them all back to Villa. He reloaded quickly; then he pulled back the trigger and, aiming at my forehead, said:

"Now say something to me."

The mouth of the barrel was about two feet from my face. Above the sights I could see the feline glitter of Villa's eyes. The iris was like an agate: full of infinite minute dots of fire. Tiny golden lines radiated out from the pupil and on reaching the white turned into fine reddish filaments that disappeared under the lids. The vision of death seemed to come from that eye more than from the dark little orifice of the barrel. Neither the one nor the other moved the least bit; they were fixed; they were of one piece. Did the barrel aim so that the eye could fire? Did the eye aim so that the barrel could fire? Without looking away from the pistol I could see that Aguirre Benavides was calmly smiling, that the officers were watching us, curious and unmoved, and that Domínguez, at my side, was hardly breathing.

I cannot say which was greater in me at the moment, fear or indignation. Nevertheless I controlled both feelings—successfully, I think—and answered Villa:

"What do you want me to say? Something good or bad?"

"Whatever comes out of your heart."

"Well, I hope this isn't going to be a fluky pistol, too," I said.

But Villa wasn't listening to me. He looked at Domínguez and slowly let his arm fall as he asked:

"Now, which of you two is the braver?"

As I had just had a horrible fright, I answered without a moment's hesitation: "Domínguez."

And Domínguez, who rightfully had a good opinion of his own bravery, said: "Neither one."

"Well, it's my opinion," Villa answered, "that the civilian is braver than the soldier."

For that unjust and inexplicable remark Domínguez never forgave Villa, nor me either.

Chapter XVIII

A Forced Loan

ON our way from Mexico City Domínguez and I had made the acquaintance of Colonel Ornelas, aide-de-camp of one of the generals who was campaigning in the interior of the Republic. He was young, intelligent and outspoken, and a great talker. All the time we were together he related to us episodes of his life in the service, and on one occasion, when we had a long wait on account of locomotive trouble, he regaled us with a full-length portrait of his general.

We were sitting along the railroad track with some other revolutionary officers that were on the same train. The autumn afternoon was fading beautifully into twilight. The near-by mountains seemed slowly to wrap themselves in the violet vapours that rose out of the bottom of the valley, which was already half-dark.

"This time," said Ornelas, "we were confronted

with the problem of getting supplies for the troops as soon as we took the town. The general sent for me and said:

" 'Do you know that there's not a cent in this brigade's treasury?' "

" 'That's what I've been told.'

" 'Well, no need to get downcast about such a trifle. This little town will give us a lift for a few days. We're going to try out a plan which is infallible for getting loans on a big scale; it's a plan that tames the strongest wills.'

"And then, after spouting along some more in the same pedantic fashion—which in no wise detracted from his shrewd, cool, efficient manner of going straight after what he wanted, and getting it at any cost—he held out to me a paper with several names in his own handwriting and said:

" 'Here are the names of the five richest men in the town. Some have land, some land and a store, but they are all stuck-up reactionaries, and supporters of Huerta. They are to report at headquarters immediately if they do not want to be shot for giving aid and comfort to the enemy.'

"The general and I were in a room of the house that had been selected for the brigade offices. Through the window we could see groups of soldiers in the streets unsaddling the horses. As we talked, orderlies came in and out of the room loaded with equipment and other baggage.

>>>>>>>>>>>>>>>>>>>>>>><<<<<<<<<<<<<<<<<<<<<<<

" 'About this order,' I said; 'shall I have it delivered or shall I carry it out myself?'

"The general reflected for barely a second and then answered quickly:

" 'That's right; you attend to it yourself.'

"I took ten soldiers of the guard and started off, though as soon as I got outside the door, I hesitated, for I did not know which way to go. Left? Right? The town was strange to me. Where did they live and who were Don Carlos Valdés and Don Ciriaco Díaz González, who headed the list of the victims selected for the loan? But an obvious idea occurred to me and I headed for the little public square where on subsequent afternoons I should while away my hours watching the flight of the magpies among its venerable leafy trees.

"In the square I soon obtained the information I needed. But as I had to traverse several streets and stop at various houses in the company of my detachment of soldiers, alarm began to spread through the town. The sinister air of my men and the uneasy look of those who followed us revived the fright produced by the morning's skirmish.

"Fortunately it didn't take long to find four of the prominent citizens chosen by the General. Everybody in town knew them and their families, their homes and their places of business. But there was one exception, the first man on the list, Don Carlos Valdés. At first nobody knew whom I meant.

" 'Carlos Valdés? Which Carlos Valdés?'

"Finally I managed to find out that there was a Carlos Valdés in the town; but I was told that this couldn't be the Valdés on my list; that I must mean Don Vicente Valdés.

" 'But why can't it be Don Carlos Valdés that I'm looking for?'

" 'Because Carlos Valdés,' I was informed, 'isn't one of the leading people in this town, like the others you are after, and Don Vicente is. He's not one of the richest, but he's not one of the poorest, either.'

"But as my orders called for Don Carlos Valdés and not Don Vicente, I asked to be shown where he lived, and when I had located him, I brought him in with the other four authentic, or at least undisputed, magnates.

"My general received the candidates for the forced loan with all the paraphernalia of ceremony prescribed for such cases. He was standing behind his campaign table, his jacket buttoned to the throat, his chest thrown out, freshly shaven, and the points of his moustache waxed to turn up like those of the Kaiser. At each end of his table, on stools, were the cashboxes of the brigade, open to reveal their emptiness.

"He allowed several minutes to elapse in silence, the better to intimidate his victims, and then began:

" 'I greet you, gentlemen, though I cannot bring myself to clasp your hands; for you are traitors, cowards, disloyal citizens, enemies of your country

157

and its free institutions, while I . . . I am a worthy representative of the brave revolutionary army—'

" 'General!' one of the five tried to interrupt.

"But the general, it goes without saying, pulled him up short.

" 'Oh, no,' he said, 'under no circumstances. Under no circumstances am I to be interrupted.'

"And to leave no doubt as to the meaning of his remark he turned to me and repeated emphatically:

" 'Under no circumstances am I to be interrupted!'

"I still had the guard of ten soldiers with me, and I ordered them to present arms and stationed them behind and alongside the prisoners.

"Meanwhile the general had taken from his pocket a copy of the list he had given me a little while before and read it over to himself. Then without raising his eyes, but addressing the prisoners, he went on:

" 'Don Carlos Valdés. Which of you is Don Carlos Valdés?'

" 'I am, sir,' said the one in question.

" 'Don Ciriaco Díaz González. Which one is Mr. Díaz González?'

" 'I,' answered a sharp, dry voice.

" 'Oho! So you are! Delighted. . . .'

"And then: 'Don Pedro Salas Duarte. Which one is Don Pedro Salas Duarte?'

" 'Your humble servant, General.'

" 'All right, we'll see about that. And Don Marciano de la Garza?'

" 'At your orders, General.'

" 'Then you, I suppose,' said my general turning to the only prisoner whose name he had not pronounced yet, 'are Don Ignacio Muriedas.'

" 'I am,' agreed the other, with a marked Spanish accent.

" 'Very good, gentlemen,' went on the general, in his oratorical tone; 'now, the revolution requires funds which we, her noble, her pure, her unsullied servants cannot call up out of the thin air. And it is only fair that you—the classes and the individuals responsible for the present state of affairs—should defray the expenses of the war which you alone have caused. You are in duty bound to fill the empty coffers so my troops can be paid, and that is the reason for this interview which you have so graciously honoured with your presence. The forces it is my privilege to command, which this morning freed this town from the ignominy of continuing under the sway of the reactionary troops, expect you to supply, without pretexts or delays of any sort, the modest sum of thirty-five thousand pesos in cash. In spite of everything, I don't want to be unfair; we will not consider the advance of the thirty-five thousand pesos as punishment for helping the enemies of the liberty and laws of the Republic—I don't want to set myself up as judge—; we will simply consider it as an obligatory loan, for which you will be given a receipt, and reimbursed when the cause triumphs. But there are two points on which I must be inflexible: the first is that the quota assigned to each of you will not be lowered by a single cent; and the second, that the time allotted for each one to make his payment cannot be extended one second.'

"The five men condemned to the loan had been feeling an acceleration in their heart-beats as the general advanced in his speech. They kept swallowing; the veins on their foreheads bulged out; they stood as though rooted to the spot, but their hands kept working nervously in their pockets. Only one of them, Don Carlos Valdés, seemed to take the situation with relative calm. He kept looking at the General, and an almost imperceptible smile, half ironical and half melancholy, played around his lips.

"The general made a slight pause and then went on, looking at his list:

" 'Mr. Carlos Valdés: the forces I command grant you a period of twelve hours, beginning this minute (it is now'—looking at his wrist-watch—'7.47 p.m), to supply the brigade's treasury with the sum of five thousand pesos. If you do not comply with this demand, you will be hanged, without further preliminaries, tomorrow at 7.47 a.m.'

"The row of the five rich men stopped breathing. From red, they turned white. Valdés tried to talk and opened his mouth, but before he could emit a sound, the general was saying:

" 'Mr. Ciriaco Díaz González: you have been

granted a period of fifteen hours, beginning this minute (it is now 7.49 p.m.), to supply the treasury of
my troops with the sum of six thousand pesos. If
this demand has not been complied with, you will be
hanged at 10.49 tomorrow morning, without further
proceedings. Mr. Pedro Salas Duarte: you have been
granted a period of eighteen hours to furnish our
treasury with the sum of seven thousand pesos. It is
now 7.51 p.m. If you do not comply with the orders
just received, you will be hanged tomorrow, without
further formalities of any sort, at 1.51 p.m. Mr.
Marciano de la Garza: you have been granted a
period of twenty-one hours (it is just 7.53 p.m.) to
supply our treasury with the sum of eight thousand
pesos. If you do not comply with the order, you will
be hanged, without further formalities than making
sure that the clock is right, tomorrow at 4.53 p.m.
Mr. Ignacio Muriedas, you have been granted
twenty-four hours to supply the treasury of my brigade with nine thousand pesos. It is now 7.55 p.m.
If you do not obey this order, tomorrow you will be
hanged, without further preliminaries, at this same
hour and minute. Just one more word. While the
orders you have just heard are being carried out
either one way—as I hope—or another—as I should
lament—you may consider yourselves prisoners here
at headquarters, under my surveillance. Nevertheless, you will be given every opportunity to com-
municate with your friends and relatives.'

>>>>>>>>>>>>>>>>>>>>>>> <<<<<<<<<<<<<<<<<<<<<<<

"My general, having finished, twirled the points of his moustache, drew over a chair, and called me to him to give me instructions about putting up the prisoners.

"They had not yet recovered from their astonishment and stupefaction. Don Carlos Valdés, who had seemed so courageous a few minutes before, made vain efforts to regain his poise. Finally they all tried to talk at the same time, but the general, who had been keeping an eye on them all the time, brusquely cut them short:

" 'It's quite useless, gentlemen; you're wasting your time trying to tell me anything. Orders have been issued, and time moves fast. You either hand over the money or you hang. You couldn't have a clearer-cut choice. At any rate, I can permit no arguments.'

"There followed a long, painful silence. Valdés began to breathe deeply, and suddenly, spurred on by his imminent peril, he broke out, in spite of the stern gesture with which my general endeavoured to silence him.

" 'I shall be quiet in a moment, General, but first I must tell you what perhaps you do not know, and what my safety and my duties demand that I inform you. As the honourable gentlemen here with me can testify—and I deplore their fate as much as my own —I am very poor; poor myself, poor in relatives, and poor in friends. I am not lying to you. I am telling you the truth. I have no houses, no land, no money, no store, no bonds, no bank accounts. Twelve hours to bring together five thousand pesos! I can't help thinking I must be dreaming. A year would be too little, I assure you. So, as far as I am concerned, you don't need to make your executioners wait. You might just as well hang me now as tomorrow at 7.47.'

" 'The revolution, Mr. Carlos Valdés, has no executioners, nor does it need them,' replied the General, and added: 'You will regret those words.'

"Everybody kept silence."

Chapter XIX

The Hangman's Noose

WE lighted a bonfire, for the sierra was sending its cold night breath down on us, and gathered around it. The flames threw a ruddy glow on our faces, and cascades of burnished gold over our sarapes. Behind us the shadows grew thicker, forming a dense hostile mass at our back; around the blaze of light in front ran a circle made up of pairs of gleaming eyes and tightly wedged bodies, which were toasted on one side and half-frozen on the other.

By the light of the fire the story extended the scope of its interest. Colonel Ornelas paused a few moments to relight a cigarette and then went on in the same tone of voice as before—dry, outwardly indifferent, but tinged with an emotion that he hated to reveal.

"I told the General what was being said about town: to judge by the most reliable opinions, Don Carlos Valdés couldn't scrape up five hundred, one hundred pesos, let alone five thousand.

" 'You're new to this work,' said the General, 'and anybody can fool you. Take my word for it, of the five prisoners we have here, the most valuable one from our point of view is Don Carlos Valdés. Wait and see.'

"Meanwhile the news had run like wildfire through the town. People talked of nothing but the forced loan that had been demanded by us, and of the critical situation of the five men picked out to furnish the money. A host of relatives and friends of the prisoners came to headquarters to bring them help, sympathy, and advice. Several delegations from the poorer classes managed to get in to see the General and tried to convince him that Carlos Valdés was not and never had been a man of means. But the General became furious; he said that neither he nor the revolution ever made a mistake, and that he would make an example of those who deceived him or were a party to concealing the true state of affairs. Nor did he show himself any more tolerant with those who came to plead for an extension of time.

" 'You must remember, General,' they said, 'that this is a little town and it has been ruined by the war. Only yesterday, before you entered, the Federals carried off everything they could lay their hands on. Just stop and think, it is beyond our powers to raise a sum like thirty-five thousand pesos. We haven't got it and we can't raise it in a few hours. Give us at least time to get in touch with people we know around here, four days, or three, or two. Accept our word of honour that we will pay. We are honourable men, who are in the habit of keeping our word. That's why we are called supporters of Huerta and foes of liberty. . . ."

"But my General, brisk and to the point, twisting the ends of his moustache, merely replied:

" 'Our orders have been given and the limits are set. You people who are cowards and traitors are going to find out that you can't fool with the revolution or with me, who represent it with a dignity in keeping with its glorious ideals, its heroic and just ambitions. If Don Carlos Valdés has not handed over his five thousand pesos before the hour that has been set for him, tomorrow morning at 7.47 you will see him swinging from the end of a rope. Gentlemen, don't waste any more time.'

"My general retired at ten that night, leaving orders that he was not to be called until seven the next morning. Quiet settled down over headquarters, except in the rooms occupied by the prisoners, where a muted agitation kept up. Friends went in and out of the rooms; messages were sent; letters were written. The prisoners were horribly nervous; every five minutes they looked at their watches. Only Don Carlos Valdés seemed oblivious of all these anxious efforts. Calmly he sat talking to a group of women that had gathered around him:

" 'I haven't got five thousand pesos, and I never

shall have. If I should try to borrow this amount, everybody knows I could never pay it back. I know that if the town could, it would try to save me. But how can I expect it to save me when it isn't going to be able to find the money to save my four companions from the noose, and they're really rich and can pay back with interest later on whatever is done for them now? Let's hope that this general who talks so much about bravery, justice, and heroism will come to his senses and realize that I am a poor devil. Then he won't carry out his threats. And if he does, well, his crime be on his head. . . .'

"All night long, attempts were made in the town and in the vicinity, for messengers were sent out in different directions, to save the five men selected as victims by the general from their terrible situation. But in spite of all these efforts it struck seven the next morning and not a cent had been turned in. My general called me as soon as he woke up:

" 'Has Don Carlos Valdés got his money here?'

" 'No, General. His isn't here, nor anybody else's. And as far as Don Carlos Valdés is concerned—'

" 'Very well,' he cut in. 'We have to hurry and get things ready.'

"After reflecting for a few minutes he went on:

" 'Look here. Out in the yard there's an old live-oak tree. For lack of anything better we can use that for a gallows. Have them tie a stout rope to the strongest branch of the tree, with a slip-noose at the end, and get ready whatever else may be needed. Not an ordinary knot, you know; a regular hangman's noose. You'll have to attend to everything quickly because it's after seven already and we've just got a little more than half an hour. Oh, as you go out, would you mind telling Juan to bring in my breakfast, please.'

"I immediately left to carry out my orders, though it wasn't so easy as might have been expected. For the only strong branch on the tree was a very low one. We had to measure Don Carlos Valdés's height to make sure that if he were put on a chair, which was to be taken away when the time came, there would be enough room between his neck and the bough for the rope and the noose. In this way, when the chair was jerked away, the body of the condemned man would swing clear of the ground, and his own weight would hang him.

"The general finished dressing at 7.30, and came out in the yard to see what I had done. He stood up on the chair that was under the tree. He hung on to the rope with both hands to make sure the branch would hold. He observed the distance from the ground, and finally he picked up the noose and examined it very carefully.

" 'This knot,' he finally exclaimed, 'is no good at all. I told you it was to be a regular hangman's noose, the kind meant specially for this purpose, which never fails. Why didn't you obey me?'

"I answered him: 'General, this is the best kind of noose I could manage. I don't know how to tie the special kind for hanging, and none of the officers or soldiers here knew how either. I sent for two soldiers who have been in jail, and they couldn't give me any information about it.'

" 'Well, none of you knows very much,' he answered, 'and you don't deserve the confidence I repose in you. Give me that rope, and I'll teach you how to tie the knot.'

"One of the soldiers climbed into the tree and untied the rope and threw it to me; but the General, agilely stepping ahead of me, caught it in the air. He tucked his riding-crop, which he was carrying in his right hand, under his arm and put his cigarette in one corner of his mouth so it would be out of his way. And there in the middle of the yard, under the curious gaze of officers and soldiers, he set dexterously about tying the sinister, complicated death-noose. The smoke of his cigarette got into his eyes and gave his face, contorted to strange angles, a satanic, Mephistophelian expression. With rapid, skilful movements of his fingers he brought one end of the rope over the rope itself, twisting it so as to form at the end the strangling noose. It was a long, closely wound cylinder, on the inside of which the rope ran freely, and which was as stiff as iron, so as to break the prisoner's neck at the vertebræ below the head, when the chair was jerked away.

" 'There you are,' he said, handing me the noose. I took it, looked it over, and threw it to the soldier in the tree, who caught it and tied it to the bough again.

"At 7.40 the general sent to ask Don Carlos Valdés if he was ready to hand over his share of the loan. Valdés answered that he was ready enough, but that he didn't have the money or any hope of getting it. Thereupon the general ordered a squad of twenty men to bring the prisoners into the yard. Then he said to me:

" 'Order all the officers in the building to report here at once.'

"When I returned, profound silence reigned in the yard. Fifteen feet from the live-oak stood the rich men sentenced to the loan or the noose, forming a parallel line with the branch from which dangled the rope swollen with its monstrous knot. At the right, at a right angle to them, stood the twenty soldiers in double column. At the left the officers formed a semicircle around the general in the order of their rank. The general was giving orders in a low voice to the sergeant and corporal of the squad.

"The sergeant immediately went over to his company; the corporal walked over to a chair that had been placed beside the one exactly below the noose.

"It was 7.45. The prisoners were deathly pale; they tried to avoid seeing anything, but they saw

>>>>>>>>>>>>>>>>>>>><<<<<<<<<<<<<<<<<<<<

everything. Valdés was the calmest of them all. But he was not wholly serene. One touch revealed his sub-conscious anxiety: the way he kept rubbing his dry lower lip with his left hand.

"The General drew from his pocket the list he had made up the previous evening, and read in a voice that reverberated solemnly:

" 'Don Carlos Valdés.'

" 'Present,' answered Valdés.

" 'Are you willing to obey the orders the revolution has dictated to you through me?'

" 'As I told you, General, and I don't see how you can have any doubts about the matter, I am perfectly willing to obey, but I have no money, nor any way of getting it.'

" 'Very well, Mr. Valdés. You will have only your own stubborn refusal to obey legitimate orders to blame for the consequences. You have two minutes in which to make up your mind. As the revolution must be prepared to carry out its orders, we will proceed with certain preparations. . . . Sergeant, you have your orders!'

"The sergeant took two soldiers and went over to Valdés. He tied his hands behind his back and then, taking him by the arms, led him over to the chairs and made him climb up on one of them. Then leaving the two soldiers with the condemned man, he stepped back to his place with his squad.

"In the mean time the corporal had climbed on to the other chair and, raising his arms, brought the noose around Don Carlos Valdés's neck.

"The sergeant called out: 'Present—arms!'

"The fellow-prisoners of Valdés were in a state of mortal terror. Their legs shook, and their eyes, almost popping out of their sockets, were glued to the rope. He was very pale, but very quiet, and he kept his eyes fixed on the general, who in turn had his fixed on his wrist-watch.

"Several seconds went by. Suddenly the general raised his head to look at Valdés and said:

" 'Don Carlos Valdés: it is now 7.47. Your time is up. Are you ready to hand over the five thousand pesos, yes or no?'

"Valdés kept looking at the general without answering a word. The general then turned to the corporal.

" 'Carry out your orders!' he said.

"The corporal jerked away the chair on which Valdés was standing and left him hanging from the rope.

"The noose instantaneously closed up, and the knot held tight. Don Carlos Valdés threshed about in the air with frightful contortions and a horrible fluttering of his tied hands.

"The other four prisoners gave a scream of terror and, clinging to each other, turned towards the wall.

"The officers shuddered.

"The general did not move an eyelash.

"At nine o'clock that morning Don Ciriaco Díaz González handed over his six thousand pesos. Don Pedro Salas Duarte paid his seven thousand before eleven. And the two other leading citizens paid their quotas before noon.

"A little while later the general, looking at the money stacked up in orderly little heaps on his campaign table said to me:

" 'See how this system never fails to bring results. They all paid up.'

" 'All except Valdés,' I answered.

" 'Valdés? Of course. But I knew he wouldn't pay. He didn't have a cent to his name.'

" 'But then . . . why did we hang him?'

" 'Why? God, you're green. Because if we hanged him, there was no doubt that the rest would pay.' "

Chapter XX

Shades of the Prison-Cell

BACK in Mexico City again, I threw myself whole-heartedly into the anti-Carranza movement.

Luis Cabrera used to come almost every day to the house where Lucio Blanco lived in Héroes Street —the beautiful mansion that had belonged to Don Joaquín D. Casasús. He often lunched or dined there, and afterwards he used to embark on long discussions with Lucio, which we, the latter's friends, avoided interrupting even by our presence.

One morning shortly after Cabrera's arrival, Lucio took me aside and said:

"I think it's time to come out in the open with Cabrera. Nevertheless, we can't take too much of a risk, so I think it would be better if you spoke to him in my name. Be as clear as you can without going into details—above all, don't mention any name but mine—and ask him, for me, to say where he stands."

So I went over to Cabrera and, taking him by the arm, led him into one of the rooms at the rear of the house where we could talk without anybody's interrupting or overhearing us.

There was a little corner-sofa in the room, and we sat down there and began to talk. Our conversation flitted from one topic to another, and when finally a favourable opportunity presented itself, I entered on the subject without any hedging.

"Carranza," I said, "is nothing but a self-seeking politician who is devilishly shrewd at turning to his own advantage his training in the old school of Mexican politics. There is no real sense of civic duty or ideals of any kind in the man. Nobody that is not a flatterer and boot-licker, or that doesn't pretend to be for what he can get out of it later on, can work with him. He corrupts people on system; he fans the evil passions, the petty intrigues, even dishonesty, in those who surround him, so he can better manage and hold the whip-hand over them. There is not a revolutionist with any personality, or even sincerely devoted to the cause, who, if he has not been willing to let himself be used as a tool, has not been obliged to break with him or accept an insignificant, humiliating role. And those who have not yet openly broken with him are on tenter-hooks and don't know what attitude to take. You know as well as I do that many of our friends are in one of these two situations. This is what has happened or is happening with Maytorena, with Angeles, with Villarreal, with Blanco, with Vasconcelos, with Bonilla, and even with you. You remember the way he treated you in Nogales. The truth is that Carranza dreams of the possibility of becoming another Porfirio Díaz, a bigger and better Porfirio Díaz, for at heart he admires and venerates his memory. Isn't it apparent that Carranza is trying to turn everything to this one end, and that he doesn't care a rap about the good the revolution might bring to Mexico? You know perfectly well that from the first moment Carranza has systematically kept the revolution divided against itself. When he came to Sonora, he was defeated, helpless, without resources of any kind. He knew what a poor military leader he had in Pablo González, and he wanted to take refuge in a remote corner of the country where nobody would dispute his command. Nobody else would have behaved so nobly with him as Maytorena did. He put himself at his service and recognized him as leader, because he thought his first duty was to preserve the unity of the revolution. But as Carranza knew that the only person who would have the right to dispute his leadership when they triumphed was Maytorena, the minute he felt himself strong again, he set about widening the breach between the two Sonora groups, those of Maytorena and Pesqueira, and paid him back with treachery for saving him from failure and ridicule. As soon as he saw that Felipe Angeles was a good and able man, all uprightness and unselfishness, made for big things, not for the mean tricks nor the underhanded wirepulling of selfish, ambitious fakers, he shoved him to one side, tormented him until he made him lose his head. Finally, when he realized that Villa was responsible for the revolution's military victories, he hampered him in every way he could. Carranza and his followers cannot forgive Villa for the big victories from Juárez City to Zacatecas, for they all know that they owe their success to those victories. As long as Carranza is in control, the revolution will never have the ambition nor the vision nor the ability to carry out a program that would justify it. Carranza's only idea is to get rid of all those who do not accept and submit to his dictatorship, and once he has done this, you may be sure that he'll let those who back him up do whatever they please. With Carranza the country and the revolution are headed straight for destruction: it will become a series of personal struggles, disguised as the conflict of principles; it will become a state of anarchy in which scoundrels will stop at nothing to get power and riches, and will not feel the least scruple at plunging Mexico into a situation still worse than under Victoriano Huerta. For this reason we believe that if Carranza doesn't go, we'll have to give up hope of any good coming out of the revolution. General Blanco knows that you do not belong to the servile group of Carranza-followers, and so he has asked me to lay these ideas before you in his name and tell you about our plans. We are determined to oppose Carranza's selfish and unprincipled domination. Do you want to join us?"

Cabrera had interrupted me several times in the course of my talk, either to make sure of my meaning or to approve and assent to what I was saying. When I had finished, he said that, offhand, he agreed with what I proposed to him; but, still, he wanted to take time to think things over before he definitely said yes or no. So we agreed to take up the matter again two or three days later.

Cabrera's answer did not please Lucio Blanco. "I'm very much surprised," he said; "for, from what I had talked with him, I imagined he would accept at once without hesitation. I regret now that we took this chance."

I did not feel the same way. Cabrera might or might not be on our side; but, in any event, the matter was a serious one and he couldn't be expected to plunge into it head first, without thinking. Besides, looking at things *a posteriori,* from the point of view of his personal success, Cabrera would seem to have been right. At that time, when he said he agreed with me, if he had also said that he would join us, perhaps afterwards he would not have been able to go back on his word when he changed his mind, and he would have suffered the same fate as all the other opponents of Carranza at the time: death or exile after the failure of the Convention. The other way he did achieve his

>>>>>>>>>>>>>>>>>>>>>><<<<<<<<<<<<<<<<<<<<

personal ambitions; he won back consideration and
power, he became influential, was made minister. Of
course, one could say that if at the time all the revolutionists of Cabrera's standing and ability had stood
out against Carranza, he couldn't have done what
he did and Mexico would have been spared this
visitation and all its demoralizing consequences. But
then there comes another question: if it had not been
Carranza, could we be sure things would have been
any better? This becomes a matter of opinion. Some
of us say yes, and some no, but neither side can prove
its point. The only thing is that we who say yes have
the satisfaction of not having taken part in the work
of destruction.

And I did not feel with Lucio that we had exposed
ourselves by talking with Cabrera. I had then—and
still have—a very good opinion of Cabrera. My
dealings with him, which were not only of a political
nature, had given me reason to believe in his loyalty,
or that he would at least keep quiet like a gentleman.
Even now I do not think I was mistaken.

Nevertheless, subsequent events took the course
that might have been expected. Two or three days
after my conversation with Cabrera, Colonel Domínguez and I met Alfredo Breceda at Blanco's house.

"Well, well," he said, "I'm certainly glad to see
you, and especially the two of you together. I was
looking for both of you. The Chief wants to have a

conference by telegraph with Villa, and he wanted
you to be there, since you are acting as his agents
here. Don't you feel that we all ought to make an
effort to smooth out these petty quarrels that are
dividing us?"

Domínguez, always uncalculating and impulsive,
immediately accepted Breceda's proposal. And he did
it in such a way that when I tried to interfere, it was
too late. Breceda had already affectionately linked
arms with both of us and was leading us towards the
door, bubbling over with flattery and pleasantries.

We all got into the automobile that had brought
Breceda, and started towards the palace. On the way
I kept thinking what an idiotic thing we had done.
That morning Breceda oozed treachery from every
pore. One had only to look at him to see it: his face
was greener than ever; his lips were more livid and
shapeless than usual, and his eyelids, half-smooth and
half-lined, like a bat's wing, drooped still farther
over his dull eyes to conceal their expression. And
how could anybody that knew Carranza at all believe
Breceda's lies about the conference with Villa by wire,
and all the other nonsense he chattered on the way?
Carranza would tolerate and forgive anything except not bowing down to him completely and not looking on him as the very embodiment of divine inspira-
tion. It was ridiculous to think that he was suddenly
going to accept Domínguez and me, who took no
pains to hide our lack of respect for him, as Villa's

>>>>>>>>>>>>>>>>>>>>>><<<<<<<<<<<<<<<<<<<<

representatives, and wanted us to help him to placate the warrior's anger.

When we got to the palace, Breceda led us into a waiting-room in the private offices. There was nobody there.

"Please wait for me a minute here," he said. "I'm going to let the Chief know you're here, and then I'll come back for you." And he went out.

"You're not dry behind the ears yet," I said to Domínguez as soon as we were alone. "Breceda will soon be back for us, but he won't be alone. Get ready to see a squad of soldiers come through that door for us. I don't say we should have refused to come, but we shouldn't have come like this."

Domínguez didn't say anything at first. On the way from Lucio's house to the palace he had had plenty of time to see how I felt about the situation.

Then he said: "You're too suspicious." And he began to pace up and down the room.

I opened one of the French windows that over-looked the street and leaned over the balustrade, watching the bustling crowds of people below. Ten, fifteen, twenty-five minutes went by like this.

"One of two things," I thought as I stood there: "either Alfredo Breceda hasn't been able to get in to see Carranza, and that's keeping him, or he is having difficulties managing the details of getting us away without any fuss."

I tried to take my mind off our plight by watching the sights in the street, which afforded a continuous panorama of bright, unexpected, amusing scenes of local colour. Little by little, however, this very spectacle, a dazzling blend of light and sound, made the image of freedom seem more beautiful and desirable than ever to me. The most trivial of the incidents taking place before me awakened in me the horrible sense of oppression that a lack of liberty produces. It was as though the noise from the sidewalk and the shouts of the fruit-venders were tearing from my soul the apathy that had settled over it half an hour before in the presence of the inevitable.

"Why let oneself be caught like this?" I thought. The idea, vague at first, and somehow mixed with the sight of piles of bright oranges for sale and the push-carts of the pastry-pedlars with their heaps of glossy, sugared cakes, suddenly grew clear. And once clear, it immediately transformed itself into action. I turned quickly into the room where Domínguez was pacing like a caged animal, for he already felt himself a prisoner. He looked at me inquiringly.

"Let's go," I said, lowering my voice. "It's foolish to stay on here. If Carranza really wanted to talk to us, I wouldn't care how long we had to wait. But they're making us wait too long to catch us. Anyway, I'm going, if you don't want to."

Domínguez was in enthusiastic agreement with me, and we began to consider the best way to get out of there. We had to keep the employees of the offices from seeing us. So we opened one of the doors leading to the corridor that encircled the inside court, and slipped through it. Then we walked calmly down the stairs to the other courtyard and out of the front door. In a minute we were lost in the crowds in the street.

How bright the sun seems when one has been on the point of losing it!

We went back to Lucio Blanco's house and told him what had happened. He absolutely agreed with me that Breceda had laid a trap for us.

"I'd advise you not to leave here," he said, "until I can find out how things stand. I'm going to sound Carranza out. We'll see if this comes directly from him, or if it is one of that busybody Breceda's machinations. Anyway, it's a good thing to get to the bottom of it if we can. After Guzmán's talk with Cabrera, this looks bad to me."

Chapter XXI

Requisitioned for the Service

DOMÍNGUEZ and I stayed and had dinner with Lucio Blanco that day. The servants of the Casasús family, whom Lucio had kept on, served us. The dining-room furniture, naturally, belonged to the Casasúses; likewise the dishes and the silver. And if I am not mistaken, we even saw a bottle or two on this occasion from Don Joaquín Casasús's cellar, which was abundantly stocked when Blanco billeted himself in that magnificent house.

The cellar, as well as everything else in the house, was a constant source of worry and annoyance to Lucio Blanco rather than of sybaritic satisfaction. At first, so nobody would touch the wine, he had the cellar padlocked. And with the same idea in mind he got hold of good grooms to take care of the splendid horses in the stables. He had a scrupulous respect for the belongings of others—in so far as respect was possible under the circumstances. For this same reason he raised the housekeeper's salary, putting her in charge of the house and everything in it and making her personally responsible for its care. But as he heard afterwards that in spite of all the precautions and all the locks the precious liquor was disappearing from the cellar without anybody's knowing how, he decided to use it himself for the table.

"I'll have to choose the lesser of two evils. If the wines are going to be stolen, it's better for me to take them and use them for my guests. In this way I'll be openly responsible and will have to pay for them, and nobody can say I sneaked them out to send to my relatives. We might as well face the facts. The revolution is not all idealism; we have our black-guards, too, and unfortunately they are the ones who give the tone here. To these rascals the revolution means a chance to steal and destroy everything they can lay their hands on."

It was the same with everything else in the house. Blanco had the worst kind of a time to keep the library of the translator of *Evangeline* from being sacked to the last volume. The half-educated Coahuilans were such fast workers that two or three days after the troops entered Mexico City, they had secured an order from General Headquarters to take to Saltillo whatever volumes they wished from Don Joaquín's library. A more predatory order was rarely issued, and if it was not carried out—or at least not while Blanco was living in the house—it was thanks to the efforts of this revolutionary general, who stood out

>>>>>>>>>>>>>>>>>>>>><<<<<<<<<<<<<<<<<<<<<

against the robbery when freebooting was the law of the day.

For the explanation of what took place while Carranza was in power is to be found, better than in anything else, in the voluntary confusion that sprang up between *meum* and *tuum,* the confusion existing in taking, not in giving. Without this peculiarly characteristic detail his rule becomes an almost unintelligible political phenomenon. One cannot otherwise understand the historical significance—as apart from the merely individual—of the private acts of many of Carranza's close followers, nor the culminating moments in the political events of these days and shortly afterwards: the official looting of the banks, the paper-money scandal in Vera Cruz, and the standardization of the currency.

It is curious how the public, so prone to make mistakes—notwithstanding what is said to the contrary —and so inclined to attribute heroism and grandeur to clay-footed gods, hit the nail on the head in this case from the very first. From Carranza the popular fancy coined *carrancear,* and "to carranzaize" and "to steal" became synonymous. Stealing became a categorical imperative in the adherents of Carranza, in part because it was a safe, quick way of getting what they wanted, and in part as a sport and amusement. Besides, it was an arm against their enemies, or those they considered their enemies, and friends and relatives of these. It became the system to wipe out opposition by kleptomaniac methods. This was what unprincipled leaders had made of a popular uprising that at first had wanted only to restore the political and moral balance which had been destroyed by the assassination of Madero. This systematic thieving explains what happened in the wealthy homes that had been taken over in Mexico City. It also throws light on certain seeming contradictions. For instance, the actual occupants of the house did not, as a rule, take anything for themselves, or very little. But at the same time it was almost incredible how they tolerated, or even encouraged, the slow looting of property that was not theirs, furniture, bric-à-brac, even clothes. There were many cases of this, like that of the young officer who was quartered in a beautiful mansion in Tacubaya. The fancy girls that used to call on him almost never left with empty hands. The dialogue that preceded the thieving always ran something like this:

"Oh, boy, what a stunning lamp!"

"Do you like it, sugar?"

"Do I like it! I'll tell the world! Aren't those three girls the best-looking things?" (It was a beautiful alabaster lamp, with the three Graces for a base.) Just look at their arms and their legs! And what a precious shade! Honestly, I don't know which I like better, the lamp or the shade."

"You know," answered the officer, thus made

aware of the beauties of the lamp, "it is a pretty lamp."

"Listen, honey, why don't you give it to me? Come on, give it to me!"

"Why, chicken, you must be crazy. How'm I going to give away a lamp that isn't mine?"

"Well, then, don't give it to me; let me take it."

"That's a different matter. Take it if you want to. But I don't promise that they won't come and take it away from you afterwards."

And "Chicken" or "Baby" or whoever it might be would leave the house carrying off in her car whatever she liked best.

Things of this sort did not happen in the house in Héroes Street. There Lucio Blanco, out of a sense of honesty and fair play, tried to act as a faithful custodian of the beautiful furnishings and fittings that chance had put in his hands. But it must be admitted that he was only partly successful. There was such a spirit of rapacity in the air that it affected the very ones detailed to combat it. Did not the woman who had been recommended to Blanco as scrupulously honest and reliable, whose one duty was to see that nothing was stolen, force the locks on the closets to make it seem that certain things she had taken had been stolen? That day Lucio forgot his gallantry, and the lady, who had entered the house a few weeks

before surrounded by a halo of uprightness, was literally kicked into the street.

But the poor house could not be saved. Blanco's
efforts fell helpless before the very nature of things.
The only way to have protected the house would have
been not to occupy it. Once quartered there, and with
soldiers around, the consequences had to be what they
were. The troops would leave in this mansion what
they left everywhere: dirt and destruction. The appearance of the beautiful entrance hall a few days
after the guard had been stationed there was an indication of what might be expected. Everything was
dirty, neglected, stained, on the verge of falling to
pieces.

The very drawing-rooms, where the soldiers rarely
entered, gave mutc evidence of the treatment they
had received. The visitor who did not drop ashes or
matches on the priceless rugs, scorched the beautiful
wood of the floors, or stained the draperies and curtains with his dirty fingers, or left the muddy imprint
of his shoes on the silk-upholstered chairs. Lucio had
stationed an orderly there just to watch out for the
cigarette butts: as soon as one was thrown on the
floor, he was to pick it up; or when one was left on
the furniture, he was to take it away. Useless precautions! Man's capacity for destruction, if no internal force restrains him, is unlimited. With a few
exceptions nobody came to Don Joaquin Casasús's

house who did not leave a trace of his visit. There was every degree: from those who stood up on the delicate little tables to those who entertained themselves for hours at a time by letting themselves drop with all their weight into the easy chairs again and again to see how the cushions regained their resiliency as soon as the weight was removed. After doing this long enough a moment arrived in which the cushion stayed flat.

This was all a depressing indication of what was to be expected. On the one hand ideals were degenerating, and on the other inanimate objects and instruments, worn out and abused by unappreciative or perverse hands, seemed to lose their properties as though convinced of the futility of trying to serve mankind.

Chapter XXII

An Ambush in the Palace

LUCIO saw the President and brought away from the interview a fairly encouraging impression. Carranza, to be sure, had avoided any reference to Villa or Breceda or us; but, at the same time, he said nothing to confirm our suspicions that Breceda was plotting something.

"In a word," Blanco wound up, "either Carranza already suspects me and has approved what we think are Breceda's plans, or there isn't any plan. The worst part of the whole situation, as I see it, is that you fellows aren't going to want to keep out of sight until the doubt is cleared up. Why don't you play safe and go with Villa?"

And, in truth, Domínguez and I could not bring ourselves to stay shut up. That same afternoon we went out for a walk in the hope that everything would be all right. One comforting thought buoyed us up: we did not doubt that Breceda would stop at nothing, no matter how low it was, for he was capable of everything. But, pretending to be friends with us, as he did, why should he double-cross us like this when he could so easily get somebody else to do it?

So we set out from Blanco's house seeing everything in a rosy light.

About five o'clock that afternoon on Plateros Street we met General Saucedo and General Santos Coy. Saucedo asked us to come with him to "La Esmeralda."

"There's something I've been wanting to do for several days," he said. "First of all, I want to buy Lucio a present. I owe it to him. And I want to give each of you a little token to remember me by. This is a good time, come along with me. I'll get your remembrance and you help me pick out something nice for General Blanco."

It took a long time in "La Esmeralda." Saucedo wanted something out of the ordinary for Lucio, and nothing they brought out satisfied him. He even selected the souvenirs for Domínguez and me with meticulous care. We took a long time to look over and consider the various things that Blanco might like, and while we were about it, Breceda suddenly appeared in the store. How in the world had he happened to run across us? It was astonishing.

He walked straight over to Domínguez and me and began in a half-friendly, half-indignant tone:

"A nice mess you made of things this morning! You

certainly got me in bad with Don Venustiano. He
made an appointment with Villa for the conference by
telegraph; Villa was there on the dot; the Chief was
waiting in the telegraph office; and when I went to
get you, you were gone. Don Venustiano was furious
with me, but he put off the conference till this afternoon and he expects you. I've been looking everywhere for you for three hours. So please come with
me, for I won't face the Chief without you."

Could he be telling the truth? Anyway he got
the better of our suspicions.

"This morning," Domínguez answered, "we
waited three-quarters of an hour. Then, as you didn't
come back, we supposed the thing had fallen through
and we went home."

"Well, the important thing is for you to come now,
right away. Do it for my sake."

"All right, we'll go whenever you want us to."
And turning to Saucedo, I said: "General, you see
that Don Venustiano has sent for us. So you'll have
to excuse us. Many thanks for the 'remembrance,'
and I hope you'll soon let me return the compliment."

Domínguez and Breceda also made their adieus to
the two generals, and the three of us left the jewelry-
shop. As soon as we were outside, Breceda said:

"Listen, fellows, if it's all right with you, I'm going
ahead in the car and you can walk over. That way
there'll be time enough to get things ready so
you won't have to wait as you did this morning. I'll

be in the private office. You come right up there."

He got into the car and drove off.

Domínguez and I followed along the avenue to the square. We hardly spoke a word all the way. Only as we crossed the market-place, he said to me:

"Well, what do you think now?"

"I don't think anything," I answered. "But anyway it's better to take the bull by the horns."

We entered the palace by the main gate. As we passed by the flag of the company on guard, we respectfully removed our hats. In front of the stairway leading to the private offices stood an automobile; strangely enough, it was pulled up so close to the door that there was barely room for one or two people to get by. I paid no attention to it at the time; it was only later on that I thought about it. The chauffeur had a military bearing. It seemed to me that behind a pillar near the car and the entrance I caught a glimpse of the brim of a hat very much like the one Breceda was wearing.

Domínguez and I went to pass between the car and the door. I was going first and he after me. But just as we were pushing the door open, eight or ten soldiers appeared on the stairs, covering us with their rifles, which had the bayonets fixed.

"Hands up!"

Our first instinct was to step back and reach for our revolvers. But before we could try it, we discovered that two sergeants, who had stepped out of the other side of the car, were resting the muzzles of their pistols against the middle of our backs. Domínguez, smiling, put up his arms. And I, who could feel that one of the soldiers was doing more than merely threaten me with his bayonet—it was going into my stomach—took hold of the gun with both hands, though offering no resistance, and I did not mince words telling the brute what I thought of him. Another minute and he would have run me through.

"Hand over your weapons!"

"Either 'Hands up' or 'Hand over your weapons,'" Domínguez answered. "We can't do both things at the same time."

The sergeants settled the argument by taking our pistols out of our pockets, and after making sure that we had no other weapons, they made us step back to the door of the car.

The poor soldiers and the two sergeants looked terrified. They must have been told that we were dangerous, and that it would be a hard job to arrest us. They eyed Domínguez and me like a pair of wild animals. This explained the very elaborate plan and everything else, including the vigour with which the soldier had handled his bayonet.

The sergeants indicated with their pistols that we were to get into the motor. One of them came inside with us and sat facing us so he could cover us both with his pistol. The other, in front with the chauffeur, had his gun ready, too. And the car started off, followed by the curious glances of the few people who had witnessed the scene. In my last recollection of the courtyard, as I saw it that day from the inside of the car, there appears again behind a pillar the brim of a hat like Breceda's.

The car went by the company on guard, drove round the Palace, and turned into Correo Mayor Street towards Lecumberri.

"To prison," I said to Domínguez.

"It looks that way," he answered.

And as the sergeant sat there with his pistol cocked and his eyes glued on us, Domínguez said to him:

"Put your pistol down, brother, and put it away. We haven't any intention of escaping, among other reasons because it doesn't suit our plans. If it did, you may be sure your pistol wouldn't stop us."

The unmistakable note of authority in Domínguez' voice so cowed the sergeant that he obeyed. He first lowered the pistol and finally put it into its holster.

Chapter XXIII

In Prison

GENERAL CARLOS PLANK, the warden of the prison, always had a smile on his lips, and in the smile a pipe. He was like an overgrown child, all rosy, fair, and bright.

That afternoon when he saw Domínguez and me brought into the prison by two sergeants and a considerable escort, his astonishment knew no bounds. His smile faded away for a minute; his pipe came out in his hand.

"You prisoners? How's that?"

And while the necessary preliminaries for our entrance were being attended to, he kept looking at us again and again, with a growing expression of incredulity on his childish, smiling face. When he was left alone with us, he said:

"Boys, I just can't get it through my head that you're here as prisoners. And as nobody can make me believe it, I'm going to treat you like guests, not prisoners."

Plank installed us in his own house; that is to say, in the quarters he occupied as prison warden. He gave us several large, airy, sunny rooms. The largest of these had windows on the street and on a court-yard. What a temptation to a prisoner those windows were, fifteen feet from the ground! A sheet tied to the railing, and a horse waiting below, were all we needed. But I must say that it never entered our mind for a minute to pay back Plank for his courtesy and consideration towards us in such a way.

We spent our first hours of captivity as people do when they move, fixing up our new house with a view to making it comfortable. Plank put a boy at our serv-ice immediately, and he helped us arrange the fur-niture as we wanted it. We decided to use the large room as a sitting-room, the one next to it as a bed-room, and the other as a dining-room. To see us so busied with all these tasks, anybody would have said that we were delighted to be in jail.

The fact is that this seclusion which had been forced on us, far from seeming the harbinger of some tragic denouement, was to us more like a game or one of the trifling ups and downs of our political adventures. Don Venustiano still preserved among his scant virtues a very praiseworthy one: not to kill. So it was possible to be in his clutches without feeling oneself in mortal danger. And, knowing this, we promptly consoled ourselves with the small amenities of our prison life. Two hours after we reached the

penitentiary, we received our first visit, from Miguel
Alessio Robles. He came to express his sympathy and
offer us his help.

"That stubborn old fool," he said, "is going to be
the ruin of the revolution, with his vanity and his
treachery."

And he went from Don Venustiano to his most intimate colleagues, flaying them in his best style; he
was already a formidable orator, and with time he
was to launch his ideas from loftier platforms than
the comfortable prison sitting-room where we were
at the time.

He talked vehemently with us on his constant theme
of how the revolution could be freed from personal
intriguers, and when he left, an hour later, he was
overflowing with active plans. He went off determined to do away with Carranzaism and every other
ism that departed from the pure constitutionalism
which should restore the law and avenge Madero's
assassination. Towards the end of his visit Plank
came in, and in a burst of enthusiasm Alessio Robles
said to him:

"See here, Charlie, why don't they arrest me? Just
tell me why. For I am absolutely anti-Carranza."

And he went down the stairs repeating this so that
everybody who had ears could hear him, from the
jailers and officials to the Yaqui soldiers on guard.
Good, generous old Miguel! From the windows I
watched him disappear in the grey twilight. A kind

of murmur accompanied his uneven footsteps: probably the wake of his vociferations in defence of his imprisoned friends. And he did not stop at merely defending us, as we should learn later. For that night we received from the Café Colón, in his name, a delicious dinner, complete from entrées to cigars, and during the whole time of our captivity the same thing was repeated morning, noon, and night, without a single exception.

Don Venustiano's efforts to stamp out opposition did not stop with us. The day after our arrest other politicians connected, or supposed to be connected, with the dissident groups of Sonora, Sinaloa, and Chihuahua were taken into custody and sent to the penitentiary. These were Luis G. Malváez, Don Manuel Bonilla, Enrique C. Llorente, his brother Leopoldo, and two or three days afterwards José Ortiz Rodríguez and Luis Zamora Plowes, at the time editor of *ABC*. Apparently Carranza was now throwing off all pretence and had completely yielded to the temptation of becoming a despot, which is irresistible to the redeemers and liberators of Mexico. But so far all he got by this was to inflame the opposition in the street by the very prestige that he himself gave to the opposition in prison. The truth is that, prisoners though we were, we did not waste our time. On the one hand, Carranza put his opponents out of the way in prison; on the other, Domínguez and I, with these same politicians, formed a colony there in the penitentiary that in activity could be properly compared with a beehive. Plank made no objection to our request to have Luis G. Malvácz come and live with us, and it wasn't hard to have Don Manuel Bonilla and his companions assigned to the rooms next to ours. In this way we were all together on the first floor of the main building, and our rooms opened on to a hall that overlooked the garden.

Our political activities could bear fruit, thanks, on the one hand, to the kindly tolerance of Plank and Martínez Urristra, the assistant warden, and, on the other, to our unbroken contact with the outside world through our continual visitors. For there wasn't a revolutionist that didn't visit us then, from the most daring to the most indifferent: Lucio Blanco, Alberto J. Pani, Luis Cabrera, Obregón, Acosta, Saucedo, Villarreal, Vasconcelos, Santos Coy, even Alfredo Breceda himself, who had the brazenness to pretend that he hadn't the slightest idea why we were in this situation, and who offered to do everything he could for us with the First Chief. If my memory does not fail me, the only one of our friends who forgot us at this time was Isidro Fabela; this was especially hard on Enrique C. Llorente, who loved him like a brother and who almost wept at the thought of his indifference.

But the visits of these exalted personages were not the only ones that interested us. There were others, like those of the secret police agents, that while less agreeable were more interesting. Domínguez and I—especially I—had had a hand in organizing the first police service in the city under the revolutionary régime, and as, after that, we had seen to it that we should be informed daily about what we wanted to know, it became a habit in several of the agents to report to us. Even though we were in prison, this custom was not interrupted; the agents came to see us every morning to tell us what they knew. In this way we learned about all sorts of schemes and plans, some of them pretty shady, like the one to have the "Gaucho Mújica" kill Villa, and we were thus enabled to take a hand in the game ourselves. The plan for the gaucho was typical. Mújica was to go to Villa, win his confidence, and then, when a favourable moment came, strike. (This plan was similar to the one which with certain military touches was to be used later on to assassinate Zapata.) But we had time to interfere and spoil the plot against Villa, as will be seen further on.

Nor did we suffer for lack of other distractions, not political. Every afternoon Lucio Blanco used to send us a military band. The musicians gathered in a circle under our windows and played for hours on end whatever we asked for. We also liked to have them come inside and play in the corridors, and the wardens, out of pity for the prisoners, were always very glad to allow it. The metal framework and gratings of the cells echoed with the reverberation of the brasses and the cymbals and the shrill vibrations of the flutes and clarinets. And to see the miracle which *Adelita* or *Valentina* worked in the most hardened criminals brought to mind the myth of Orpheus.

Some mornings we used to stroll through the corridors and inside courts and we often discovered scenes and details that were interesting or moving, even if not pleasant. We would spend a long time trying to decipher inscriptions on the walls; we would enter into long discussions with the most dangerous prisoners on themes of human conduct and problems, and sometimes they would tell us the story of their lives. And occasionally we would observe from a distance and with a strange curiosity—as though they were creatures from another planet—the followers of Huerta and the reactionaries imprisoned there. Among these were men of high standing: Nacho de la Torre, always ailing, stretched out on his cot and covered with rich blankets and comforters; General Mondragón, aged and pale; and any number of officers and civilians of every origin, appearance, and type.

We could not help feeling a certain sympathy for these adherents of Porfirio Díaz and Huerta who were prisoners there like ourselves. And for two of them we even felt gratitude—a very peculiar kind of gratitude—for, without knowing it, they were responsible for the best moments in our penitentiary existence. We owed them what I used to call the "pathetic hour" and the "Dionysiac hour," both so significant, though in different ways, that we used to look on them as the most outstanding event of each day that passed, and look forward to them as the supreme happening of the day to come.

The "pathetic hour" was the daily arrival of Doña Amanda Díaz de De la Torre, who came to see her husband. At first her frequent visits met with certain difficulties, as they were against the rules. But afterwards, as a result of Domínguez's and my efforts, about which she knew nothing, Plank and Martínez Urristra, like the excellent fellows they were, smoothed out everything, to our great satisfaction. Our efforts were more than repaid by the sight of the beautiful lady.

She always arrived in a cheap hired cab, and her whole being radiated an air of serene, profound melancholy, which charmed and captivated us. Her dark slender silhouette combined dignity and grace in the perfection of its lines. From our windows we would watch her descend from her carriage and, inside the building, cross the courtyard, enveloped in an atmosphere that she created as she moved. There are supreme majesties, in nature as among mankind, who triumph by their mere appearance. Thus the swan is itself the herald of its grace; and when Doña Amanda Díaz appeared, everything around her seemed to

fade into shadow that she might shine alone. Ten
years before, I had seen her arrive, dressed in red
velvet and sparkling with rubies, at a fashionable ball
given by the School of Mines; now she walked alone
and in mourning through the sinister court and corridors of a prison. But she was not a whit less under
these circumstances than she had been before. On her
beautiful Indian face, half hidden by a simple, becoming hat, grief and suffering had left no trace;
there was only a calm, melancholy dignity, so assured
and poised that something of it was left in the atmosphere that surrounded her.

The "Dionysiac hour" was the daily morning appearance of the daughter of one of the Huerta generals who was imprisoned there. Her coming was like
that of spring; the most hidden sources of life and
desire sprang into being at her approach. We used to
crowd out on to the balcony for her coming. We
would watch her come walking across the square, and
then, as she went into the hall, we would all rush
across to the corridor, as though our lives depended
on getting there. From here we could contemplate
the conflagration lighted by her brief transit through
the courtyard. I used to think that a sixth sense had
been born in all of us, for without anybody's an-
nouncing it everybody knew when she was going to
arrive, and became all expectancy: jailers and prisoners, criminals and law-abiding men. Up in the corridor we would hang over the railing, and our glances

formed an inverted cone, the tip of which moved with her from one end of the courtyard to the other.

She moved with the most extraordinary cadence of soft, flexible rhythms. Her feet as she walked seemed to follow along one straight line, with the most exquisite movement of the ankles. Her body was like a flexible wand, and shed about it the fragrance and vigour of her youthful beauty, which as she passed seemed to flow from her into the ground and from there up the walls with the sole object of bringing to life that great stone organism and all the little organisms within it, bound during those moments with double chains.

Chapter XXIV

Prisoners on the March

THE Military Convention in session in Aguas-calientes ordered Carranza to set us free. He did not obey the command, however, but decided on his own authority to put us on the train and send us to General Nafarrate, the military commander of Mata-moros, with orders to take charge of us until we reached American territory. Don Venustiano was trying to kill two birds with one stone by doing this: first, not openly to disobey the Convention; and, second, to administer to us his favourite punishment. For Carranza, who used the death-penalty sparingly, had a great predilection for exiling his enemies, especially personal ones. It was he who re-established the system of ostracism (so contrary to the spirit and the letter of the Mexican code) to which our revolutionary governments since him have adhered so enthusiastically.

Naturally, we did not in the least mind being taken to the other side of the border. Once we were in

Brownsville, nothing could stop us from going to El Paso and entering Mexico again by way of Ciudad Juárez. And Ciudad Juárez meant Villa and Villa meant the Convention. But the thing we did not like so much was that General Nafarrate was to see us over the border. His fame as assassin rather than general was too great not to make us uneasy. Besides, there was another obvious question that added to our worry: what was the reason for expelling us by way of Matamoros when Laredo was much nearer?

The enigma puzzled us very much, and our attractive sitting-room in the penitentiary became more animated than ever and then settled down to meditation. Everybody turned the matter over in his mind, and we all agreed that what Don Venustiano had up his sleeve was to get rid of us through some one of the many resources at the command of the large and small Nafarrates in the country. (Nor were these suspicions unfounded. It was this same Nafarrate who a few months later was to shoot Aguirre Benavides, Bolaños, and the other delegates from the Convention who gave themselves up to him, trusting to the safe-conduct Pablo González had given them.)

In view of these fears some of our friends—particularly Pani and Lucio Blanco—tried to have our route changed. But their attempts proved fruitless, as was to be expected. Besides being stubborn, Carranza was despotic, which made it impossible to argue with him once he had reached even the most trifling decision. There were few things he enjoyed more than being surrounded by supplicants and ignoring them. As a matter of fact, of all the revolutionists produced in Mexico up to that time—since him there have been worse—he was the most profoundly and sincerely hostile to the rights of man. (Naturally, I am referring to those revolutionists who had some sense of responsibility for their acts and their obligations.)

At last the moment came to leave that prison, where, thanks to the kindness of General Plank and Martínez Urristra, we had not had such a bad time. To tell the truth—perhaps, in a measure, because of the fears that assaulted us—we felt a parting pang. Our imprisonment had not been without certain pleasant features, a certain novelty, and had taught us certain lessons. While there we had plotted successfully, we had acquired a first-hand knowledge of the mysterious, sometimes terrible prison world. Our acquaintance with the imprisoned followers of Huerta had taught us to weigh better the responsibilities of the politician of second rank—in a word, we had learned to be more tolerant, more understanding, more human. And we were filled with a sense of melancholy at the thought that all this, whatever it was, lay behind us now forever.

Half an hour before we left, Plank came to the rooms we had occupied, and said to us:

"Nafarrate is a bandit. You want to be careful with him. For safety's sake I'm returning your revolvers. Hide them carefully and don't give me away. If Don Venus finds out about it, I'll lose my job."

And he laughed with the sunny laugh of a blond, pink baby.

Carrying arms under those circumstances was a knife that might cut both ways. They might serve for our defence, or they might serve as a pretext to apply the escaping-prisoner law or some other similar law. Still, Plank's advice seemed good, and we followed it. Plank had always been our friend, but on this occasion he was more than just that. He talked to us like an experienced revolutionist, one who knows all the tricks of the trade. It was he who advised us not to leave Mexico alone, but to take our families with us.

"The more women and children, the better," he said. "That way there can be no doubt about your peaceful intentions, and Nafarrate can't say afterwards that you got rough and he had to teach you manners."

It was late afternoon when we left the penitentiary, to the excitement and astonishment of the neighbourhood. The less the spectators could understand all this movement of soldiers and civilians in a strange promiscuity, the more interested they became. And from the point of view of a spectacle the affair was not devoid of a certain profound and typically Mexican interest. Carranza had ordered that we be taken to the station on foot, and for greater pomp and safety—whether his pomp or ours I cannot say—he had sent an escort large enough to take care of twenty criminals.

From our big middle window, where we stood looking out for the last time, we had watched the soldiers approaching, followed by a crowd of people. When we came downstairs, the soldiers stood in formation to the right of the street-door. There Plank went through the formalities of turning us over to the Captain who had been detailed to take charge of us. The latter, for something to do, looked us over first, and then counted us off, like heads of cattle, pointing to each of us with his finger as he said:

"One, two, three, four. . . ."

But once we were in his charge, he did not know what to do with us. It seemed to embarrass him to have to conduct a string of prisoners that didn't look like prisoners; he could not screw his courage to the point of issuing orders to people before whom he felt submissive. He could not get any further than saying to us: "All right, now let's get into formation and start off."

But he gave no order. He was a man well along in years, and he had a humble, almost servile air. His uniform, like most of those of that period, displayed more dirt and patches than martial attributes—which was quite as it should be, for, aside from his pistol and the three bars on his broad-brimmed hat, there was nothing martial about him, either in his words or in his bearing.

For the third or fourth time he repeated: "All right, now let's get into formation and start to the station."

But what he did was to take a cigarette out of his pocket and light it.

Evidently he was overawed by us. We were something new in his experience and he was reluctant to proceed. Finally we grew impatient. Domínguez exchanged a few words with us and then turned to the Captain and addressed him in these impressive terms:

"You know that I am a Colonel?"

"Yes, Colonel."

"You know what the rules provide for a case like this? I am referring to my prerogatives, my rank, my rights. . . ."

"Yes, Colonel."

"Then, Captain, you won't object if, in spite of the fact that I am under arrest, I take command of the squad?"

"At your orders, Colonel!"

No sooner said than done. Domínguez took command and did not relinquish it. His first act of authority was to order eight or ten taxis. Then he put the prisoners in some, the soldiers in others, he and I got

>>>>>>>>>>>>>>>>>>>>>><<<<<<<<<<<<<<<<<<<<

in with the Captain, and in this fashion we set out towards the station.

Mexico then was not the desolate city it has become in later years. San Francisco still preserved much of the gentle but imposing tranquility of the years 1905 and 1906. As we rolled slowly down the avenue, our cars plunged into the rising tide of brilliant joyous existence. After our long imprisonment it was like feeling a breeze from the sea or the mountains in our faces.

Lucio Blanco and other friends were waiting for us at the station and with them our families, ready to accompany us into exile. Altogether we were going to form a numerous caravan.

The train was already filled with passengers. Domínguez advised the Captain to give orders that room was to be made for us. And the Captain, who bristled with energy when somebody else was in command, ordered a first-class coach vacated "for the needs of the service." The passengers made vigorous and noisy objections. But in five minutes the coach was empty, and all of us, escort, prisoners and families, got in and made ready to settle ourselves. Our thirty soldiers immediately made the car reek with their customary odour. The ladies of the party could not stand it, and Domínguez took steps to remedy the difficulty. It was not much trouble to persuade the

Captain to make certain modifications in the plans
for the trip; the "needs of the service" made it necessary to distribute the soldiers through the second-
class cars, with the exception of the Captain, who was
to stay with us.

The train finally started. We hung out of the windows to wave good-bye to Lucio Blanco, who bran-
dished his gold-headed riding-crop above the heads of
the crowd on the platform. As the train rolled out of
the train-shed, I heard the sound of music. I listened
attentively; on the other side of the fence they were
playing *La Golondrina*. Lucio? Of course, Lucio had
thought of it. He had stationed a band there to send
us off in good revolutionary style.

Chapter XXV

In the Shelter of the Convention

NOBODY would have believed that our car was in reality a travelling prison of politicians who had fallen on evil times. General Plank's advice had met neither deaf ears nor refractory wills. We were accompanied by our mothers, our wives, our children, our sisters; and their presence created such an atmosphere of domesticity and contentment that it was hard for us to remember the origin of our journey and its possible outcome. Besides, the contrast between the seclusion in which we had been living the preceding days and the sense of freedom we felt as we rushed ahead in the train, masters of mountain, plain, and valley, was so vivid that it took away the sense of a journey into exile. The train rolled on for hours, days; and we, so recently emerged from the narrow prison horizon, gave ourselves over to the delight of drinking in the scenery, feasting our eyes on the luminous purity of the immense perspectives. No doubt the lack of anything better to do contributed to the popularity of this form of amusement.

For, aside from a few more than ordinary inconveniences, this trip in itself was not very different from others we had made, or if there was a difference, it consisted in the fact that there was less novelty to it. Naturally, the prolongation of our association, after the long days together in captivity, could offer us few surprises. Only an occasional one of us—gifted in certain aspects with a richer personality—could now and again evolve something worth noticing; as for instance, Enrique C. Llorente, for whose impeccable neatness my admiration reached its climax on this occasion. He gave proof of how great and mysterious was his capacity for the exquisite grooming of his person, of the unalterable poise of his manners, and of his marvellous ability to look at all hours as though he had just stepped out of a bandbox. In the course of the trip all of us, sooner or later, grew hopelessly dirty, and our interpretation of the rules of travel etiquette grew more and more lax. Not so Llorente, however; just the opposite happened with him; his clothes seemed to press themselves, his collar whitened instead of darkening, his bearing grew steadily more erect, his hair lay smooth, and the points of his moustache bristled, blacker and stiffer than ever. And everything else the same way. To rest or sleep, we others used to lie back or stretch out on the seats; Llorente was never seen to vary by an angle of ten degrees, to the right or left, backwards or forwards, from the most ceremonious sitting position. This was true even when sleep, closing his lids, gave his face the anatomical dignity of a statue instead of the laxness of muscles it produced in the rest of us.

There was one thing that Don Venustiano had overlooked when he ordered us into exile, and that was the authority, fleeting, it is true, but great, of the Convention at Aguascalientes. And even less had he allowed for the fact that it was presided over by an upright man: Antonio I. Villarreal. Carranza thought himself so strong that he believed his arbitary orders were going to be respected even in the sections under the control of generals sincerely in favour of the Convention. But Villarreal showed him in our case how ridiculously mistaken he was, for he made short work of Carranza's disregard for his and the Convention's orders. Villarreal was still imbued with his early revolutionary spirit; he had not yet been bitten by the tarantula of presidential ambitions. He preserved—not yet clouded as in 1922, or completely obscured as in 1923—his sound human and political criterion and the strict sense of justice that made him one of the fairest, if not the most brilliant, of the leaders of the Constitutionalist revolution.

Villarreal commanded that the orders to put us at

liberty be carried out as they had been issued, and this was done when the train we were on reached Monterrey. Nothing was further from our minds, and at first we were surprised and alarmed to see a large detachment of soldiers stationed on the platform, who surrounded our car as though they meant to take it by assault. But the smiling air with which Colonel Alfonso Vázquez (Poncho Vázquez, everybody called him) jumped on to the steps, opened the door, and came in quieted our alarm.

"Nothing to worry about, gentlemen," he said, shaking hands with us; "my soldiers are here only to protect you, even if it doesn't look like it. We had to do things this way to keep your escort from putting up any resistance."

He was young, friendly, and enthusiastic. His voice rippled gaily as he talked.

"Let's see, now," he went on, assuming a more military tone, "who's in command here?"

"Colonel Domínguez," answered the Captain in whose custody we had been placed.

Vázquez looked puzzled. "You?" he said, turning to Domínguez.

"Yes," the latter answered. "I'm in charge, but only by chance and for reasons of expediency. Don't pay any attention to that, though; the real commander here is the Captain."

Vázquez then turned to the Captain. "What are your orders?"

>>>>>>>>>>>>>>>>>>>>>>><<<<<<<<<<<<<<<<<<<<<

"None, Colonel. I mean, nothing special. Just to escort these gentlemen to the border, and if I am requested to do so, to leave them with General Nafarrate at Ciudad Victoria or Matamoros."

"Very good, very good," interrupted Vázquez, laughing heartily, as though the Captain's orders were extremely funny; "but now things have changed. General Villarreal, president of the Convention at Aguascalientes, has ordered me to relieve you so that you may return at once to Mexico City with your men. As you know, he is the highest authority in the Republic. Your prisoners are now under my orders."

"Just as you say, Colonel," answered the Captain, "only I'd like to have it in writing."

"Of course; you go right over to headquarters and they'll give you the official documents."

As we did not understand exactly what this change of custody might mean, we bombarded Vázquez with questions. He explained the situation in a few words:

"Nothing, except that Don Venus just reckoned without his host this time. General Villarreal ordered me to assign you an escort to accompany you to Aguascalientes, not as prisoners, but as free men. He just told me to ask you, when you got there, to present yourselves at Convention headquarters. If you want to, you can stay here tonight and rest; otherwise you can take the train that will be coming by in a little while."

We had been shut up in the discomfort and dirt of our car for forty-eight hours, and it had been very hard on the women and children. But we were so overjoyed that we decided not to stop off in Monterrey, but to go straight on to Aguascalientes. We communicated our wishes to Colonel Vázquez, who gave the necessary orders.

Soon afterwards our car was uncoupled from the north-bound train and coupled to the south-bound, and a few minutes later we began our way back by night, as far as San Luis Potosí, over the same road we had just covered by day. But now our escort was from the Convention's troops, not from Carranza's, as before.

San Luis Potosí seemed to us, the day we spent there between trains, little short of an enchanted city, especially watched over by the good fairies. Was it because the revolution, still in its beginnings, had not yet stamped its destructive seal on it, as it did afterwards on practically all the cities of Mexico, which before had been beautiful and flourishing? Or was it rather because of the unique glow that everything takes on when one has recovered his lost liberty? Be that as it may, San Luis Potosí seemed to me a species of urban paradise: such clean, well-paved thoroughfares; such intimate, inviting squares; such well laid-out streets; such pleasant architecture! At night it gave the impression of a city covered by

a great transparent roof through which one could
see the stars. And this same sensation of something
protected from the inclemencies of the weather was
not dissipated by daylight. There was something
urbanized and domestic in the surrounding country,
a certain refinement which seemed to radiate from the
city to the country-side, from the city to the sky,
which had a civilizing influence on all alike. Even the
vegetables in the near-by gardens seemed to acquire
a degree of perfection unknown elsewhere.

Our impressions in Aguascalientes, as we finally
got out of the train, were different, but not less pleasant. The slow dimming of the afternoon, the faint
twinkle of the stars above, the slow lighting of windows and street-lamps on the street, the walk
from the station down the long, tree-lined avenue to
the city, all tended to submerge the spirit in a gentle
melancholy. And in this sensation of autumnal
warmth, of twilight well-being—neither dark nor
bright, neither sad nor joyous, the remoteness of the
limbo—lies the essence of all Mexico. . . .

Leaving our families for the moment where best
we could, the whole group of us went straight to the
theatre where the sessions of the Convention were
being held. Just as we went up the stairs, a clock
somewhere struck eight.

We waited for a few minutes in the vestibule to
be announced. In a little while we heard a burst of

applause from the room, and then a commission of three delegates came out to welcome us and invite us in. As we walked in through the middle door, all those present got to their feet and turned towards us. The orchestra, the boxes, the gallery were a blaze of light and people. Once inside the door, we stopped, somewhat embarrassed, for we did not know what it was all about. But we saw that the members of the committee in charge got up from their seats, and one of them walked over to the footlights, making signs to us to come ahead. We then walked down the aisle to the front row. The commission of delegates and the officer in command of our escort had accompanied us.

Villarreal, who was presiding, tapped the bell for silence; he was about to speak. One had only to look at him to see that more or less the same thing was happening to him as to us: he was bewildered by all this ceremony. For the moment he could not find anything to say. His handsome head was bent forward for a few seconds; the intense blackness of his thick hair, of his heavy moustache, of his eyes gleaming darkly from their deep-set sockets, shadowed by heavy brows and surrounded by unbelievably deep circles, seemed to catch all the light in the room.

Finally, with perfect simplicity of word and gesture, he said: "Gentlemen, the Convention has ordered that you be put at liberty. That is all: you are free."

The Convention broke into applause of an uncertain nature. Some seemed to applaud this sovereign decision; some, I do not know why, seemed to applaud us, the outpost of the Carranza opposition. When the applause died down, Don Manuel Bonilla, as the oldest of the group, expressed our thanks for the act of justice that had been done us. And next, amidst further applause, we mounted to the platform to shake hands with General Villarreal and the delegates around him.

Chapter XXVI

Early Convention Days

AGUASCALIENTES led a troubled existence in those days, owing to the excesses—unbelievable at times—of the revolutionary troops. *Revolution* and *the revolution* became synonymous, and probably for this reason the names of certain figures of the Constitutionalist epic sowed panic by their mere sound. "Bañuelos" or "Domínguez" was heard, and people rushed to take refuge in the most hidden nooks, especially if there were handsome virgins in the family or other equally desirable treasures. The wealthy inhabitants or even those in moderately comfortable circumstances would have given a great deal to have been able to hide their property, their stores, their homes. To combat the danger of losing everything they tried one of two plans: either they hid everything they could, or else they made open display of it, in order to ingratiate themselves with the new group in power, and in this way save their possessions through their new friends.

Thanks to this latter attitude, Aguascalientes, which normally could not have accommodated two or three hundred outsiders without overflowing, on this occasion managed to make room in its small hotels and its not too spacious houses for the thousands of people the Convention brought with it. The rooms for rent were all taken in a minute; but no sooner had this happened than offers of comfortable rooms, of whole houses, of mansions, began to pour in, all *gratis et amore,* merely out of enthusiasm for the cause.

At first I was puzzled by this phenomenon, so contrary to my notions on political economy. It represented a depreciation of capital and an indifference to interest so sudden and spontaneous that I could not make it fit in with what I had studied on the subject. The law of supply and demand did not work at all. And, as is customary with me, in search of a ray of light to illuminate the mystery I let my imagination run away with me. Apparently—so I reasoned with myself at first—we were preceded wherever we went by the fame of our opposition to Carranza, and this made us very popular and assured us a warm reception from those who shared our attitude. This is to say, without expecting it or deserving it we were beginning to be looked upon as great men—a typical revolutionary occurrence—and to enjoy the advantages connected with a reputation of this sort, even though we were not and did not feel like heroes.

The fact is that not less than six prominent citizens came to call on us the morning after our arrival, and each of them, vying with one another in hospitality, placed his home at our disposal with such cordiality that we could not say no. These were moments of great political satisfaction to us. We felt popularity dropping on us like manna from heaven, and the revolution and its hopes seemed to open before us in an infinite horizon. The brief springtime of the ideals we had so long cherished bloomed in our hearts, and it touched us deeply to see how these ideals—by the mere strength of their altruism and purity—were triumphing among people who did not even know us.

But the spell was of brief duration, for very soon our eyes were opened once more to the true state of affairs, and political economy resumed its normal channels. The truth, the sad truth, was that the well-to-do residents of Aguascalientes, than whom there are no better economists, sized up the new revolutionists as they arrived, in search of the least suspicious-looking faces, and as soon as they found a man that made a good impression on them, they overwhelmed him with attentions in the hope of making use of him afterwards. Thanks to this, we found lodgings in less time than it took to ask for them. I do not recall where my eight companions and their families stayed; I had a beautiful room in one of the central streets, not far from the Morelos Theatre, where the Convention met.

As we were not generals or generals' delegates, we were not entitled to sit on the platform during the Convention. But our role as early victims of Carranzaism surrounded us with an aureole and we were treated with great deference; from the night we were declared free, those in charge of the assembly had assigned us a box so that we could be present at the sessions. It was an orchestra box next to the stage, and from there we could see all the theatre. The speaker's table, which was at the extreme left of the platform, was right beside us, and a few feet away was the chairman's table.

I had only to take one look at that military assembly to be convinced that nothing would come of its deliberations. It may be that the moral and cultural level of the Convention was not so low as in some of the congresses we have since had in Mexico—congresses in which the deputies sold themselves to the highest bidders, where friends and companions were sold out, where legislators who could barely sign their names plotted and passed laws. But, nevertheless, the Military Convention revealed at a glance that it lacked the civic consciousness and the far-seeing patriotism that was needed at that moment. The problem it faced was to save the revolution by ridding it

of two perils: Carranza—the greater—and Villa—
the lesser. The first represented the betrayal of the
purpose of the revolution and the return of a struggle
of personal ambitions in the fight for leadership. The
second represented unrestrained brutality, which
could be controlled only by wise guidance. But the
majority of the generals who had gone into the revolution, on a vague though noble collective impulse
(and backed up by personal ambitions, not so vague
or so noble), were not as a rule capable of convert-
ing into a disinterested idea what had been a nebulous
urge in them. To the voice of patriotism the majority
responded with their little personal ambitions, so
petty and so mean that, as one looked at them, it did
not seem possible that they could have been the authors of the revolution, and less still that they deserved to be.

Eduardo Hay, who was one of the best men there
—at least as far as intentions were concerned—ut-
tered a phrase at one of the early sessions which revealed the dominating spirit of the assembly. "We
are here," he said amidst resounding applause, "on
our honour." The instantaneous popularity of these
words showed up to what point the sentiment they
expressed was false—not on the part of Hay, who
spoke from a sincere conviction, and who would hold
no traffic with the chicanery and combinations of those
who sold themselves for power—but on the part of
the military politicians who took it up with such dis-

play of enthusiasm. It was evident that the rarest thing at the Convention was honour, and this would be clearly seen a little later on when nearly every one of the generals, some for one reason, some for another, would go back on his agreements on the most trivial pretexts. The sincere efforts of some of the outstanding men at the Convention were doomed to failure, as in the case of Villarreal and Angeles and Obregón. It must be admitted (though some of us do not relish it) that at the Convention there were few who could compare with Obregón in generosity, and no one so ready as he to conciliate opposing groups. His lack of success may have been due to the fact that he was too ready, or his tone was too humble, and this detracted from the prestige he had acquired on the field.

The Convention underwent a serious moral and cultural decline with the arrival of Zapata's delegates and his aides-de-camp. They arrived one morning, accompanied by Angeles and the other officers who had gone after them to the "mountains of the south." Their appearance aroused, not enthusiasm, but a positive frenzy. They were received as though they bore the truth and the Gospels, and as though, once Chihuahua and Morelos were united, the rest would take care of itself. Yet there were those who felt, just from looking at them, that they would be harmful rather than helpful to the work of harmony.

The group was headed by Paulino Martínez, Díaz Soto, and Serratos. The first was in politics a snake; the second affected a plebeianism that was unexampled, even among the humblest figures of the revolution; and the third was a strange mixture of a good man at heart and a politician without any guiding principles, who was at swords' points with his own better impulses. For a cheap audience the three were good speakers, better, on the whole, than those of any of the other groups in attendance, better than those of Carranza, Villa, or those representing the tendency personified by Villarreal, Eulalio Gutiérrez, and Lucio Blanco. But the oratory of the three of them—this was evident in their first speeches, acknowledging the ovation they had received—was inspired in a negative passion, a hatred of everything that did not mean an inversion of values so that the most barbarous, the most primitive, the most uncivilized elements should become the leaders in the progress of mankind.

Díaz Soto used to wear at that time the tight trousers of the Mexican *charro,* a cotton jacket, and a broad-brimmed hat. Anybody who did not know him would have taken him for the driver of a pulque-wagon. But those of us who were familiar with his connexions, his profession, and his education had the sensation, when we saw him make this deliberate, unnecessary show of himself, that he was trying to act as a symbol, an allegory of Zapatism, by giving it, in his own person, a local habitation. Was he a faithful symbol of the real Zapatism? Zapata is still an enigma, but an enigma that admits of only two answers: it is either the white cotton trousers and the palm-leaf hat of the *pelado*—which the depth of his suffering makes worthy of respect—or it is the tight trousers and broad-brimmed hat of the *charro,* which (outside of the theatre and the ranch) stand for the degradation of all cultural values, having all the spiritual poverty of the *pelado,* but without the humility and the resignation that redeem him; having the insolent material ambitions typified in trousers and shoes, but without the higher aspirations that would justify them. And the Zapatism that spoke through Díaz was the second and not the first, and the same was true of Paulino Martínez, though one could also hear the small-town lawyer in him, as well as of Serratos, although in him it was overlaid by an agreeable simplicity of manner.

Chapter XXVII

Convention Scenes

BUT if the Convention was doomed to failure as a political achievement, as a show it was a brilliant success. I used to sit down in my box in the same frame of mind as if I were going to see a performance of one of Reinhardt's productions or some other theatrical offering in which all of us—actors and spectators—would soon be taking part in the action, though the emotion was more intense and absorbing in this case, as one felt here that it was a question not of feigned but of real truth. At times the show provoked laughter; at times it left one perplexed and bewildered; at other times it produced its catharsis, for it was a tragedy in fact if not in form, with its fatal struggle between two irreconcilable forces. Two profound aspects of the same nationality were locked here in a death-struggle: one, the diffuse but desperately earnest and noble longing for a better social fabric; and, as opposed to this, the deep-rooted incapacity to direct the turbulence of this aspiration and convert it into something feasible, organic, and co-ordinated. The visible dramatic motive was the political passions, untrammelled, brooking neither let nor hindrance; and the presiding power at the cross-roads of action was the pistol—here elevated to the role of fate in the classical tragedy, or of character in the modern drama.

The leading man of the Convention show was usually Roque González Garza. Villa had appointed him his personal representative, and his choice would seem to have been shrewdly made, for with his friendly manners and his honourable intentions he offered the military gathering a softened replica of the too crude figure of his master. Roque possessed other virtues besides. He was loyal to the core and honest in his convictions, and, for an affair of this sort, he possessed no end of parliamentary tricks, which were no less useful because they provoked the amusement of the more serious-minded and learned.

One morning Roque arrived at the Convention absolutely convinced that he had found the solution to the Villa-Carranza dilemma. He radiated satisfaction and mystery and, though bursting to confide in his friends, nevertheless restrained himself. He got several of us who were unquestionably anti-Carranza into a corner in the hall and intimated to us the importance of his idea, though without going into details.

"It will be," said he, "the test. Carranza either goes or he is done for in politics."

"And what about Villa?" we asked.

"Villa doesn't matter here. The important thing is that if Carranza tries to hold on, it's all over with him."

How or why Carranza was done for if he did not retire was not explained. And so when we saw him go into the room where the meeting was in session, we followed in a few minutes, skeptical and smiling. For Roque was so good-hearted and so eager to find a solution for every difficulty that even his best friends often had their doubts as to his mental capacity.

With fervid phrases Roque described the great civic generosity of General Villa, and his readiness to make every sacrifice for his country. And he wound up by reading aloud a document in which the Chief of the Division of the North, in his eagerness to remove every obstacle from the path of the revolutionary enterprise, offered to take his life with his own hand if Carranza would commit suicide together with him.

This heroic proposal brought down the house.

But from the point of view of dramatic interest nothing could compare with the tempests that Antonio Díaz Soto used to stir up. His unbroken stream of oratory made this possible, and the corrosive ideas he was championing almost made it a duty. Díaz Soto did not believe in God or the Devil, in good or evil, in country or family, in mine or thine. He did have a feeble belief in the divine, mysterious origin of the Zapata gospels and in Emiliano Zapata as a super-human being. He used to describe him, among his mountains in the south, at the moment in which he revealed to a few faithful the Ayala Plan. His descriptions of these scenes were couched in biblical terms that evoked Moses and Mount Sinai, and if the four hundred leaders there assembled did not fall to their knees at the sound of this strange oratory, half lay and half religious, Díaz Soto flayed them in spirit, upbraiding them for their ignorance, their inconsistency, and their servile submission to stupid prejudices unworthy of the revolution's anointed.

One day it came to his mind that there was such a thing as socialism, and that Karl Marx had written the Communist Manifesto and *Capital,* and that patriotism and other similar inventions were but ruses invented by the classes in power to weld more tightly the chains of the proletariate. And as the poor Convention generals were not very well up on this, he decided to enlighten them, with the vehemence of gesture and the vigour of phrase characteristic of him.

Somebody (Angeles, perhaps, or some other revolutionist uninitiated in the mysteries of the International) had placed a Mexican flag on the stage near the speaker's table, that it might fan the patriotic ardour of the orators. The three colours of the Independence and the pre-Cortés eagle presided like a tutelary divinity over all that was thought and expressed in that tribune. From time to time, at the voice of the orator or the breeze set in motion by his gestures, the folds of the national ensign rippled as though affirming his statements or emphasizing his gesture.

Up to that morning Díaz Soto seemed never to have noticed the flag. But this time, as he was marshalling his ideas to begin his speech, he began toying with the cloth, lifting it, and letting it fall again. I cannot recall exactly what his speech was about that day, but as usual it had to do with the excellence of Zapata's ideals and the imperative need for bringing them down from the mountains of the south to the central and northern plains of the Republic—all this delivered with the pyrotechnical eloquence in which Díaz Soto was unrivalled. There was one beautiful passage, with sweeping historical touches, demonstrating that mankind is one in origin and destiny. In another he led in magnificent procession before the rapt gaze of the Convention the great leaders of humanity who had admitted no distinction of nationality, race, or colour; Buddha, Jesus Christ, Saint Francis, Karl Marx, and Zapata. This was followed by a veritable paroxysm of oratory denouncing the perverse division of humanity into countries and nations, flagellating imperialist ambitions, refuting the ideas of a fatherland and repudiating those childish

emblems that men in their folly invent to make war
on each other.

During the latter part of his speech Díaz Soto tried
to suit the action to the word, and, gripping the folds
of the Mexican flag that hung beside him, he began to
apostrophize it with exclamations and rhetorical
questions.

"Now, what is the good," he asked, shaking the
flag and sweeping the front rows of his audience with
an impassioned gaze, "of this dyed rag, bedaubed
with the image of a bird of prey?"

Naturally, nobody answered. Shaking the tricolour
banner once more, he asked, or shouted:

"How is it possible, gentlemen of the revolution,
that for a hundred years we have been venerating this
silly mummery, this lic?"

At this point the revolutionary gentlemen, as
though slowly shaking off the spell Zapata's best orator was weaving around them, began to doubt the
evidence of their eyes and ears and to look round at
one another in astonishment. A tremor ran through
their ranks, and, to a man, they got up just as Díaz
Soto, on the point of tearing the flag from its staff, to
judge by the way he was tugging at it, was rounding
off his idea with these words:

"This rag and all it represents is but a mockery,
an empty show, against which we must all . . ."

Three hundred pistols flashed out of their holsters.
Three hundred pistols gleamed on high, their bright

fingers of light pointing straight at Díaz Soto's breast. The room became a babble of scraps of phrases, fierce insults, and vile interjections:

"Let go of that flag, you dirty . . ."

"Zapata, son of a . . ."

"Take your hands off that flag, or . . ."

Díaz Soto was never more admirable than at this moment. Under the aim of the revolvers and the rain of the vilest insults, he stood pale but firm beside the table, his arms folded, waiting for the storm to wear itself out. All he said was:

"When you have finished, I'll go on. . . ."

Chapter XXVIII

The Death of the Gaucho Mújica

WHILE we were still in prison, Berrueco had come to us one day with a long story of how "Gaucho Mújica" had been released from jail a few days before.

Berrucco was one of the various secret agents that I had put on the police force. He seemed so insignificant that at first I had paid scant attention to him; but he showed himself so faithful and active that little by little he completely won our confidence. Of all the group to which he belonged he was the most assiduous visitor Domínguez and I had while we were locked up. General Plank knew perfectly well the capacity in which Berrueco was employed, and, besides, we ourselves had told him that he was the channel through which we received most of our political information. Yet Plank never interfered with his coming up to our cell, and much less did he inform

Carranza of the frequency and nature of his visits. When Plank had to choose between duty and friendship, the latter always won.

"I know you won't believe me," Berrueco told us on this occasion, "but it's the God's honest truth. One of the generals that is closest to Carranza has fixed it up with Gaucho Mújica to go and assassinate General Villa. The gaucho is already out of jail (and you know he was held for murder), and the general I'm talking about has promised him a big sum of money and his complete freedom if he carries out their agreement. He must be on his way to Chihuahua already, and what he plans to do is to worm his way into Villa's good graces and, the first time he gets a chance, kill him."

Berrueco did not tell this in the calm way I write it; he was in a state of great excitement, stammered even more than usual, and was so pale and nervous that one only had to look at him to see the importance he attached to his discovery. His nervousness was at least partly justified; because, in view of the gaucho's reputation as a killer, the plan really represented a danger to Villa's life, and this touched our agent in a sensitive spot. Berrueco, to be sure, did not know the Chief of the Division of the North, and owed him no personal allegiance; but he never forgot—on this he based his hopes for the future—that it was I who had given him his job in the secret service, not to serve Carranza, but, on the contrary, to further

our own plans, and the trump card in our game was
Villa. For this reason, through his loyalty to us, Berrueco came to feel almost the same concern as we
about anything that referred to this formidable warrior.

Domínguez laughed heartily at what Berrueco was
telling us. And, to be sure, heard offhand like that,
it did sound too silly to take seriously. Only when one
stopped to think that the person selected to carry out
the plot was the Gaucho Mújica, and recalled the
man's daring and his criminal astuteness, did one realize that the thing might not be so incredible as it appeared at first blush.

"Berrueco, old man," said Domínguez, "you're
just seeing things. It's plain you don't know
Villa. . . ."

"Well, neither does the gaucho," answered Berrueco, who was nobody's fool.

"That doesn't make any difference," Domínguez
answered. "Either the gaucho isn't so smart as they
say, or he ought to know that the gaucho hasn't been
born yet who can pull the wool over Villa's eyes. You
can't fool round with Pancho Villa."

"Well, Colonel, you can think what you please. But
I swear to you that everything I've told you is so, and
if you don't believe me, just wait and you'll see." So
great was Berrueco's solemnity as he took his oath
that for the moment he stopped stuttering.

It seemed to me that the first thing to find out was

where he had got his information, whether we believed it or not. So I began to question him.

"Now, first of all," I said, "tell us who this general is."

He answered without a moment's hesitation: "Don Pablo." [1]

It was my turn to be skeptical.

"Don Pablo? I don't believe it. Don Pablo isn't capable of such a thing. . . ."

"Don Pablo," Berrueco insisted.

"Well, but how do you know it?"

"From two different sources, two of the best."

"What are they?"

"We know it (I'm not the only one, there are other agents who know it, too) first from a person who is close to Don Pablo, and then from another person who's in touch with Mújica. . . ."

"Who are they? What are their names?"

"I can't tell you any more about the first one. The second is a woman."

"A woman?"

"Yes, sir. A woman who is on intimate terms with the gaucho. Please don't make me tell you her name; we, too, have our professional secrets."

Berrueco departed and we were left perplexed and troubled. Domínguez's first impression had changed. Now it did not seem so improbable that somebody

[1] Pablo González, one of Carranza's most important military leaders.

might have been found bold enough to make an attempt on Villa in his own territory. On the contrary, now it seemed to him perfectly logical. "That's the only way they'll ever get Villa," he said, "some coward assassinating him by surprise. A man with a heart in him would never do it." But my skepticism remained unshaken, more as regarded the supposed intervention of Don Pablo than about the gaucho. I could not bring myself to believe that one of the leading generals of the revolution—in rank if not in achievements —would descend to such low, cowardly plotting, and against the very man to whom the revolution owed its most important military victories. To accept this meant to renounce the noblest revolutionary hopes and ideals, everything that Carranzaism was openly to repudiate later on, when it planned and exulted over the assassination of Zapata.

We finally came to the conclusion that it was our duty not to judge Berrueco's report too far-fetched, and, on the strength of the possibility, to send word to Villa about the reputed intention of the gaucho and his accomplices. It would not do to send a letter or a telegram, so we decided to have one of our friends, Cabiedes, a brave, loyal young chap, deliver the message in person. He was to repeat to Villa word for word our conversation with Berrueco.

Now that we were free in Aguascalientes, we decided at once to go to see Villa, among other things, to find out how the matter of the gaucho and his plans had worked out. It was three weeks since Cabiedes had left, and he had not returned nor sent us any word as to the outcome of his mission, and we had heard nothing from Villa.

So Domínguez and I started out towards Zacatecas, and about evening we found the Chief of the Division of the North in his headquarters, a little beyond Guadalupe. He seemed greatly surprised to see us.

"Well, where did you boys drop from? I thought the old man had had you shot. . . ."

"No, General, not yet. . . ."

"And how about Nafarrate?"

"We haven't even seen him."

"You can thank your lucky stars that you got off safe, believe me. To tell the truth, I was sure something was going to happen to you, especially to this fellow," and he pointed to Domínguez as he said this.

Domínguez asked: "To me, General?"

"Yes, to you, my boy, to you. Because you talk too much."

Domínguez turned red with rage, but Villa, who had intended no offence when he said this, but merely a friendly warning, went on talking—fortunately for us—without noticing Domínguez's anger. He was in good spirits, almost jovial, and it showed in his eyes, which were less bloodshot and restless than usual, and in the gentler movements of his lower jaw. His expression was almost human.

Patting Domínguez on the shoulder with his left hand, he said:

"And thanks for the warning. That devil of a gaucho! If he wasn't on my trail already!"

"Did he actually get here?" I asked.

"Twice, partner. The first time he fooled me good. He said he admired me without knowing me, just by my reputation, and he wanted to join me. He was telling me how many men he'd killed (to win my confidence, you know), and finally he got me to give him money for a trip to the north, saying he'd soon be back. Then that friend of yours came along—what's his name?"

"Cabiedes."

"That's it, Cabiedes. Well, he came and told me what was up. You can guess how I took it. I almost put a bullet through Cabiedes to teach him to travel a little faster. But after a while I calmed down, thinking that the gaucho would soon be back, and that's just what happened."

"And then what did you do?"

"What did I do? Oh, everything was tended to. I've got him buried now."

"Buried, General? Where?"

"What do you mean 'Where'? Why, where would

>>>>>>>>>>>>>>>>>>>>>>>> <<<<<<<<<<<<<<<<<<<<<<<<

it be? In the ground. And would you believe the son of a bitch almost got away from me? Because these lawyers around here told me that as he was a foreigner we couldn't just up and kill him like anybody else. But I said I'd like to know why this dirty double-crosser of a gaucho shouldn't get his just because he was a foreigner. So we held what they call an international trial. He confessed every last thing, for I told him I knew everything, and that if he lied to me I'd let daylight into him, but if he told the truth, we'd see about it. Mr. Carothers, the United States consul, heard the confession and signed the declarations. Then we read them over again and I had some more seals and signatures put on them, and then I ruled that it would be only justice to sentence the gaucho to the same punishment he had wanted to give me. Mr. Carothers said he'd do the same thing in my place. When the gaucho found out that I was going to do him in, he went all to pieces, and he began to offer me things. He promised over and over that if I'd only let him off, he'd go and kill Carranza. But I asked him since when he thought I needed traitors to kill my enemies. 'You dirty skunk,' I said to him, 'I'm a man and I can do my own killings.' He soon saw it was no good; so he shut up. We shot him right on the spot."

After a long pause Villa added:

"Where's Cabiedes now? You know, I'm kind of sorry for the way I treated him because I thought he'd been too slow about getting here with your message. Tell him to come to see me. I want to give him a present. He's a nice fellow. Who knows?—maybe if it wasn't for him I wouldn't be here now."

Chapter XXIX

Pancho Villa on the Cross

THE Convention was still in session when war broke out again. That is to say, the attempts at conciliation failed in practice before they failed in theory. To tell the truth, the reason they failed was that this was what the majority on both sides wanted. They had armies, and they were close at hand, so how could they resist the temptation of putting them to fighting?

Maclovio Herrera, in Chihuahua, was one of the first to begin hostilities again, flouting Villa's authority.

"The damned son of a bitch," the Chief of the Division of the North fumed; "why, I made him! All he knows about fighting he learned with me. How does the treacherous, ungrateful cur dare to turn on me like that?"

His wrath was such that only a few days after Herrera's rising the troops Villa had sent in pursuit of him were hemming him in. The encounters were bloody, desperate. Both sides were Villa men, and it was a case of hurricane against hurricane. It was kill or be killed.

One of those mornings Llorente and I went to see Villa. It made our blood run cold to look at him. The glitter in his eyes made me realize suddenly that mankind is not of one species, but of many, and that these species are separated by limitless space, have no common denominator. An abyss cleaves them, and it may cause vertigo to look from one of these worlds to the other, which lies opposite. As fleeting as a ripple on water there passed over my soul that morning, face to face with Villa, the giddiness of fear and horror.

To our "Good morning, General," he replied in a sinister voice:

"Not good, my friends. There are more hats around than we need."

I did not understand what he meant by the expression, nor do I think Llorente did, either. But whereas he selected the part of wisdom, keeping quiet, I asked with stupid, almost crime-provoking tactlessness:

"More whats, General?"

He took one step towards me and answered with the deliberation of a person who can barely control his anger: "More hats, my learned friend. Since when don't you understand the language of real men? Or don't you know that on account of Long-Ears (the damned son of a bitch, if once I get hold of him!) my boys are killing one another? Now do you understand why there are too many hats? Do I talk plain?"

I didn't say a word. Villa paced up and down the car, as if keeping time to the internal rhythm of his wrath. Every three steps he would say between his clenched teeth: "The damned son of a bitch. The damned son of a bitch."

From time to time Llorente and I exchanged glances, and finally, not knowing what to do or say, we sat down, close to each other. Outdoors the morning shone bright, its perfect harmony broken only by the distant noises and shouts of the camp. In the car, aside from the palpitations of Villa's rage, nothing was heard but the ticking of the telegraph apparatus.

Bent over his table, facing us, the telegraph operator worked on. His movements were precise, and his face as expressionless as his instrument. Several minutes elapsed in his fashion. Then the telegraph operator, who had been transmitting before, said, turning to his chief:

"I think they're here now, General."

Taking his pencil from behind his ear, he began to write slowly. Villa came over to the little table where the apparatus stood. His air was at once agitated and icy, impatient and calm, revengeful and indifferent.

He stood between us and the operator, in profile, leaning forward. On one side of the dark blotch of his silhouette against the wall the energetic line of his under jaw and of his arm folded across his breast stood out, and on the other, concluding the powerful angle that descended from his shoulder, the curved, dynamic outline of his pistol-butt. This morning, instead of his slouch hat, he wore a grey sun-helmet, with green facings on the brim. This head-gear, always odd on him, seemed to me more absurd than ever that day. Strangely enough, instead of taking away from his height, it seemed to add to it. Seen close to, and against the light, his stature seemed to increase enormously; his body stopped all the light.

The operator tore off the pink pad the sheet on which he had been writing, and handed the message to Villa. He took it, but handed it back immediately, saying:

"You read it to me, friend, but read it carefully, for I think this means business now."

There was a sinister inflection in his voice, so portentous and threatening that it was reflected in the voice of the operator. Separating the words carefully and pronouncing every syllable, he began in a low tone: "I have the honour to inform you. . . ."

As he read on, his voice grew stronger. The message, which was laconic, gave notice of the defeat that Maclovio Herrera had just suffered at the hands of the troops pursuing him.

Villa's face seemed to pass from the shadows into the light as he listened. But instantly, as he caught the final words, his eyes blazed again, and his face flamed with his most terrible rage, his uncontrollable, devastating wrath. The commander of the troops, after giving the list of his casualties, had ended by asking instructions as to what to do with the hundred and seventy of Herrera's men who had given themselves up.

"What to do with them?" shouted Villa. "What a question! What should he do except shoot them? I honestly believe every one of my men is going bad, even the best ones I absolutely relied on. And if they're not, what in hell do I want with these generals that get friendly even with the traitors that fall into their hands?"

He said all this without taking his eyes off the poor operator, through whose pupils, and then through the telegraph-wires, Villa perhaps hoped to make his anger reach the very battle-field where the corpses of his men lay.

Turning to us, he went on: "What do you think of that, gentlemen? Asking me what to do with the prisoners!"

But Llorente and I hardly returned his glance, and, without answering a word, looked off into space.

This did not disturb Villa in the least. Turning to the operator, he ordered him:

"Come on, friend. You tell that damned fool I don't want him using up the wires on nonsense. He's to shoot the hundred and seventy prisoners immediately, and if he hasn't notified me in an hour that the order has been carried out, I'll come there myself and put a bullet through him so he'll know how to manage things better. You understand?"

"Yes, General."

And the operator began to write out the message. At the first word Villa interrupted him:

"What are you doing, not obeying me?"

"I'm composing the message, General."

"What do you mean, 'composing'? You send that off the way I said it to you and that's all. Time wasn't made to be lost fooling with papers."

At this the operator put his right hand on the transmitter and, pressing the lever with his little finger, began to call: Tick-tick, tiqui; tick-tick, tiqui.

Between a pile of papers and Villa's arm I could see the knuckles of the operator's hand, tense and vibrant from the contraction of the tendons as they produced the homicidal sounds. Villa did not take his eyes off the movements that were transmitting his orders seven hundred miles to the north, nor did we. I kept wondering—with that stupid insistence we have in dreams—at exactly what moment the vibrations of the fingers were spelling out the words "Shoot immediately." For five minutes that was a horrible obsession that blotted out every other reality, every other sensation.

After the operator had sent off the message, Villa seemed to grow more calm and sat down in an armchair near the desk. He sat there quietly for a little while. Then he pushed back his sun-helmet. Then he buried the fingers of his right hand in the reddish tangle of hair that hung over his forehead, and scratched his head as though he were trying to get at some inward itching of the brain, of the soul. Then he sat quietly again. Perhaps ten minutes had elapsed.

Suddenly he flung round towards me and said: "What do you think about all this, friend?"

I answered evasively: "Were you talking to me, General?"

"Yes, to you."

Hedged in like this, I tried to turn it off using the language of real men: "Well, there are going to be a lot of extra hats around, General."

"Maybe I don't know that. That wasn't what I asked you. What about the consequences? Do you think it's right or wrong, this business of the shooting?"

Llorente, braver than I, cut in ahead of me: "General," he said, "to be frank with you, I don't think that order is fair."

I shut my eyes. I was sure that Villa was going to get up—or, without even getting up—and whip out his pistol to punish this criticism of his conduct in a matter which had flicked him on the raw. But several seconds went by, and then I heard Villa ask, without getting up, and in a voice whose calm contrasted strangely with the storm that had so recently preceded it:

"Well, let's see. Why don't you think my order was right?"

Llorente was so pale that it was hard to tell his skin from his collar. Nevertheless he answered firmly:

"Because, General, the message says the men surrendered."

"Sure. What of it?"

"When they are taken that way, they shouldn't be killed."

"Why not?"

"That's why, General. Because they surrendered."

"You're a funny fellow. That's a good one. Where did you ever learn such things?"

My shameful silence had become unbearable. I broke in:

"I feel the same way, General. It seems to me that Llorente is right."

Villa enveloped us both in one glance.

"And what makes you think that, friend?"

"Llorente explained why: because the men surrendered."

"And I say again, what of it?"

As he repeated it this last time, a certain uneasiness was apparent which made him open his eyes still wider to take us both in with his restless glances. From the outside I could feel the pressure of this look of his, cold and cruel, and from the inside, an irresistible impulse to talk, which was pricked on by the vision of the distant executions. I had to hit quickly on some

255

convincing formula. "The person who surrenders, General, by doing so spares the life of others, since he renounces the possibility of dying fighting. And this being so, the one who accepts the surrender has no right to order the death-sentence."

Villa looked at me steadily, and his eye-balls stopped rolling from one to the other of us. Jumping to his feet, he shouted to the operator: "Listen, friend, call them again, call them again."

The operator obeyed. Tick-tick, tiqui; tick-tick, tiqui.

A few seconds went by.

Villa inquired impatiently: "Do they answer?"

"I am calling them, General."

Llorente and I could not sit still, and we too came over to the instrument table.

Villa asked again: "Do they answer?"

"Not yet, General."

"Call louder."

The operator could not call louder or softer, but it was plain from the contractions of his fingers that he was trying to make the letters clearer and more exact. There was a short silence, and in a little while the receiving instrument began to tick.

"Now they're answering," said the operator.

"All right, friend, all right. Now you transmit as quickly as you can what I am going to say to you. Pay attention: 'Hold up shooting of prisoners until further orders. General Francisco Villa.' "

Tick, tiqui-tick, tiqui. . . .

"Finished?"

Tick-tiqui, tiqui-tick.

"All right, General."

"Now tell their operator that I'm right here be-side the instrument waiting for the answer, and that I'll hold him responsible for any delay."

Tiqui, tiqui, tick-tick, tiqui-tick, tick. . . .

"Have you told him?"

"Yes, General."

The receiving instrument began to tick.

"What does he say?"

"He says he is going to deliver the message him-self and bring the answer."

All three of us stood beside the telegraph table: Villa strangely restless; Llorente and I weak with anxiety.

Ten minutes went by. Tick-tiqui, tick, tiqui-tick.

"Are they answering?"

"It's not them, General. It's another station call-ing."

Villa took out his watch and asked: "How long ago did we send the first order?"

"About twenty-five minutes, General."

Turning to me, Villa asked: "Will the counter-order get there in time? What do you think?"

"I hope so, General."

Tick-tiqui, tick, tick. . . .

"Are they answering, friend?"

"No, General, it's somebody else."

Villa's voice was husky with an emotion I had never heard in it before, and it grew deeper each time he asked if the call was the answer to his counter-order. His eyes were riveted on the little lever of the receiving apparatus, and every time this made the slightest movement, he asked as though the electricity of the wires were reaching through to him:

"Is it him?"

"No, General, it's somebody else."

It had been twenty minutes since telegraphing the counter-order when finally the operator said:

"Now they're calling," and picking up his pencil, he began to write.

Tick, tick, tiqui. . . .

Villa bent farther over the table. Llorente, on the contrary, seemed to stiffen up. I walked over beside the operator to read what he was writing.

Tick-tiqui, tiqui, tiqui, tick-tick. . . .

After the third line Villa could not curb his impatience and asked me:

"Did the counter-order get there on time?"

Without taking my eyes off the paper, I nodded my head.

Villa pulled out his handkerchief and mopped the sweat off his forehead.

We stayed and had dinner with him that afternoon, but he made no reference to what had happened that morning. Only as we were leaving, late that evening, Villa said, without any preamble:

"And thanks, friends, for that thing this morning, that business of the prisoners."

Chapter XXX

A Perilous Sleep

THE natural gifts that made Villa a vivid and entertaining talker were revealed to me one night in the little town of Guadalupe, in the state of Zacatecas.

Enrique C. Llorente, José Vasconcelos, and I had reached Guadalupe that afternoon. All three of us had come to talk with Villa about a number of different things and we planned to leave again in a few hours. Llorente was going to Washington, Vasconcelos to Aguascalientes; and I had to make a short trip to Chihuahua. After we had finished the official business, Villa said he would keep us company until our departure. But as the trains from Juárez and from Mexico City did not come through until one o'clock in the morning, in order to do this he had to give up his invariable habit of going to bed early. Such a delicate attention on his part surprised me beyond expression, for I knew him so well that I could not understand it. Partly because of his rude upbringing and partly because of his disposition, he was never polite to anybody. What was behind this unusual amiability? My astonishment and my suspicion—I could never free myself from my distrust of Francisco Villa—put me somewhat on my guard, and I watched the General with more than ordinary attention. I analysed his least movement, I watched his gestures, I studied his expressions, his words.

Our conversation took place in a special car that Villa used for travelling or campaigning. The servants had cleared the table where we had had dinner. Villa's desk was closed. Every now and then the telegraph instrument clicked with what seemed, to us, idle messages going by. Through the little windows of the car we could see the pleasant valley, with its pools of water here and there, as it lay blue and mirror-like in the light of the moon. On the other side the silver of the moonlight and the ochre of the abrupt, barren lands gave touches of enchantment to a landscape devoid of all beauty by the light of the sun.

The miracle of the autumn night finally took possession of us, and we stepped out on the platform to contemplate the vague dreamlike confines that lay limitless beneath the nocturnal covering of the glittering sky. It was chilly. On one of the steps a sentinel stood guard, all wrapped up in a dark sarape, and humming an endless, melancholy air in a voice as light as the glow of his cigarette. Another, half stretched out on the platform, was sleeping with his head rest-

ing against the brim of his hat, which he had bent
down to make a pillow. His breathing was so smooth
and rhythmic that it seemed to be keeping time to
the light-flooded night. The moonlight was so bright
that we could see his chest rise and fall as he breathed.
Villa had been looking at him ever since we came out,
and he had not taken his eyes off him while Llorente,
Vasconcelos, and I were admiring the view.

"What a mystery sleep is!" said Villa as we went
back into the room. "What a mystery sleep is!"

And his restless eyes, always roving about as
though possessed by terror, suddenly came to rest;
they seemed to fix on some vague, distant point.

"Sleep is the strangest and most mysterious thing
there is."

Vasconcelos had pushed the back of his chair up
against the desk. On the other side, to the left, Llorente's bust rose from behind the telegraph table. I
sat directly across from Villa, and to be more comfortable I had tilted my chair back against the win-
dow-sill. As he talked, Villa seemed to be looking at
me; through my eyes there passed that invisible ray
by which he contemplated the images he was calling up.

"One time," Villa began, "when I was escaping
with my pal Urbina, I found out that sleep is the
strangest and most mysterious thing there is. For a
week the mounted police had not let up for a minute

in one of those brutal pursuits of theirs in which we came within an ace of being killed. My pal and I were hiding in the Durango sierra, and every day we thought they'd surely catch us as we slipped from one of our caches of provisions to another. We had left the last settlement we knew far behind us, the last wood-chopper's cabin, the last shelter of the forest-guards. And yet it took us longer to dismount than for the mounted to appear again and make us start our cruel journey over again. In all this time we had hardly rested or slept, and when we did, it was only for a few minutes. Our horses were ready to drop. Urbina was getting so worn out he'd doze off on his horse until he slipped out of the saddle. Several times I had to wake him up and talk to him and scold him so he wouldn't give up. In spite of my powers of resistance, I was getting utterly exhausted, and I couldn't get over my surprise that we couldn't shake the mounted off our heels. How did they do it? Had they planned it all out beforehand and sent men on ahead? Didn't they sleep, either? Didn't they rest?

"Finally one morning we thought we were safe. From the peak where we had managed to work our way through the heavy woods and thickets we could see the whole plain below, and there wasn't a sign of our pursuers. Two hours before anybody could find us we could see the approach, not only of a troop, but of a single rider, and we'd have time to climb farther into the sierra.

>>>>>>>>>>>>>>>>>>>>><<<<<<<<<<<<<<<<<<<<

"We unsaddled. We fed the horses. We got ready to go to sleep.

" 'Look pal,' I said to Urbina, 'I guess there's no danger now. Still, I don't feel easy. One of us had better watch while the other sleeps, and then we'll change. You can go to sleep first while I watch. In two hours I'll wake you up and then I'll go to sleep.'

"All Urbina said was: 'All right, pal.'

"He couldn't keep his eyes open. He lay down, put his head on his saddle, and went straight to sleep.

"What a mystery sleep is! My pal slept just as calm and easy! There was nothing but peace and rest about him as he lay there. As I looked at him, I couldn't believe that for a week he had been within an inch of being killed or taken prisoner several times. It seemed to me that either I was dreaming then or I had been dreaming before. His breathing was even; his face had the repose of a man who has never known any danger. I remember he had on a pink shirt, and the button was off at the collar—I can still see it— and the folds of it would open and close with every breath. The light moving of the pink cloth on my pal's hairy black chest seemed to be such a part of the loneliness of the mountain, the quiet rustle of the trees, the steady munching of our drowsing horses, that I began to be afraid. The peace of his sleep terrified me, it was so different from that struggle to the death we had been mixed up in for so many years, God only knows why. And yet I couldn't take my eyes off that regular movement of Urbina's shirt, just as though I had been bewitched. Maybe I was beginning to go to sleep, too.

"But I came back to myself. To get away from that obsession I looked up. Away off, in the distance, down the mountain, where the mounted police might come, I saw a little white speck moving. But as I was still bewildered by the drowsiness that was overcoming me, I had to make an effort to realize what I was looking at in the valley. 'That's what it must be,' I said, and I jumped right up. Sure enough, it was the mounted. They were on our trail again; they'd soon be up to us!

"I shook Urbina.

" 'Hey, pal, wake up, they're coming. Wake up, the mounted are after us.'

"But sleep is the queerest thing there is. My pal didn't hear me. His pink shirt kept on moving the same as before. There was the same peaceful expression on his face.

"To make time I went and brought up the horses and saddled mine. All the time I kept calling my pal and shaking him with my foot. When I had my horse saddled, he was still asleep. I took hold of his head and shook it hard. He went right on sleeping just the same; his breathing didn't change at all, and to look at his face you would have thought that instead of pulling his hair and rubbing his ears I was smoothing his pillow so he would sleep better. When I saw that he wasn't waking up, I pulled the saddle out from under his head and started to saddle his horse. And all the time I kept yelling at him. When I had finished, I gathered up our guns and the sarapes. I rolled up our saddle-bags. I fastened everything to the saddles with the straps. . . . My pal didn't wake up. Then I began to call him as loud as I could. I yelled so loud that I didn't recognize my own voice. I had never heard my voice like that before and I never have since. And still my pal didn't wake up. Then I pulled out his pistol, lifted up his head with one hand, and with the other I fired off two shots right beside his ear. Urbina kept on sleeping. His breathing was just the same as when he went to sleep an hour before. His pink shirt barely moved.

"Afterwards, when I remember what an agony I went through that morning, I often think I should have lighted a match and held it in his hand until he woke up. But I didn't think of it then. The dark spot that was the mounted was getting clearer and clearer down below, and I couldn't think straight. Dimly I compared the helplessness of my pal with the danger that was flying towards us, and it seemed to me like a dream when your knees give way under you and you want to run and can't.

"Sleep is the most mysterious thing there is! I picked up my pal, threw him face down across his horse, and tied him tight. Then I got on my horse and made for the sierra.

>>>>>>>>>>>>>>>>>>>>>>> <<<<<<<<<<<<<<<<<<<<<<<

"That's the most terrible day I ever went through in my life. I had to look for the worst path I could find so as to throw the mounted off the track, and at the same time I had to watch out on those bad trails to keep my pal from getting hurt against the rocks and tree-trunks. Several times I had to double back on a trail and take another. Again I had to travel long distances on foot and open the way for Urbina's head, which was hanging over the side, or half carry his body in my arms. And I fled like that for more than three hours, more than six, more than eight. Finally, late that afternoon, I reached a place that offered some protection. I felt safe there and made camp.

"When I took my pal off the horse, his face was black with dust, and purple, for all the blood had rushed to his head. Yet he went right on sleeping, just as easy. I unsaddled the horses. I threw myself on the ground. I slept."

A long silence left Villa's last words echoing in our ears. Llorente, whose admiration for the guerrilla leader was boundless, smiled with an expression half moved, half triumphant. "What do you think of my man?" it seemed to say. Vasconcelos, who was always quick to show appreciation and respect for every manifestation of real humanity, whether fleeting or enduring, was pale with emotion. I just watched.

In a little while we heard the whistle of an engine.

We got ready and went out. We said good-bye along-side the train.

A few minutes later from one of the train windows I saw Villa pass by at a distance, with a woman who, I believe, had come in on the train from Juárez. To judge from her bearing and her silhouette she was young, perhaps pretty. Villa had an arm around her waist and was leading her towards his car.

Had he not said he would keep us company until the trains came in? So that was the real reason!

Chapter XXXI

A New President

I WAS up Chihuahua way when I heard that the Convention had named Eulalio Gutiérrez president *pro tem,* and not Villarreal, as we had all expected. Apparently Eulalio had appeared as a dark horse (as the Yankees say) at the last moment, a compromise candidate who satisfied the different factions because he did not represent any one of them too strongly.

At a time like this, when the most absurd ideas—such as trying to save the situation by appointing a president for twenty days—ran riot, Villarreal might have seemed to many a better and less spectacular choice than Eulalio. Villarreal was really popular and respected by everybody. In a way he was the type of civilian hero of the revolution, a private citizen who had become a soldier in response to the exigencies of the situation and had taken up arms without any taste for military glory, though all his life he had been a man who had fought for his ideas. He used to say: "I have been in many a quarrel, but I can say without

ᐳᐳᐳᐳᐳᐳᐳᐳᐳᐳᐳᐳᐳᐳᐳᐳᐳᐳᐳᐳᐳᐳᐳ ᐸᐸᐸᐸᐸᐸᐸᐸᐸᐸᐸᐸᐸᐸᐸᐸᐸᐸᐸᐸᐸᐸᐸ

boasting that I have never fired a pistol or a rifle."
His words were in keeping with his appearance, for
his whole being radiated goodness and honesty; and
his frank, open look and sincere smile bespoke the true
and generous man.

But at the same time it cannot be denied that it
would have been hard to find a braver, cooler,
shrewder person than Eulalio. In spite of his ironic
smile and gentle voice, in those days Eulalio represented the ideal of the Mexican revolutionist, whose
last thought is of saving himself. He used to give me
such a feeling of actual and potential bravery and
audacity that my imagination adorned him with the
prestige of some fictitious character, one of the heroes
of the daring exploits of the Spanish Main. He, too,
would have been capable of carrying with his own
hand the lighted torch to blow up the powder-maga-
zine of a ship or fortress.

If, then, he was so brave—one queries—why did he
name Villa Commander-in-Chief of the Convention's
armies at a moment when to do this was nothing but
cowardice? This at least was the contention of all
those who wanted to wriggle out of their Aguascalientes compromise, the conventionists who found it
more convenient not to honour the signatures they had
affixed with great solemnity a few days before between the serpent, the eagle, and the cactus of the
Mexican flag. But Gutiérrez could have answered
them that if he appointed Villa, it was because of the

defection of those very ones who were later to cen-
sure him bitterly, at the same time that they backed up
Carranza in those wily tricks of his which made all
solutions impossible.

The Convention had voted, on the one hand, to do
away with the presidency, and to this end had appointed a provisional president; and, on the other,
had voted that Villa should give up his command of
the Division of the North. But whereas the independent generals and the enemies of Carranza obeyed
the edict, about whose meaning there could be no
question, the generals in favour of Carranza decided
to support him—which was an open act of insurrec-
tion—until the terms he laid down for his retirement
had been observed. Now Carranza had no right, in
the face of the sovereignty of the Convention, to lay
down terms of any kind, and he never would have
done it if he had not counted on the support of the
generals who would back him up. He would simply
have been deprived of his office, and that would have
been the end of the matter.

Nor was there any possibility for Villa to interpret
or twist to suit himself the order about giving up the
command of his troops. What, then, was the duty
of the generals who were sincerely opposed to such
factiousness? Would it not have been better to stand
behind Gutiérrez so he could have enforced orders?
But instead of doing this Carranza's partisans left
Aguascalientes and then sent messages from Mexico

City or Orizaba notifying Eulalio that they would support Carranza and not him until he had obeyed the order to remove Villa. This was not only disloyalty and an injustified rejection of the agreement that they had just signed, but a piece of low trickery. They were trying to hold Gutiérrez and the few who supported him to an agreement that had been made on the understanding and basis of unanimous cooperation, which was only feasible this way. By the same token the enemies of Carranza could have refused to support Eulalio as long as he did not put out Carranza. And this would have put the provisional President in the grotesque position of having to fight alone the two opposing factions.

Whichever way one turned it, it was evident that the problem of putting out Carranza and getting rid of Villa resolved itself into a military question, because there was no doubt that both would offer armed resistance. But this problem which the Convention had unloaded on Gutiérrez's shoulders could not be undertaken without the immediate aid of the majority of the generals in the Convention. United, these would form the strongest group, but divided—each group hanging back until the other was brought into line—the old personal contentions would begin all over again. Inasmuch as Carranza's backers had destroyed the unity of purpose of the Convention by demanding that Gutiérrez dismiss Villa when he counted on **no other support**, Gutiérrez did what anybody else would have done in those circumstances: he temporized with Villa, even did everything he could to lull his suspicions until a favourable moment when he could come out in the open with him.

Those were the days when each of us rode round in his private train as though it were a cab. The majority of our political conversations, weighty or trivial, took place to the accompaniment of moving wheels and scenery and were permeated with the smell of smoke and hot-boxes. The trains of generals and the trains of civilians ran up and down the main lines, passing each other at the stations or on the sidings. The freight service had practically disappeared and the passenger service barely existed. There was nothing but military convoys or engines pulling a drawing-room and a caboose, transporting with lightning speed the armies and the ideas of the revolutionary tempest. When the trains met at the stations, the engines greeted each other, the train-crews joked together, and if the passengers were politicians of rank, they would get down and talk importantly with one another.

That was the way Vasconcelos and I met one morning somewhere between Torreón and Fresnillo, or Fresnillo and Zacatecas, and I learned through him that General José Robles was impatiently waiting for me at Aguascalientes to offer me a post in the new government.

"But Robles hardly knows me," I demurred.

"That doesn't matter," said Vasconcelos. "Eulalio and I aren't acquainted and still I'm to be Secretary of Education. Whatever it is, you ought to accept. We all have to pull together now."

In Aguascalientes Robles informed me that he would probably be made Secretary of War and invited me to be his assistant. I laughed and then, in a more serious tone, I explained my reasons:

"A year ago," I said, "General Iturbe offered me, the day after the capture of Culiacán, the rank of lieutenant-colonel on his staff. If I had accepted, by this time I should be a general and I could, without blushing, consider your proposal. But as I did not accept then, I am still a civilian and I lack the necessary rank to act as your assistant in the War Department."

"That doesn't matter in the least," answered Robles, "because it's as a civilian that I need you."

"If that's so, you'd regret your choice in twenty-four hours. Take my advice as a friend, General: make another general your assistant secretary, who has troops of his own, and if possible let him be a friend of yours and a man you can trust."

Fortunately for me, Robles took my advice, or at least acted as though he had, for shortly afterwards he selected for the post General Eugenio Aguirre Benavides, an intimate friend of his. But still he did not want to deprive himself altogether of my supposed services, and he finally persuaded me to accompany him on his cabinet adventure as adviser. For this purpose he invented certain official functions *sui generis,* designed specially for me, which were neither those of a private secretary (these had been entrusted to poor Bolaños) nor those of chief of staff (which were discharged with great flourish and good sense by General Serratos).

I do not know whether Eulalio Gutiérrez knew about the proposal Robles had made me. But, once our arrangements were made, we immediately went to see him, and I soon found myself forming part of the intimate clique where the weightiest problems of the new government that was coming into existence were discussed. Gutiérrez was surrounded at this time by the pick of the anti-Carranzaists, both military and civilian—that is to say, the best of Villa's and Zapata's followers, made one through the miraculous waters of the Convention. But the truth is that nobody was willing to abate a jot or tittle of any personal claims he might have, and in consequence the new government was born sickly, premature, feeble; and nobody seemed to know what to do with it. The one who seemed to know most and say most was Díaz Soto, though when one listened closely, it was evident that he was as ignorant as the rest.

Chapter XXXII

A Secretary of War

CARRANZA and his generals fled towards Vera Cruz, and Eulalio Gutiérrez, with the burden the Convention had placed on his shoulders, made ready to transfer his government to the capital of the Republic.

It was a sight to behold how all the railroads were jammed with interminable cordons of military and civilian trains, hurrying on, not because of strategic or political needs, but because of our impatience to take possession of the magnificent booty that the Carranzaists had left behind in their flight—the city of Mexico. Of course we had a feeling (or, to be more exact, the certainty) that Eulalio's government was sure to go on the rocks; but we also knew that in Mexico's national sport, civil war, Mexico City is like the cup in an athletic tournament: the one who has it savours the joys of victory and feels himself the winner in the political contest; he maintains his title against his rivals, though he be in constant danger of losing it to the many opponents who long to snatch the prize from his hands.

My close friendship with José Isabel Robles began on that trip of conquest to the capital of the Republic. Robles was more set than ever on having me with him and had given me the room next to his in his own private car, and for several days we were together at all hours except to sleep. And this association, at least for me, was a revelation and laid the foundation for a deep, intelligent understanding.

Because, judged superficially, Robles seemed a centaur, a somewhat mythological incarnation of primitive warlike and equestrian virtues. But at close range one immediately discovered, under the epidermis of his ignorance, a certain quiet austerity, a certain delicacy of perception, which in anybody else would have seemed acquired traits, but which in him could only be innate and spontaneous and had the effect of seeming to raise him above himself. The semifabulous hero of the cavalry charges, whom I had been able to imagine only galloping at the head of his brigade of horsemen, sowing terror with his glance, his hat fallen back, his arm brandishing a smoking pistol, was, without any effort on his part, transformed into a gentle, serene, sensible man, more than willing to judge everything calmly and to settle all disputes and difficulties without any other consideration than the justice of the case.

277

This dual aspect of his personality was forcibly revealed to me one day when I surprised him reading nothing less than Plutarch's *Parallel Lives*. And I say surprised, for he was so absorbed in his book that he did not notice me for several minutes after I had come into the room, and it embarrassed him considerably.

"That's a good book, General," I said, somewhat mechanically, for I was thinking less of what I was saying than of the fact that one of Villa's right-hand men should be reading Plutarch, the moralist, with such absorption.

"It is a good book, isn't it?" he answered.

But as I had not yet recovered from my astonishment, I merely nodded.

He went on:

"I found it the other day when we took Torreón from the Federals. Aguirre Benavides and I went into a house where there were lots of bookcases, and just out of curiosity I picked up some of the books; some were in Spanish and some were in foreign languages. After I had looked through a lot of them that I didn't understand or didn't like, I found this one, and I put it in my pocket. I'm sorry now I didn't take the other volumes, for there were several of them. If a person could only have lived in the days of Greece and Rome!"

"To a man that's a man, General, all times are alike."

≫≫≫≫≫≫≫≫≫≫≫≫≫≫≫≫≫≫≪≪≪≪≪≪≪≪≪≪≪≪≪≪≪≪≪≪

"No, my friend, don't you believe it. Why, right now, while we were in all this mix-up of the Convention, I kept thinking to myself: 'Among all these speechifiers, there's not a single Demosthenes. And that's why we're in the fix we are.'"

This serious, sober side of Robles's character, which was not immediately apparent, explained the sway he had over Villa. One could understand why the Chief of the Division of the North, so brutal of word and deed towards his subordinates, except towards Angeles, for whom he felt a superstitious sort of admiration, should treat Robles as a father treats a son. Robles was as brave as a lion in the hour of danger, and austere as a hermit afterwards, and thus he seemed to Villa twice perfect. This made him immune to all criticism and gave him every privilege.

Robles was permitted by his chief to counsel, advise, reprove, and even protest in situations where others had to keep quiet. That "fluky" pistol of Villa's, so ready to punish at the least suspicion, for the most trifling mistake, would have pardoned real disloyalty in Robles. It was a pistol that had learned to bow its head before Robles, as was proved on the occasion when Obregón was on the point of being shot by Villa. Obregón got off with his life that time not merely because two or three of Villa's generals intervened for him, but because Robles came to his aid, and Robles's moral force, his valour, his evident superiority in qualities that Villa could appreciate,

turned the coarse balance in which Villa weighed his
responsibilities.

But it must not be thought that, away from the
field of battle, Robles altogether renounced his somewhat primitive virility. When necessary, he knew how
to impose his will and make himself obeyed in peace
as well as in war. Despite his small stature and his
slight frame he could on occasion behave like a gang
boss or the quartermaster of a brigantine. But always
his violence was tempered by a sense of justice, which
without detracting from the severity and efficiency
of the punishment, purged it beforehand of the possibilities of hatred.

What happened in San Luis Potosí the afternoon
we left for Mexico City is an instance in point. One
of the staff officers was drunk, and for several hours
he had been trying to pick a fight with several of his
brother-officers. When Robles heard about it, he ordered him put under arrest. But instead of submit-
ting, the officer barricaded himself behind one of the
pillars in the station and, pistol in hand, and more
insolent than before, threatened to shoot anybody
who tried to lay a finger on him. Under other circumstances his defiance would probably not have pre-
vented the execution of the order, but as the station
was full of people waiting for trains, the officers who
had been ordered to take him into custody thought it
more prudent not to provoke an encounter that would
surely cost somebody's life.

>>>>>>>>>>>>>>>>>>>>>>>><<<<<<<<<<<<<<<<<<<<<

It was about four o'clock in the afternoon, and our train was ready to start as soon as General Robles should arrive. From that time on until six o'clock, when Robles and the group of persons that was to accompany us to Querétaro got there, that drunken officer was the lord and master of the station: he hugged and kissed the women, insulted the men, and the minute he saw or thought he saw anybody make a move towards him, with the astuteness of the drunk he quickly got into a position where he could drop the first person who should take a step. And while he stood there with his pistol levelled, not a soul for two hundred feet around moved a finger.

Robles had been informed about what was going on before he reached the station, but when he saw with his own eyes the spectacle one of his men was making of himself, his wrath knew no bounds. I saw him as he passed by me, and his face was colourless, though his eyes glittered and his hand trembled as he pulled down the chin-strap of his hat.

He walked straight over to the nearest group of officers. One of them was wearing his sword, and Robles pulled the blade out of its scabbard, while he shouted:

"Everybody stand still!"

And then, holding the sword in a position for striking, not for thrusting, he started straight over to the rebellious officer. When the latter saw that someone was finally taking up his challenge, he raised his arm and took aim. The other officers, without moving from their places, called to him:

"Don't, Martínez; it's the General!"

Martínez's eyes grew as big as saucers; he swayed for a minute and then took two steps forward, ready to hand over his pistol. But Robles was not to be deterred by this gesture; carried away by his sense of outraged justice, he brought the sword down with all his might on the officer's back.

The officer lowered his head, and bent double with the pain. Robles struck him again.

"Down on your knees, this minute," he said as he struck him.

The officer flinched as he bent over, but did not obey the command.

"On your knees, you hound!"

The officer, still on his feet, covered his eyes with the hand in which the pistol still gleamed. He was trembling and sobbing with pain. In a low voice, he said:

"No more, General."

From the row of officers came sympathetic voices: "Let him off now, General!"

But far from paying any attention to their pleading, Robles redoubled the fury of his blows. Every time he struck, he repeated:

"On your knees! On your knees!"

And he did not stop until Martínez finally dropped

to his knees and then fell full length, in a faint, on the stone floor of the platform.

When Robles got into the train, he was his calm, pleasant self again. But there was a trace of bitterness in his voice as he said, sitting down beside me:

"You see the kind of things we have to do. This isn't much like what we were reading about last night."

And, in truth, it did not resemble it, for we had been reading the life of Cicero in Plutarch.

Chapter XXXIII

Military Justice

A LARGE number of military convoys had gathered near Tacuba on the eve of the official entry into Mexico City of the Convention government. On the railroad tracks near the town, the trains of Villa, Eulalio Gutiérrez, Robles, Eugenio Aguirre Benavides, were lined up in parallel rows. The assemblage of passenger coaches that had been converted into headquarters and offices, and of freight cars that were used for the troops—with cradles swung between the wheels, and primitive shelters on top of the cars—made up one of those typical camps of the Mexican Revolution which day and night afforded the most varied scenes and noises.

A little after dark I left the small office I occupied in Robles's car and went to see Villa, without any other object than to talk with him. It fascinated me to listen to him, and his remarks, which were often original and unexpected, interested me very much. On the way from my train to his I stopped several times to look at the stars, which have a peculiar brilliance in the valley of Mexico. Farther down along the slopes of the railroad embankment the soldiers were scattered in little groups, sitting round their camp-fires with their women, their cookery, and their songs.

When I came in, I found Villa absorbed in making roses with a lariat. The chairs and tables had been moved out of the way, and Villa was standing in the middle of the car in his shirt-sleeves, his hat pushed back on his neck, holding in both hands, at the height of his thighs, a design resembling a rose, which the bright line of a new lariat had drawn in the air. It was a highly complicated figure of exact geometrical proportions, which stayed in place because of the stiffness of the rope. Villa's secretary and four or five others were sharing in the warrior's amusement, and they were all standing with their backs to the wall of the car so as to leave him as much room as possible. When I came in, Villa said to me:

"How do you like this rose?"

"Which rose?" I asked, as I did not grasp what he meant.

"This one here in my hands."

"Oh, is that a rose? It's pretty, all right."

"Isn't it!" And he studied it complacently for several seconds. Then he went on, explaining to me:

"Yesterday when I was in San Juan del Río I bought these lariats"—and he indicated with a gesture of his head a number of lariats on his desk, all rolled flat, and as white as the one he had in his hand. "I bought them to see if I had forgotten how to use them, but you can see I haven't. Say, are you any good at this?"

I smiled and was going to say I had never thrown a lariat in my life, but he went on without pausing:

"I'll bet anything you want that you can't make a rose like this. I'll bet you five thousand pesos that you can't make even the simplest one of my roses."

"It can't be done, General, because, among other reasons, I never bet."

"All right, then, we won't bet. Or rather I'll be the only one that bets: I lose five thousand pesos if you can do this same thing with a lariat."

While he talked, he took apart the design he had in his hands, and as he finished the last words, he gave two or three quick turns to the rope and it made another rose, not so complicated as the first, but quite as pretty.

"That's really very difficult, General," I answered; "I'm sure I can't do it. Anyway, it wouldn't be fair for you to bet five thousand pesos without my risking anything."

"That doesn't matter. You risk your reputation."

"My reputation?"

"Yes, your reputation as a lariat-thrower."

"Very well," I said, "I accept, but with the condition that you make the rose again so I can see you."

"All right. Now watch."

He straightened out the lariat and took hold of it in two different places with each hand; he made two wide loops without a knot, turned them upside down, crossed them, pulled out the two loops they formed in the centre, and, putting his hand between them, opened them out into a large, beautiful rose. The whole thing had not taken him more than two or three seconds. I watched every single move he made, for I had set my heart on winning that bet of five thousand pesos on my ability as a lariat-thrower.

"Now you do it," said Villa, handing me the rope.

I don't know how I did it, for I have never been able to repeat that night's achievement since. What I did was to imitate like a monkey everything Villa had done. I adopted the same posture as he, took the lariat in my hands just as he had done, and followed detail for detail, imitating even their rhythm, the movements he had made. And, without quite knowing how, out of my hands there emerged a rose just like his, though not so perfect.

"And this is the fellow," he said as he looked at it, "who pretended he didn't know how to handle a lariat!"

And turning to Luis Aguirre Benavides, he said, in the most unconcerned fashion:

"Luis, my boy, give this gentleman five thousand pesos."

Aguirre Benavides went into one of the inside compartments of the car and returned in a minute with a sheaf of bills, which he put in my hand. They were new and smelled of printer's ink. I was still looking at them when the door opened and an officer came in. He was tall and of a muddy colour, and there was a strange air of sinister humility about him. His grey uniform might have been part of his skin, and the same was true of his shoes, his leggings, and the dirty handkerchief that was knotted around his neck. When he took off his hat, it revealed a thatch of lank, black hair which grew back from his forehead as though his skull ran up to a point. He included all in his salute and said, turning to Villa as he handed him an envelope:

"Here's the list of my prisoners, General."

"What prisoners are you bringing in, friend?" asked Villa, without looking at or opening the document.

"Those five counterfeiters, General."

"Oh, the counterfeiters. Listen, Luis, those prisoners are to be taken to the court-martial car, and I want them tried this very minute and shot tomorrow."

Aguirre Benavides went out to give the necessary order.

A little later, by putting my face against the window-pane, I could make out the outlines of the group of prisoners and their guard moving towards the

>>>>>>>>>>>>>>>>>>>>>><<<<<<<<<<<<<<<<<<<<<

train where the offices of the military court were located. I could not see their faces. I wondered who
they were. By this time they must have learned from
the lips of the unpleasantly meek officer the fate that
was in store for them. The supreme will had sentenced
them to death without even finding out what their
names were, and for a crime which he himself, the
judge, committed: manufacturing money for his personal use. And sentenced to death beforehand, as they
were, they were now going through the farce of a
trial, at midnight, as is the practice in our troop mu-
tinies and revolutions. Summary trials to cover up
assassinations!

That was one of the most horrible nights I ever
went through in my life.

When I got back to Robles's train, I found a group
of women from Mexico City waiting for me beside
the car steps, weeping and lamenting. They were the
wives and mothers and sisters of the five counterfeiters, some of whom belonged to the better class.
They had heard of the punishment that was going to
be meted out to their relatives and they were desperately knocking at the door of anybody who might
be able to help them. In some way they had found
out about my friendship with Villa and my intimacy
with Robles and Gutiérrez, in whose hands they imagined the final decision rested, since the one was the
Secretary of War and the other the President of the

Convention government. They all surrounded me and
tried to talk at the same time.

"You, sir, you can save them."

"Aren't you the person who was with Villa just
now when they brought our husbands in prisoners?"

"Won't you please ask General Robles or the President. . . ."

I was startled out of my own melancholy reflections, and at first I did not know what to answer. For
a few moments I had the horrible feeling that I was
an accomplice or an accessory to the crime that was
going to be perpetrated, and, like a criminal caught
red-handed, I felt the little package of bills that
Aguirre Benavides had just given me scorch my
fingers. It seemed to me that in that instant the conscience of the revolution had become personified in
me. To be sure, the revolution had not falsely coined
the money to pay its troops to overthrow Huerta. But
what about that which its generals threw away on
their extravagant whims, their gambling, and their
orgies?

But I pulled myself together and tried to answer
them:

"Ladies, you don't know how sorry I am. . . ."

"Oh, no, no, don't refuse us, for God's sake, don't
say no!"

"You look like a good son!"

"We know that if you just speak a word with General Villa . . ."

"Ladies, please, try to calm yourselves a little, and I'll try to do anything I can for you."

At this, one of them, controlling herself by an effort, spoke for the group. By the light that came from the train windows I could see how her face was swollen with crying. She had a black shawl over her head, and where the ends crossed on her bosom, the colour contrasted with the yellow silk of her dress. It was plain that the poor soul had dashed out of her house, snatching up the first things she found.

"For your mother's sake," she said, "we beg you to intercede with General Villa not to shoot Daniel or his companions."

"But, madam, what you ask of me is impossible, or, at any rate, useless. If I go to him now to ask him to revoke an order he issued in my presence, the only result will be that he may order me shot, also."

" 'Also,' you say? That means that it had been decided already? Then you know they're going to shoot them?"

"I don't know anything, ladies, but I cannot deceive you, either. You have to take what I say literally."

The weeping and wailing and lamentations knew no bounds. And all that suffering seemed to me so unnecessarily cruel and senseless that if I had not been completely surrounded by the women I should have taken to my heels. Besides, a crowd of soldiers and women and children of the camp had gathered around us, attracted by the noise of the women's grief. I noticed, too, that several men had come with the prisoner's relatives, but none of them spoke a word. They probably realized that it would be useless for them to try to secure with words what the women had been powerless to win by their weeping.

With her voice broken by sobs, the woman with the shawl spoke again:

"At least, let us see the Secretary of War or the President."

"I'll be glad to do that," I said, and I drew over to the steps of the car, inviting them to come up, with the idea that Robles should see them at once. But just as I was going to help the first woman up, the officer on guard on the platform bent down and whispered to me:

"General Robles has ordered that no stranger be admitted to his car. If the ladies are coming in, you'd better see him about it first."

All my efforts to convince Robles were futile. And not because he was indifferent to my arguments or in favour of Villa's decision, but because he knew that it was impossible to argue with his chief on matters of this sort, and therefore it was better not to try it. In a word, in spite of his position as Secretary of War, and in spite of the fact that he was Villa's best and most trusted general, he was in exactly the same situation as I. The only thing he agreed to do was to help me to get Eulalio Gutiérrez to intervene.

Meanwhile the tribulation of the prisoners' families had penetrated the whole camp and had even pierced the ingrained unconcern of the non-commissioned officers and the soldiers. Nobody talked about anything but the shootings that were to take place the next day.

Eulalio Gutiérrez vented his indignation even before we began to talk.

"Everything you are going to say to me," he began, "I've already thought myself. Villa is bringing off an assassination, and you and Robles and I and everybody else who is mixed up in this business is going to seem like an accomplice. You say I'm president. President! President in name is what I am! Who has the power here? Who has the troops here? Who has control of the railroads? Villa. We might just as well admit it: we are more insignificant to him than to that autocrat of a Carranza. At least one could talk with him!"

"Well, then we'll be a pack of fools and cowards if we go on like this," I answered, looking at Robles, who nodded his approval.

"No, we won't," answered Eulalio, "because we won't go on this way; you leave that to me. But just now all we can do is bear it. What would you have me do? Make a fool of myself telling these women that I do not approve of the execution of their sons or their brothers or whatever they are, and then have Villa shoot them, snapping his fingers in my face?

The world is full of ups and downs, and these poor
devils struck a bad moment, and there's not a soul can
save them."

When I heard Eulalio talk like that, I realized it
was useless to try to do anything, for I knew, both
from hearsay and personal experience, that he was
neither stupid, nor cruel, nor a coward, but, quite the
contrary, a man of exceptionally keen intelligence and
kind heart, who did not know the meaning of fear, as
he proved a few days later when he broke with Villa.

But I wanted to do all I could to satisfy my conscience and I went over to Villa's car. I wanted to see
if it was really some immutable law of God or nature
or history that our revolution should be directed only
by assassins and their henchmen. At the steps of the
car one of Villa's soldiers blocked my way. An officer then appeared on the platform, who said:

"The General has retired for the night. He has
given orders not to be disturbed under any circumstances. If you want to talk with him, come back tomorrow at nine o'clock."

"But tomorrow morning at nine o'clock there'll be
nothing left of the counterfeiters," I replied.

"That may be, but I don't think the General will
be up before that time."

I spent that night in Mexico City and deliberately
kept away from the camp at Tacuba until late in the

morning of the next day. It must have been close to eleven when I got back there. The gracious sun of November threw a kindly veil over the drought-cracked earth and the stubble of the surrounding cornfields. Had the execution been carried out? I wondered when they had got rid of that tragic group of women.

Robles was not in his car. I sat down and was absent-mindedly staring out of the window when I saw a group of soldiers followed by a throng of spectators coming up through one of the cornfields. The soldiers' muskets threw back the rays of the sun. The furrows made walking difficult, and the soldiers were not in formation. They formed two uneven rows, and between them came five men whose arms were tied behind them with ropes that passed from elbow to elbow, and who tried to keep as close together as possible. Some of them stumbled at every step; others walked with the precision of marionettes. They all had a dazed expression, as if they were perceiving everything about them too acutely or too faintly. Some seemed engrossed by the very stones their feet encountered; others seemed not even aware of the dazzling sunlight that enveloped them. One of them —fair and of a ruddy complexion—looked in my direction with such wild eyes that his look hurt, like the pain produced by a sharp instrument. They were on their way to the cemetery. The sensation they left with me was that they were bearing their own corpses on their backs to the open graves in which they would be buried as soon as a couple of bullets had been put through their bodies.

Chapter XXXIV

Zapata's Troops in the Palace

Eulalio Gutiérrez wanted to visit the National Palace before he installed his government there.

One afternoon he, Robles, and I went there. Eufemio Zapata, who was in charge of the building, came out to the main entrance to receive us and began to do the honours of the house. To judge by his air, he was taking his momentary role of receiving the new President in his government abode and showing him the splendours of his future drawing-rooms and offices very seriously. As we got out of the automobile, he shook hands with each of us and spoke like a rough but affable host.

While the greetings were being exchanged, I looked round me. The car had stopped under one of the arcades of the large *patio*. A short way off, a group of the Zapata soldiery stood observing us from the sentry chamber; others peered from between the columns of the massive white arches. What was the attitude of these men? Meek or suspicious? At the time, they produced in me more than anything else curiosity, because of the setting of which they formed a part. That place, which I had seen so many times and which always seemed the same, gave me on that occasion, practically empty as it was, and in the hands of a band of half-naked rebels, the effect of something new and strange.

We did not go up the main stairway, but used the staircase of honour. Eufemio walked ahead of us, like a janitor showing a house for rent. He was wearing the tight trousers with a broad fold down the two outside seams, a cotton blouse tied in front, and a huge broad-brimmed hat; as he mounted step after step, he seemed to symbolize the events that were taking place, in the contrast of his person, not meek, but uncouth and clumsy, with the cultivation and refinement presaged by the staircase. A flunkey, a coachman, an official, an ambassador would have been in place there; each would have had the dignity, small or great, that went with his position, and that had its place in the general scale of dignities. Eufemio looked like a stable-boy who was trying to act like a president. When his shoe touched the carpet, there was a clash between carpet and shoe. When his hand rested on the banister, there was an immediate incompatibility between the two. Every time he moved his foot, his foot seemed surprised at not getting tangled up in brush and undergrowth. Every time he stretched

out his hand, it seemed to feel in vain for a tree-trunk
or boulder. One only had to look at him to see that
everything that should have formed his setting was
lacking, and that everything that surrounded him was
superfluous as far as he was concerned.

But at this moment a terrible doubt assailed me.
What about us? What kind of impression would the
three of us who followed Eufemio have made on anybody who saw us—Eulalio and Robles in their Stet-
son hats, unshaven and with their unmistakable plebe-
ian aspect, and I with that everlasting air of the
civilian in Mexico who goes into politics, a mere
instrument assuming the attitude of intellectual adviser to a successful military leader, at best, or of
criminals passing themselves off as leaders.

Eufemio took great pride in showing us one by one
the different rooms of the palace. Our steps alter-
nately were echoed on the waxed floors, so polished
that we could see ourselves dimly reflected in them, or
were hushed by the velvet of the carpets. Behind us
we could hear the soft slapping of the sandals of the
two soldiers who followed us at a little distance
through the empty rooms. It was a meek, gentle
sound. Sometimes it ceased for a long time while the
two soldiers stopped to look at a picture or examine a
piece of furniture. Then I would turn back to look at
them through the long perspective of the rooms. They
formed a double figure, strangely quiet and remote,
as they stood very close to each other, looking at

things in silence, their heads with their lank heavy hair uncovered, and their palm-leaf hats humbly clasped in both hands. Something sincere and worthy of respect was unquestionably represented in their rapt, embarrassed, almost religious humility. But we, what did we represent? Was there anything fundamentally sincere and serious in us, who were making joking remarks about everything we saw, and had not bothered to take off our hats?

Eufemio made some remark about everything we passed, and his comments were often primitive and ingenuous. They revealed a cheerful, childlike conception of the gubernatorial functions. "This is where the government meets to talk." "This is where the government eats." "This is where the government has its dances." It was evident that he thought a house with a roof on it a mystery to us and supposed that we had not the slightest idea of the uses of a sofa or an arm-chair or a corner-table, and he went along illuminating us. He said everything in such good faith that it positively touched me. When we reached the presidential chair, his tone became triumphant, almost ecstatic. *"This* is the chair." And then in a burst of candour he added: "Ever since I've been here, I come every day to look at it, just to get used to it. Because—can you imagine it?—I always used to think when I heard them talk about the president's seat that they meant his saddle." Eufemio laughed heartily at his own ignorance and we laughed too.

Eulalio was aching to take a dig at General Zapata, and he saw his opportunity here. Turning towards Eufemio and putting a hand on his shoulder, he said in his gentle, modulated voice:

"That's why it's a good thing to be such a fine horseman, partner. The day this chair becomes a saddle, you and your friends can all be presidents."

The smile disappeared from Eufemio's face as if by magic, and a gloomy, sinister look replaced it. Eulalio's witticism had been too cruel and too apt, and it had flicked him on the raw.

"Well," he said a few seconds later, as though there were nothing more worth seeing, "let's go downstairs now and see the stables. Then I'll take you to the rooms where my men and I are living."

We went over the stables from one end to the other, though with greater satisfaction on Eufemio's part than on ours. Amidst the array of collars, bridles, bits, and halters—all smelling of grease and leather—he displayed an amazing store of knowledge. And the same with the horses. His enthusiasm for these things took his mind off the incident of the chair, and then he led us to the quarters he and his men occupied in the palace. Eufemio had found rooms to his taste in the poorest, most out-of-the-way rear court.

"I picked this place because I've always been poor and I didn't feel right in better rooms."

Really the place was abominable. I thought I should smother as I went in. The room was not large and had only one door and no windows. There must have been from fifty to a hundred officers from Zapata's army, of all ranks, there when we came in. The majority were standing up, side by side, or with their arms around each other. Others were sitting on the table, and some were lying on the floor in the corners and along the wall. Many of them had a bottle or a glass in their hand. The air was foul and sour and a hundred different odours were mingled with the heavy pall of smoke. Everybody was drunk, some more, some less. A soldier stood by the door to keep it shut against the light or against inquisitive eyes. Two small electric lights glimmered feebly through the asphyxiating fog.

At first nobody paid any attention to us. Then as Eufemio went from group to group, whispering something in a low voice, they began to look at us and make certain signs of welcome. But they were faint, almost imperceptible expressions. We had, beyond question, fallen into a world so different from our own that our mere presence was a source of perturbation in spite of everything they and we did to overcome this. With the exception of a few, they avoided looking straight at us and watched us instead out of the corner of their eyes. Instead of talking with us they whispered among themselves. And every now and then they would turn their backs to take a long swallow from their bottles or empty their glasses.

Eufemio and those around him invited us to have a drink.

"Here, let's have some glasses," shouted Eufemio. Timid hands reached out to set five or six dirty glasses on the edge of the table. Eufemio set them in a row and poured out fresh drinks of *tequila* on the dregs at the bottom of the glasses.

We drank in silence. Eufemio poured out more *tequila*. We drank again. Once more Eufemio filled up the glasses. . . .

As we drank, Eufemio began to warm up. At first he became happy, then jovial, and then thoughtful and gloomy. At about the fifth or sixth glass he happened to remember Eulalio's joke about the presidential chair.

"This fellow," he said, addressing his men, "thinks that Emiliano and I, and others like us, will be presidents the day they saddle horses with seats like the one upstairs."

There was a profound silence, broken only by Gutiérrez's sarcastic laugh. Then the rustle of voices began again, but there was a new, vague note in it, excited and menacing. Nevertheless Eufemio went on serving *tequila* as though nothing had happened. Once more the glasses were handed round and we drank over each other's sticky leavings. But at this point Robles began to look at me hard and then, almost imperceptibly, make signs to me with his eyes. I understood what he wanted; draining my glass, I took leave of Eufemio.

An hour later I was back at the palace, and Robles's guard was with me; but just as we came up to the entrance, I saw Eulalio and Robles calmly walking out of the same door through which we had entered in the early afternoon.

"Thanks," said Eulalio when he saw me. "Fortunately we don't need the soldiers now. They were so busy drinking that they could not waste the time fighting with us. But, anyway, the precaution was thoughtful. What amazes me is how you and Robles understood each other without saying a word."

Chapter XXXV

A Form of Government

THE generals who had left Eulalio Gutiérrez
with Zapata and Villa, and, contrary to all the hopes
of the revolution, continued to support Carranza,
had not put their money on the wrong horse. The
Convention group represented the sense of moral responsibility of the revolution and represented, therefore, the real danger for Carranza's corrupt, ambitious supporters. What better policy, then, could they
have pursued than to let their enemies wear themselves out struggling with an impossible situation?
Because it was an impossibility for the Convention to
maintain its moral prestige so long as it had to put up
with Villa and Zapata to bring Carranza to terms,
and an even greater impossibility to array itself at
one time against Carranza, Villa, and Zapata, armed
only with the excellence of its intentions. And between one impossibility and the other, after a few
convulsive, useless efforts, would come dissolution,
and with it what the Carranzaists wanted: a free

hand in the struggle for power, and the chance to turn into a boss system, with certain trappings of social reforms, this revolution against the previous boss system, which in its turn had been decked out with certain adornments of scientific and economic liberalism.

Eulalio, who was far from a fool, took in our situation perfectly; three or four weeks in power (to give it this name for lack of a better) reaffirmed him in his first idea that the only thing that could be done for the moment was to play for time and look for some way of escaping from Villa without falling into Carranza. But while we waited, we had to defend ourselves against the most imminent danger, which was Villa and Zapata, and as a result we had to work out one of the most absurd and incongruous policies that could be imagined: we had to help our declared enemies, Carranza's followers, defeat our official supporters, Villa and Zapata, in order to relieve ourselves a little from the terrible pressure of these latter.

Robles, Aguirre Benavides, and I employed the system in the War Department with a cool efficiency whose success was accompanied by not a few dangers and difficulties for us. It went hardest with me because, being a civilian, I lacked the guard and the officers they had to protect them, and I had to face single-handed the countless big and little Zapata chieftains who regarded me as the cause of their defeats. And all this in days in which nobody was safe in Mexico, when every morning the city asked—as so many other

times in our long history of political crimes—how
many murders had taken place that night, when the
most cruel and treacherous assassinations could and
did occur nightly.

Robles had said to me: "As you understand, we
can't do a thing against Villa now. He doesn't need us
at all, except as a sort of emblem. But it's different
with the Zapatists. Give them money when they ask
you for it, though don't let them exceed the limits; but
under no circumstances are they to get arms, ammunition, or trains."

And it was a sight to see how furious some of
Zapata's subordinates got—mostly generals in blouse
and cotton trousers, a rifle on a bandolier over their
shoulders, and cartridge-belts across their breasts—
and how others battened on the situation, these the
generals in tight breeches, drill jacket, and silver-
studded pistol-holster.

During the days when Zapata's forces were trying
to drive Alvarado out of Puebla, I used up every pretext imaginable to keep from supplying them with
arms, ammunition, and engines. As Robles and
Aguirre Benavides rarely appeared in the office, I
was the one the leaders of the Army of Freedom of
the South besieged. They would come in to see me,
followed by their numerous staffs, and the gloom of
my office would be lightened by the white blotches of
their cotton trousers; their sandals flapped softly;
and their enormous hats, which seemed the wheels of

some invisible convoy of wagons, would set in motion a close, fetid breeze with every movement. I would have them sit down in any order, without distinction of rank, and enter on a highly technical discussion of the art of modern warfare, with and without ammunition, with and without rifles, with and without trains. Everything was fine as long as I was explaining how our factories of arms and munitions and explosives could not supply us with the hundredth part of what was needed, or when I explained that by the terms of our alliance General Villa was the only person authorized to supply them with what they needed; but as soon as they saw or suspected that I did not want to help them, they put me in the most difficult situation and sometimes almost started a riot. One group of them that did not get what it came for revenged itself on me by dancing in my ante-room, to the terror of some fifty people who were waiting there, something that could be called "the dance of the rifle and the pistol." And these were among the tamest; others simply threatened to kill me, like the general who asked me for trains to go to the support of Amozoc, which was being attacked by the Carranza troops. I assured him we had no engines; he said this was a lie, that he had seen them at such and such a station, and when finally, to get rid of him, I offered him one that was so old it still burned wood and was practically worthless, it exasperated him so that he said to me, very calmly:

>>>>>>>>>>>>>>>>>>>>>>><<<<<<<<<<<<<<<<<<<<<<<

"All right, boss, I'll take it. But if I'm defeated, I know the son of a bitch that's going to pay for it."

As he pronounced the insult, I picked up a glass paper-weight and, raising my arm to throw it, said to him, my voice trembling with rage:

"Son of a what?"

"Nothing, boss, nothing, don't get excited. That just slipped out. But I mean what I said about the rest: if I'm defeated, straight back here I come, and you'll get hurt."

And, sure enough, though I did not get hurt, he did come back, not after the capture of Amozoc by Cesáreo Castro, but after Puebla had fallen into the hands of Carranza's troops. He came back with some fifteen or twenty other generals who believed us responsible for this other loss, and they were not wrong. Because, naturally, from their point of view there was no explanation, unless it was our bad management, for losing ground all the time. Perhaps they already suspected, without its being quite clear in their minds, that we were acting more as Obregón's allies than as theirs.

As Robles said, we could do nothing against Villa's forces. But they could do anything they liked, even laugh at the government they affected to support. What was not clear was just how deliberate their intention was in behaving this way. Did they have an idea that they should theoretically accept the author-

>>>>>>>>>>>>>>>>>>>>>> <<<<<<<<<<<<<<<<<<<<<<<

ity of the Convention, or did they think this authority existed like the padding in a maniac's cell, to break the violence of his frenzied blows? However this may have been, the fact is that Villa, Urbina, Fierro, and the other prominent figures of the Division of the North behaved at this time in Mexico City as was their usual custom, and their excesses, seen thus, without perspective, seemed wilder and more scandalous than ever. Against this urban background, actions that were designed for a setting of mountains and woods acquired a lurid relief.

As, for example, Villa's amorous indulgences, which lost their robust rustic harmoniousness in the city to the point of becoming at times delicate international problems. His doctrine, as he preached it to his officers, was very simple.

"You must never," he said, "do violence to women. Lead them all to the altar; you know these church marriages don't mean a thing. That way you don't have to lose your good time and you don't make them unhappy. Just look at me: I've got my legal wife that I married before the Justice of the Peace, but I've got others that are legitimate too in the sight of God, or of the law that means most to them, which is the same thing. That way they're not ashamed or embarrassed, because whatever slip or sin there may have been is mine. And what could be better than an easy conscience and a nice friendly understanding with the women you take a notion to? Don't pay any attention if the priest objects or grumbles; just threaten to put a bullet through him and you'll see how he comes round."

But Villa sometimes grew a little lax about his own rules or failed to apply them with the tact the circumstances required. Hence the terrific scandal he caused one day when he tried to marry the cashier of the Palace Hotel in his own fashion. Though, if the truth be told, there was more smoke than fire to the scandal, as will be proved the day these matters can be discussed without hurting anybody's feelings. To a few pusillanimous souls, simple folk who do not understand the workings of the feminine heart in general, and the French feminine heart in particular, that scandal seemed appalling. But compared with the other events of which it was a part, it was a trifling matter. Villa did much worse things a dozen times a day and so did Fierro and Urbina.

The efficiency and skill with which Urbina had organized his system of robbery on a large scale was extraordinary. And he completely discredited the contention of the Carranzaists—who had invented it to justify similar holds-ups of their own—that Zapata and Villa stood for the reaction supported by the rich foreigners and the clergy. Because it was exclusively against people of wealth—natives and foreigners— that Urbina directed his activities. He practised that variety of robbery which goes by the euphemistic name of "forced loan" or "immediate subsidy" with a skill nobody could imitate, though many other generals tried it. His judgment in selecting his victims was unerring, and his methods were as quiet as they were infallible. He never made a mistake and he never had to make much show of force to get his money; they used to pay him right up, "cash in hand," as he put it. He first mapped out his campaign on a large scale and then worked his territory district by district, block by block, street by street, and house by house, preparing things beforehand with a network of invisible guards so that none of his victims should escape. And he used to do it—glorying in his abilities, like a virtuoso of the art of robbery—in broad daylight, in the offices of his victims, right on the principal thoroughfares of the city, while everybody was going about his daily occupations. He did it all in such a quiet and orderly manner that nobody ever suspected a thing.

Those of us who were in charge of things did hear about it, but we, too, in view of our inability to do anything, kept quiet, like the victims, who feared worse reprisals if they made a complaint.

What days those were, when murders and robberies were like the ticking of a clock, marking the hours that passed! The revolution which had dawned four years before as a noble hope was threatening to disappear in deceit and crime. What good was it that a little group preserved its ideals unsullied? Its very equanimity and sense of responsibility had already made it the least adapted to the struggle. This was another of the great contradictions of the revolution: a movement that was essentially idealistic and generous had fallen into the hands of the most selfish and the most unprincipled.

Chapter XXXVI

The President Shows his French

IN the midst of the wreckage of the revolution's highest hopes Eulalio Gutiérrez did not forget the obligations he had acquired in Aguascalientes. He was doing everything he could to get Obregón to break away from Carranza at the same time that we freed ourselves from Zapata and Villa. We were secretly making preparations for our march to San Luis, ready, if it came to a show-down, to fight both Villa and Carranza. And it must be recognized that this decision reflects the greatest credit on the President *pro tem,* for it required almost as much faith in the ultimate destiny of the revolution to convince Obregón of the dangers Carranza represented as it did bravery to prepare the break with Villa while still under his thumb. There was no question but that Villa would soon learn what we were about, in spite

>>>>>>>>>>>>>>>>>>>>>><<<<<<<<<<<<<<<<<<<<<<<

of all our precautions, and once he knew, he would
surely fall on us with his usual violence.

The situation came to a head one Sunday morning. (Or if it was not Sunday, it was a day on which
for some reason or other the offices were closed to
the public.)

I had gone to the War Office to attend to a number
of matters that were urgent. I had been going over
papers and dictating letters and telegrams for three
hours. Ugalde, my stenographer, was sitting across
the table from me, transforming the words that fell
from my lips into forceful little tracings with his yellow pencil, which slid agilely across the paper. We
both felt happy. We were working in the quiet soli-
tude of the office in the same frame of mind as if the
overwhelming military incubus, which my words and
his pencil handled so deftly, had no significance other
than the detached reality that scientists attach to the
object of their experiments.

About one o'clock the telephone rang. Ugalde took
down the receiver and answered without raising his
hand from his note-book or releasing the grip on his
pencil. His voice was in keeping with the tranquil atmosphere of our work as he spoke:

"Hello. . . . Yes. . . . Yes. . . ."

I saw that he put his hand over the transmitter and
heard him say, from the depths of the paragraph I
was mentally elaborating:

"They want to know if you're here, and if you are, they want you to come to the phone immediately."

I took the telephone from him and answered, like him, in a tone of the greatest serenity:

"Hello. . . . Yes. . . . Guzmán talking. . . ."

But the state of affairs at the other end of the line must have been different. The voice that came from there was breathless, agitated, and catastrophic; at its sound, notwithstanding my best efforts to remain unmoved, a shiver ran over me from head to foot. I could notice the effect these words were having on me as I listened to them, more in Ugalde's face, which reflected stage by stage the expression of my own, than in myself.

When I set the telephone back on the table, the magic of our peaceful work had been dispelled. My silence bespoke my perplexity. Ugalde, without taking his eyes from my face, had put his pencil in his pocket and closed his note-book. Finally, in a tremulous voice, which was in striking contrast with the way he had answered the telephone, he asked:

"Is it anything serious, Mr. Guzmán?"

"I have just been informed," I answered in a voice that resembled his, "that Villa has just taken the President prisoner and has ordered the arrest of his Cabinet and the other important members of the government."

I went out into the yard, got into my automobile, and drove away. Outside, the bright winter sun, warm

and comforting at midday, had a placid gleam; it radiated harmony and seemed to deny the possibility of
conflict. The streets were alive with pleasant noise
and jocund passers-by, all conducive to a state of
well-being. The Zócalo was a lake of light; automobiles and street-cars seemed to move along in rhythm
without a care. But my automobile was full of worry.
And as I passed through the bustle of Plateros
Street, I felt more and more how alien I was at that
moment to the impulses that moved the crowds of
men, women, and children on the sidewalks and in the
other vehicles.

As we passed the confectioner's shop "El Globo,"
my car was moving so slowly that it seemed to exist
only in contrast with the rapidity of my thoughts:
slow motion at the service of vertigo. . . . But at
that moment I happened to see Colonel Domínguez
in the shop, taking a package from one of the sales-
girls, who was offering it to him with a smile and a
boutonnière of flowers.

Jumping from my car, I threaded my way through
bumpers and mud-guards into the store. Domínguez
was standing near the cashier's window, with his cane,
his cigarette, his package, and his flowers in one hand,
and his money in the other.

"Never mind about those cakes," I said to him in
a voice that was not so low as I should have wished,
"and come with me right this minute."

Several of the customers looked at us in astonish-

≫≫≫≫≫≫≫≫≫≫≫≫≫≫≫≫≫≫≫≪≪≪≪≪≪≪≪≪≪≪≪≪≪≪≪≪≪

ment and wonder. But Domínguez, with an air of perfect composure, put his package down on the counter and followed me.

I walked ahead, clearing a path through the crowd, until we reached the automobile, which had kept moving in the triple row of cars. Once inside, Domínguez asked:

"But what's the matter?"

"This is the matter," and I told him what had happened.

As we drove, we made our plans. We would leave the car at the door of the garage that was just across from Eulalio's house. And I would do my best to try to get some word with Gutiérrez. In the meantime Domínguez would try to telephone to Lucio Blanco, to warn him of the danger and ask his advice. If I had not returned in half an hour, Domínguez would come to look for me.

The first difficulty I encountered was the guard. Instead of the President's usual escort, I found Villa's *"dorados."* [1]

"You can't pass, sir."

"I can't pass?"

"You nor nobody, sir. Them's orders."

"Whose orders?"

"Why, General Villa's. Whose did you think they

[1] Villa's famous body-guard, whose uniforms were resplendent with gold braid and ornaments, hence their name, "the gilded men."

were? Don't you know he's the boss around here?"

It was no use to go on arguing, so I asked to see the captain of the guard. He repeated what the soldier had said; but I assured him that it was Villa I wanted to see, to consult him about certain matters connected with the troops, and he finally let me come into the vestibule at the foot of the stairs.

"You positively cannot go any farther," said the officer. "Orders are very strict."

Downstairs none of Eulalio's men were to be seen. The *dorados* were everywhere. A group of them were standing by one of the windows watching Urbina's cavalry parading beneath the trees of the avenue. I watched them, too, for several minutes. The riders were reining their horses to a slow canter, the better to impress the spectators.

"Has the General been here long?" I asked the officer.

"About an hour or so."

Then I began to walk up and down the room, affecting the patient air of a person who waits. As though sunk in thought, I prolonged my strolls into the next room. And a little later, when nobody was looking, I slipped out into the middle courtyard.

It was radiantly clear out there; the green trees seemed varnished with sunlight. In one corner there was a staircase. For a minute I studied the lay-out, and then I went up it. It led to a sort of mezzanine, which seemed to be servants' quarters. There was nobody there; I walked through and managed, with some difficulty, to get into one of the larger rooms. The doors from this room into the rest of the house were locked, but one of them opened on to a little corridor with a window, and from this window I managed, after considerable effort, to climb through the next window.

I then found myself in another empty room, like the first two, but farther ahead I could hear voices. I went forward until I got near enough to make out what was being said.

I left my hat on a table and, with a nonchalant air, as though I were a member of the household, I walked past the door to see what was going on.

The voices belonged to a group of Villa's officers, who were calmly talking in the middle of the room. Some—the majority—were sitting on the table, swinging their legs, and the others were standing. Their indifferent talk did not disguise the fact that they were alert and waiting for some important event to take place. They made a compact group before the door of the reception room, which was closed. Without a doubt Eulalio was being held in there.

With the same easy air I walked through the room towards the next one, which adjoined the reception room. The officers turned to look at me. I greeted them familiarly, my hands in my pockets:

"How's everything. . . ."

"We're here with the Chief."

I went ahead. The room next to the reception room

was a bedroom. Like the others it was empty. Here the voices in the waiting-room were drowned out by others which came through one of the sliding doors, though the heavy hangings and carpets somewhat muffled all sounds. The new voices were harsh and argumentative, but they sounded as though the worst of the quarrel was over. The better to hear, I tiptoed over to the doors through which they filtered. The two halves of the door were ajar, but the portières on the other side were completely drawn. Slipping between the doors and the velvet curtains, I could now hear Villa's voice, sharp and emphatic:

"You say Mr. Vasconcelos's life has been threatened. Well, why didn't you tell me about it? I'll give him a guard."

Eulalio's somewhat sibilant voice, high-pitched and ironic was heard: "But that's not the way things are done. If I'm president, all the troops have to be under my orders, and I'm the one to assign the guards."

Villa's voice again: "Well, sir, but who says that my troops aren't yours, too? Aren't we all one government?"

At this point several voices were heard together. I could make out only an occasional word.

I drew the edge of the curtain away from the wall a little and peeped through. I could see a part of Roque González Garza's face and uniform and a little of Vito Alessio Robles's back and head. I pulled the curtain back a little more; a hand appeared, a hand that I recognized, but which seemed very odd without the body to which it belonged. It was Eulalio's hand. Close to it stood a bottle of cognac, surrounded by three or four little glasses. Higher up and farther off between two figures I could see a lock of Villa's curly auburn hair under the drooping brim of his hat. At times the movements of the hair were accompanied by the glittering flash of an eye. Villa's face was very red and wore that set smile which accompanied his attacks of anger. By the arms and legs I could see, I judged that he formed the centre of a large group.

Eulalio's hand took hold of the bottle and poured out liquor in one of the glasses. With three fingers he picked it up, and glass and hand disappeared from my range of vision. The mingled voices went on confusedly. Hand and glass appeared again. Eulalio said something in a clearer tone. A brief silence.

Villa's voice was heard again: "I gave that order, sir. If I turn all the railroads over to your government, how will I move my troops? Look at the territory I hold."

". . . ?"

"But anyway it's all the same thing. You've named me Commander-in-Chief of your troops, haven't you? Well, I'll protect you, and to protect you I'll keep under my command all the forces the situation demands. Besides, they're my trains and my troops."

At this juncture I could make out Fierro's voice

and, a little closer by, Alessio Robles's. Eulalio answered something.

Villa's voice was heard again: "Well now, I'm telling you, sir: three thousand of my cavalrymen are on parade in front of your house, just so you can feel how strong I am. The guard I've stationed here is mine, too. You won't leave this place without my permission."

Eulalio's voice: "We'll see about that."

A buzz of voices.

Then Villa: "And if you did get out, a lot of good it would do you, because now, just so you'll know it, I'm going to leave you without a single train. How do you think you'd get away from me?"

Eulalio's voice came sharp, clear, and serene: "How? Don't you worry about the how. To get away from you I'd be willing to ride a mule."

"All right, you heard me; you try it and I'll lay you out cold."

This was followed by noises that the carpet muffled. I thought the quarrel was going to begin again, but then I realized that it was over for the time being. I swiftly drew back from the curtain into the bedroom. Voices were heard and the sound of many feet. A door opened and footsteps were heard moving down the hall. Then steps and voices died away. There was quiet in the waiting-room, quiet in the reception room. I walked over to the curtain once more and lifted it. Nobody. I walked into the room.

Eulalio, seated in an arm-chair, had just poured himself another glass of cognac, which he was lifting to his lips. He was startled to see me at first, as I emerged from my hiding-place; then he smiled, but said nothing. I could not keep from smiling myself to see him sitting there so calm and mocking.

Nevertheless I asked him: "Well, General, what do we do now?"

"Now? Why, what you fellows say who read books and went to school." And his keen, intelligent eyes sought mine as the expression that preceded laughter came over his face.

"What we say?"

"Yes, you intellectuals."

"I can't think. What is it we say?"

"Why, *malgré tout,* Mr. Scholar, *malgré tout.* Isn't that the way you say it?"

Chapter XXXVII

In the Lion's Mouth

I WAS afraid the Zapatists might lay a trap for me, so I used to change my sleeping-quarters frequently. During the day, one way or another, we civilian officers of the Convention government managed to defend ourselves from the enemies that surrounded us; but at night we were exposed to the most brutal assaults. Finally things got so that I never slept two nights in the same place after those dark days in which Vasconcelos, Secretary of Education, had to flee to Pachuca to keep from being killed.

Nobody, naturally, knew where I was going to sleep. At the last minute I would decide to leave my car almost anywhere; I would take out the pistols, rifles, and cartridge-cases I carried under the seat, and then spend the night, in the company of my military aide and chauffeur, in whatever hotel or boarding-house I had decided on. Nor did my precautions rest with this: my two companions and I used to barricade ourselves in the room or suite we occupied together, with our arms loaded and within easy reach.

This was the state of affairs when one morning the moment I stepped out into the street I felt something unusual in the air. I seemed to sense the approach or the wake of something new. Was it perhaps that I was politically hypersensitive, what with our departure from Mexico City so close at hand? Then I decided not to pay any attention to my uneasiness and put it down to imagination. But as the auto rolled along, trifles, things you could not put your finger on, seemed to multiply and took such a hold on me that I ordered the chauffeur to drive faster. And as we approached the War Office, I began to feel a touch of panic.

When we came out into the Plaza de la Reforma, I could not stand it any longer. The Trojan Horse was bathed in sunlight, but if I saw it, I did not take it in, because my eyes travelled past it to a policeman standing on the other side of the square. I ordered the chauffeur to stop.

"You see that policeman over there?" I asked my aide.

"Yes, sir."

"Well, get out and ask him what has happened."

The man looked at me blankly. And really, to judge from appearances, nothing was happening. Vehicles and people were coming and going as usual.

The policeman was leaning lazily against the corner of a building, basking in the sun.

Then my aide said: "Would you mind repeating what you said?"

"Ask the policeman what is happening."

"Happening, sir? Where?"

"Here, in the city!"

He jumped out of the car with military agility, crossed the street, and, after exchanging a few words with the policeman, turned back to the car.

"He says," he informed me, "that this morning the Convention government and its troops evacuated the city."

"What!"

"Yes, sir!"

"That's impossible!"

"Well, that's what he says, sir!"

We found the doors of the War Office bolted and locked and without the customary sentinels. We knocked loudly; nobody answered. But at the sight or the noise of the car two officers of José Isabel Robles's staff crossed over to me from the opposite side of the street.

"What are you doing here?" I asked.

"We're not doing anything, chief. You could have knocked us over with a feather. We were out on a tear last night, and when we got here this morning, if you please, the troops were gone. We'll do whatever you order."

I thought for a moment. Then I asked: "Have you got your guns?"

"The pistols."

"And where are your rifles?"

"God only knows. Last night, about ten, they were in the General's house; that is, we left them there. But who knows where they are now?"

I understood from all this that something unforeseen and imperative had obliged Eulalio Gutiérrez to leave for San Luis sooner than he had intended. I felt sure that he had left word for me at my house as to where I should join them.

"Let's all get in the car," I said to the officers, though the order created difficulties. It was a struggle to get more than three people into that auto. One of the officers had to sit on my aide's lap, and the other sat on the floor, so as not to attract attention.

When I got to my house, I found that my suppositions were correct. There had been several telephone calls for me during the night, and Gutiérrez had sent for me at twelve and at two. At about four that morning General Robles, accompanied by Colonel Domínguez, had come to the house and had made them open the doors to assure himself that I was not there. Finally he had left a message for me. It read: "I am so sorry not to have found you, and that you have to be left behind, but we have been looking everywhere for you since midnight. Things have taken a very serious turn and we have to evacuate the city immediately. I'll explain it all when I see you. We're leaving for Pachuca, where I hope you will join us as soon as possible. I only hope you will receive this in time, because I know that by morning the city will be in the hands of Zapata's troops. I'm taking your horse along so it won't be lost in the disorder that's coming. Unless some better way occurs to you, or something special comes up, the best thing for you to do will be to leave in an automobile. Watch out for Medinaveitia as well as Zapata. Hope to see you soon.—*Robles.*"

The dining-room clock was just striking half past eight as I finished the letter.

My difficulties in escaping began with the automobile. Mine was a ridiculous little coupé, which had belonged to the secretary of one of Huerta's ministers; it would not run two miles on an unpaved road. Besides, it was very small, and, to make matters worse, as I passed the park of San Fernando, I had picked up two more of Robles's officers who had been left behind. The first and most urgent thing to do, then, was to get hold of a seven-passenger car, and I set out to look for one.

Naturally, I wanted to hire one, but two or three attempts in this direction convinced me that I should never get one that way. The chauffeurs would take in at one look our revolutionary stamp, hear us say we

wanted to go out of the city, and refuse point-blank to
rent their cars. Besides, these cars that were for rent
were in a lamentable state. Of the four tires probably
not a single one was any good.

And it was getting late. The clocks had struck nine,
and in the streets one could see signs of the military
change occasioned by the withdrawal of the Convention troops.

I stood on the corner of Balderas and Juárez ave-
nues, hesitating as to what I should do. Up and down
the street, cars of every size, make, and description
went hurrying by, of American and foreign manufac-
ture, old and new. And although, no doubt, each was
serving its master's desire, nobody had such pressing
need of a car at that moment as I. I looked at my
watch; it was ten minutes past nine. Every minute
that passed whirled twenty, thirty, fifty cars past me
and at the same time made my possibilities of salvation more remote. Then I made up my mind: why
should there be laws to guarantee the property rights
of two thousand automobiles and none to guarantee
my life? I got into my car with my aide and the two
officers and said to the chauffeur:

"Drive ahead slowly, and the first Hudson Super-
six you see, turn around in the street and block its
way."

We had not gone three hundred feet when, coming
behind us, we saw exactly the car we were looking for,
brand-new and shining. Holding out his hand, my

>>>>>>>>>>>>>>>>>>>>>><<<<<<<<<<<<<<<<<<<<<<

chauffeur turned quickly, so quickly and so short that the Hudson had to jam on its brakes and stalled. The other chauffeur began to protest furiously, but he stopped as two of my officers jumped on to the running board on either side, and the third addressed himself to the owner, who was in the car.

The officer's words were brief and to the point: "This car is needed for the service. Kindly get out at once."

The owner of the car probably wondered if he was dreaming. His first reaction was astonishment, and his second righteous indignation, accompanied by unsuccessful attempts at resistance. But at this juncture my other two officers, who were armed with rifles, drew over to him, and I myself went over to try to convince him.

The attempts at persuasion were not, if the truth be told, very successful. The owner insisted that he was being the victim of a hold-up right on a public street, and on this ground resisted giving up his car, and I tried to persuade him that although it did look that way, it only went to show how we all had to submit to the exigencies of times of war.

In a frenzy of indignation he shouted: "Your reasoning sounds like that of a highwayman."

To which I replied, unruffled: "Sounds and is."

Finally the threat of taking him along with us brought him to terms, and I promised to return his car to him that same afternoon.

Scowling, he gave me his card and I handed him mine, on which I wrote out a sort of receipt, binding myself both officially and privately.

He and his chauffeur got out of the car. My officers and I got in, and my chauffeur took the wheel.

"What's the good of this?" the owner of the car asked contemptuously as he read my card.

"Not much, probably," I answered. "But keep it anyway, just on a chance."

And as the motor started, I said:

"One last favour: take my car and use it until we return yours this afternoon."

"What if I don't want to?"

"Then leave it. I meant it for your own good. A bad car is better than none. So long!"

And we drove off.

Chapter XXXVIII

González Garza, President

HAD anybody noticed the means we had employed to secure our Hudson? Not many, at any rate, for we did not seem to attract more than ordinary attention as we drove two blocks farther down the avenue and then turned towards Humboldt. There we stopped.

"Look the car over," I said to the chauffeur, who with the help of the five officers gave it a quick examination. Everything seemed to be in good shape except the supply of gasoline. There was not more than enough for fifteen miles in the tank.

And then our troubles began again, for gasoline was not to be found in Mexico City in those days at any price. After we had asked for it in a number of places and begged for it in others, finally, pistol in hand, we persuaded a garage to part with four cans that they kept on hand for emergencies. We emptied two of them into the tank and fastened the other two on the running board.

At last we were ready to start! But just then I hap-

>>>>>>>>>>>>>>>>>>>>>>><<<<<<<<<<<<<<<<<<<<<<<

pened to remember that I had two more rifles in my
house and a supply of bullets for them, and we went
back there again. I got the guns and some food, and
when everything and everybody was settled. I gave
the order:

"To Pachuca!"

It was a little past nine thirty.

As we drove down the Avenue of Notable Men, I
noticed a great crowd of revolutionary-looking people
in front of the Hotel Lascuráin. There seemed to be
a meeting going on, and undoubtedly at that meeting
the departure of Eulalio and his forces was being discussed. Should I stop to find out about things? Pru-
dence counselled me to lose no more time; but my instinct said: "Find out all you can. . . ." We stopped.
I jumped out of the car, joined the crowd, and made
my way into the hotel.

On the first floor the mass of people was tremen-
dous. There were members of Villa's, Zapata's, and
the Convention's groups, civilians and soldiers. In
the main parlour all attention seemed to be focused
on the dais. There, standing up on something that
raised him above the crowd so he could be seen and
heard, Roque González Garza was eloquently and
excitedly haranguing the multitude. "It is in moments
of anxiety and perplexity like these that the true pa-
triots . . ." Just as he reached this point he spied
me (I had just come into the room), and, breaking off

his speech, he shouted to me over the hundreds of heads:

"Have you heard the news?"

"No, that's what I came to find out. What's the matter?"

"A mere trifle: they've just betrayed us, that's all. Gutiérrez, Robles, Blanco, and the rest of their bunch ran away this morning with the troops. They've left the Convention flat, and they've broken with Villa and Zapata. They've deserted us to go over to Carranza."

As he talked, I had been coming towards him, in the midst of a general silence. But he had lowered his voice as I had drawn nearer, and private conversations had started up all over the room.

Then I said: "Well, now what do you think we ought to do?"

"First of all, keep our heads. Then make the best of whatever comes along. For the present I'm going to take charge of things. I have taken over the executive power. I haven't a doubt that General Villa will approve of what I do, and I'm going to have the Convention ratify the functions I am taking over as an emergency measure, this very afternoon if possible. And, since you are familiar with the work in the War Department, would you take charge of it right away?"

"I don't quite understand. You want to make me your Secretary of War and the Navy?"

"Secretary or whatever you want to call it. The important thing is for us to hang together and keep the government going."

I did not want to deceive him, nor did I want to give myself away, either. So I replied ambiguously:

"Very good, very good."

And after talking a little while longer with him and with some of the others that were there, I went out. Apparently, judging from Roque's invitation, my presence in Mexico City was not ascribed to its real cause, but to the supposition that I was more loyal to Villa than to Gutiérrez. The thing to do was to take advantage of this mistake.

We drove as fast as we could through Santa María la Redonda. We left the Plazuela de Santiago behind us and made for Peralvillo. The Hudson behaved like an angel. Along the Guadalupe road we began to meet scattered officers and soldiers. Some were going, others coming. Some looked tired, bewildered, or frightened and had sat down along the edge of the road or were stretched out under the trees.

La Villa revealed at a glance the recent passing of a considerable army. We drove through without stopping. A group of officers waved to us. We did not know them and pretended not to see them. We passed the Pocito Chapel and were just coming into the wide street that leads out on the road. Three hundred

yards and we should have been out on the highway.
But just as I was thinking this, a group of soldiers on
horseback trotted out to meet us. They were from
Zapata's forces. We had to stop.

The leader of the troop came over and asked:

"Where you going to?"

"You can see for yourself," I answered. "That
way."

"Well, you can't get through that way. Them's
orders."

"Nobody is allowed through?"

"Nobody."

"All right, if we can't get through, we can't.
Thanks. We'll go back."

And I said to the chauffeur: "Turn round."

But the officer interposed:

"No, sir. You can't do that either. Orders are to
arrest anybody heading that way."

There was no chance to argue with him. The soldiers crowded around us while the officer directed the
chauffeur towards a wide gate near by. They made
him drive through and then took us, car and all, into
a big yard that looked like a barn-lot. There was a
crowd of prisoners in there of the most varied classes
and appearance.

Just as we were about to get out, an idea came to
me which revealed such life-saving possibilities that,
in spite of our situation, I smiled to myself.

Assuming an air of great assurance, I said to the officer: "By the way, do you know who it is you are putting in here?"

His attitude was one of quiet contempt. "We'll soon find out."

"No," I answered, "you'll find out right now. Do you know who I am?"

"What's the hurry, chief?"

I became more emphatic. "Who are you?"

"Major Margarito Sifuentes, at your orders, sir."

"Very well, Major. I am the Secretary of War in the Cabinet of the new Convention government. The President is General Roque González Garza."

Major Sifuentes opened his eyes as wide as two saucers, and, pushing back the brim of his palm-leaf hat with one hand, he exclaimed, half incredulous and half impressed:

"You don't say so, General!"

"Exactly as I've told you, Major. And these gentlemen who are with me are members of my staff. Now you can use your own judgment about what you do."

For several seconds the Zapata officer sat motionless. Then he got down from his horse and, coming towards me, said:

"General, will you excuse me if I go and get some advice on the matter? What did you say your name was?"

I told him. He repeated it twice and then walked over to the group of houses that closed the lot on one side. In a little while he came again, accompanied by another Zapata officer, of somewhat fiercer expression.

The new officer began: "I'm the colonel of the regiment stationed here to cut off the escape of traitors on this side. Is it true that you are the Secretary of War in the new government?"

"It is."

"You won't be offended, will you, General, if I ask you for some identification?"

"How shall I identify myself?"

"Haven't you got some documents?"

"None suitable for this purpose. I was only appointed an hour ago."

"Then if you don't mind (and it isn't that I doubt your word; it's that I have to do my duty), we'll go together to see the new president, so he can back up what you say. That is, if you wouldn't rather we did something else. . . ."

"I think that's an excellent idea," I answered. "Get into the car."

The officers who were with me got up to give him their place. But the Colonel went on, without moving from where he stood:

"And I hope you won't take offence, but if you don't mind, I'd rather we left your aides here. That way we shan't need to take along an escort, and just you and I and one of my captains will be enough."

Perhaps if I had answered him short at that moment and had blustered a little, there would have been no need for trips and identifications. But at the same time I might ruin everything by violence, so I decided to select the part of meekness. I lauded the Colonel's military procedure and accepted all the conditions he laid down.

Half an hour later I was back again in the Hotel Lascuráin. There were more people than before. Roque was filled with the spirit of his office and was perorating and giving orders at a great rate. His new functions seemed to have communicated to him a new and unwonted importance; he seemed taller and more capable; the lisp that characterized him was less noticeable; and he was as active as a canary in a cage.

I walked over to him, followed by the Zapata Colonel, who was so overwhelmed at the sight of so many mirrors and so many people that he hardly knew where he was going, in spite of his rigid sense of duty.

Then in a loud voice, so the Colonel could hear, I said to Roque: "I have come to get my appointment as Secretary of War in writing, so I can accredit my position. Otherwise I'll have more trouble than I am looking for. I just had a lot over in Guadalupe Hidalgo."

"Of course, man. Right away. Here, you write it out yourself."

I sat down at the table Roque indicated, and, putting a sheet of paper in the typewriter, I began to

compose, as modestly as I could, the wording of my
appointment as Secretary of War and the Navy in
the new government. After reading it through, Roque
signed it, folded it, and handed it over to me. Then
with sudden curiosity (an inkling of suspicion) he
asked:

"What were you doing over in Guadalupe?"

Bending over until my face almost brushed his, I
whispered to him:

"I was looking for Robles. They say he's over that
way."

"Do you think it's possible?"

"I don't know, but I was looking for him on a
chance. Well, so long!"

As soon as we were outside, I said to the Colonel:
"Are you satisfied?"

"General, I'm at your orders!"

There was no question in his mind but that I was a
general.

We got into the car again to go back to La Villa
for my officers. But when I had picked them up and we
were at liberty, I turned back to Mexico City instead
of going towards Pachuca. I had learned from the
Colonel in the course of our conversation that troops
were stationed all along the road to Pachuca, and I
realized that it would be folly to try to get away. Two
hours earlier it might have been possible, but not now.

At the Zócalo the officers and I separated. "It is
impossible for us to get away together," I said. "Let

each one save himself as best he can. The best thing will be for you to leave your arms or hide them, put on citizen's clothes, and go by train as far as you can. I'll see what I had better do."

The first thing I did was to drive to the address our unwilling saviour had given me that morning. I was going to keep my promise and return his Hudson Super-six that very afternoon.

Chapter XXXIX

From Frying-pan to Fire

GONZÁLEZ GARZA did not like in the least my refusing without any satisfactory explanation the post he had assigned me in his new Cabinet. Our interview the day after what took place in Guadalupe was long and stormy. He brought it to an end with these words:

"Well, I've said all I have to say. Now you either change your mind within twelve hours or you go to the penitentiary."

It was not easy to change my ideas or even pretend that I had changed. I did not want to be locked up, either. So when the period he had set was up, I decided to take refuge with Vito Alessio Robles, who was still governor of the Federal District.

Then, as always, Vito placed above every other consideration his civic responsibilities and his honour as man and soldier. At every turn he displayed that fundamental rebelliousness characteristic of the Alessio family. He hated a coward and a flatterer and despised a fool and felt himself irresistibly drawn to the

non-conformists. He had been born to the opposition,
to act as the scourge and censor of false, lying politicians. His keen penetration and sarcasm had left
many a rancorous memory among the unprincipled
and self-seeking of the revolution. But towards the
men whom he admired and who shared his convictions and aims his kindness and devotion knew no
bounds, and he stood by them in defeat as in victory.
And if the hour was of defeat, he gave the cowards
who fled or deserted their leader and companions a
lesson by going himself in search of the dead or van-
quished friend. Wherever one touched him, one found
the man.

"But are you afraid of González Garza?" he
asked me.

"No, not of him, but of the penitentiary, which has
been turned into a Zapata stronghold. Roque, at
heart, is a good fellow."

"And now what are your plans?"

"I need three or four days so I can join Eulalio
some way."

"But if I tell Roque that, he'll have you shot."

"Don't tell him that. Tell him something else. You
tell him that he ought to let me alone, because the
proof that I'm not against Villa is that I didn't go
with Gutiérrez. And tell him that I want to go to
Aguascalientes as soon as there's a train. He doesn't
need to know that I'm on my way to San Luis, but will
think I'm on my way to see General Villa."

Vito looked at me in astonishment. "But would you risk going to Aguascalientes?"

"Why not?"

"It's dangerous. Villa is not a man to fool with, you know."

"I don't see any other way."

"Stay here."

"Here? That's worse yet. At least in Aguascalientes there's only one danger, though it's a big one: Villa. But here there are at least three: Villa, Zapata, and Carranza. Besides, from there I may be able to rejoin Gutiérrez; but from Mexico City, never. . . . Villa is a big risk, that's true; but I know him well, and I'll try to avoid the danger."

"You won't be able to avoid it, because Villa is not a man to fool with. But, anyway, I'll at least talk with Roque."

The news that I wanted to join Villa pleased Roque beyond expression. He promised Vito that in this case he would make no trouble for me. And when we met again, he said to me with a certain ironical note in his voice, which was unusual in him, who, as a rule, was ingenuous and frank:

"Yes, do go there, as soon as you can. I know you'll be well received, as you deserve."

But this did not add to my uneasiness. I felt pretty sure that since Roque had first wanted to make me a member of his Cabinet, he would not paint me too

black to Villa. Besides, it was not my intention to
convince Villa of my innocence, but to keep out of his
way. There was just one serious danger, and that was
that while I was waiting for a train to leave, bad reports of me might get to Villa at his headquarters, in
Aguascalientes.

At the last minute I found out I was not to make the
trip alone, but together with Luis G. Malváez, who
had been bottled up like me in Mexico City since Gutiérrez's departure. Then we found out that Luis
Zamora Plowes and Fernando Galván, whom I had
made managing editor and treasurer of *El Monitor,*
the short-lived daily of the Convention administration, were joining us.

The trip was long and tiresome. The train was a
peculiar mixture of a military and freight train, on
which anybody could travel that wanted to, without
the formality of a ticket. Galván had brought along
among his luggage several rolls of the paper that was
used to print *El Monitor,* and they had become public property. The passengers—everybody travelled
third-class—soon got in the habit of putting the paper
to the most varied uses. At night they improvised
paper curtains, paper sheets, paper blankets, mufflers,
shawls, capes of paper. In the darkness the multitude
of white spots gave the car the appearance of a camp
of lost souls, or of whole communities at prayer or in
an ecstasy. The bundles rustled with every jerk the

train gave, at every stop and every start. It was a
gentle frou-frou, which made a strange contrast to
the grinding of the wheels and the screeching of the
springs and axles. Every now and then the cigarette
butts put us in danger of fire.

At the station in Irapuato we had to wait over
twelve hours. The troops of Calixto Contreras and
Rodolfo Fierro were returning from Guadalajara,
where they had been defeated by Diéguez and Mur-
guía. Every half-hour a train went by. The endless
cordon of men, horses, and cannon closed the road
for us, and as the telegraph line to the north had been
cut, travel was very slow.

At midnight, when we were about ready to start,
Malváez returned from the town in a state of great
excitement and uneasiness.

"Bad news," he said to me. "The telegrams from
Mexico City for the north are being held here till the
line is fixed, and I have just found out in the telegraph
office that one of the messages is from Roque to Villa
and it's about you."

"What does Roque say?"

"It's serious. He tells Villa that we're going
through Aguascalientes and advises him to have you
shot."

"Do you think Roque would do that?"

"That's what they've just told me."

"I can hardly believe it."

"Well, I haven't a doubt of it."

There is no denying that this news upset me and gave me a shock. I recalled Vito Alessio Roble's prudent counsel. Malváez was of the opinion that we ought to change our route or else disappear and hide for a while.

"It is foolish to hide," I answered, "because we should have to stay hidden indefinitely so they would not find us out. We can't change our route either, for all roads are the same for three hundred miles around. If it's not Villa, it's Zapata or Carranza; if we take to flight, we're bound to fall into the clutches of one of them. The safest thing is for us to beard the lion in his den, in the hope that our anomalous situation may save us."

Anybody but Malváez would never have listened to me, much less followed me. Because, no question about it, I was committing an act of folly. But Malváez was always brave, and he accepted the situation and decided to risk his life with me. This was really heroic on his part, for he was not familiar with Villa's psychology, nor had he reason to cherish the hope that buoyed me up a little in spite of Roque's terrible message: the hope that Villa, when he saw me come to him, would ascribe Roque's attitude to personal animosity against me.

It took us two and a half days to go from Irapuato to Aguascalientes, held back all the way by the military convoys. The last of these was Rodolfo Fierro's.

Sometimes we caught up with him, and the General would often come to keep me company as we spent long hours seated on the embankment waiting. Those were difficult hours for me, for I was torn between two feelings. His first words brought to my mind the memory of the infamous assassination of David Berlanga and filled me with indignation and sorrow. Fierro, who must have suspected or felt the reason, exaggerated his air of a repentant sinner, which he had assumed with me ever since that day in the War Office when he confessed what had happened, and I could not help feeling sorry for him.

At the stop before Aguascalientes the engine of Fierro's train got out of order and pulled on to a siding to let us pass. Two hours later ours arrived and stopped about a mile from the cradle of the Convention. We got out. Engines and coaches crowded the tracks, still filled with the troops from Jalisco and their equipment, and made of the surrounding country a noisy, incoherent primitive little world, like all encampments of Mexican soldiers.

Making our way through the soldiers and their women, we walked towards the city. Zamora Plowes was delighted to have an opportunity to meet Villa personally and offer him his services as journalist. (How little he knew him!) Galván was determined to take the first train for Chihuahua and the United States, and Malváez and I, with the words of Roque's telegram ringing in our ears, were so nervous we could hardly breathe. The thing that worried me most of all was the necessity of an explanation with Villa, which was now inevitable, as my one defence against Roque's intrigues. This was staking everything on one card; I was risking not only my life, but, supposing I should get off alive, my future part in the revolution. The one was as important from the material standpoint as the other from the moral.

Chapter XL

At the Mercy of Pancho Villa

WHEN we got into Aguascalientes Galván and Zamora Plowes went off to look for a hotel, and Malváez and I made our way down the railroad tracks. Under the train-shed there was a still greater conglomeration of trains and troops; but not far away we soon made out the unmistakable figures of Villa's *dorados*. As we proceeded, the soldier crowd grew thinner until it finally disappeared altogether from the railway landscape, except for a few dogs and Villa's guard.

My heart began to pound at the sight of the *dorados,* a quick, noisy thumping in contrast with my feet, which, through some force alien to my will, were moving in perfect time. I do not ever recall walking with such precision and lack of effort. The ground seemed to slip away under my rhythmic feet as though responding to an impulse in which I had no share. Mine was the delight of witnessing, at once a spectator and a disembodied will, an exercise of the muscles, appreciating it to the fullest. Through my memory there floated like dim pictures the scenes of the executions in Tacuba two months before: those five condemned men walking towards the cemetery.

At the steps of Villa's car I said to the soldier who was standing guard:

"Tell the General I'm here and I want to talk to him."

I listened to my own words as to a doom that destiny had planned for me since the beginning of time. The soldier looked at me with a smile. He made no movement. His smile prolonged itself; likewise his immobility. This unforeseen obstacle in the smooth unfurling of my fate gave me a sudden sick feeling.

"Did you hear me?" I insisted.

The soldier went on smiling and staring at me. Slowly, as though from a different world than the dizzily moving one in which I was living, he answered:

"The General ain't here. He's out riding."

His voice sounded unreal. Inside myself existed the only reality.

Leaning up against the car, I prepared to wait. Without a word Malváez ranged himself alongside me.

Time went by. The grey light of the afternoon had been taking on a translucent blue and silver tone. The dust in the air was made luminous by the last rays of the setting sun. From time to time a dark bird ploughed a furrow across the sky. Little by little, like a convalescent, I grew calmer at that placid sight, and my inward rhythm began to slow down until it was in time with the exterior.

Perhaps half an hour had elapsed.

Malváez said: "The most sensible thing would be for us to leave."

"No."

"I'm not thinking about myself, but about you."

"I know it, Malváez. But I won't go."

"We've still got time. Make up your mind."

"It would only be losing time if we went. I know everything is against us; but our one chance to win lies in the way we first meet Villa. If we run away, he'll pursue us and shoot us; but if he thinks we have come to him, he's even capable of rewarding us."

Another quarter of an hour went by. It was beginning to get dark.

A little while later I began again: "What I do think is unnecessary is for you to stay here with me, Malváez. I think it would be better for us both if you went away. If your presence adds anything, it adds danger."

Malváez stubbornly refused to go, but I finally convinced him. He left; his figure was lost to view between the rectangular masses of two box cars. I was alone. The sky grew dimmer; the soldiers' voices came from far off. One of them, gazing into space, was humming:

"I told you not to go down for water. . . ."

The melancholy sound rose towards the sky and seemed to remain floating there:

"And if you went, not to go so late. . . ."

The melancholy of the song, repeated again and again, wiped out all sense of time:

"Someone may be waiting there, loved one,
Who will make you forget about me. . . ."

Song and twilight seemed blended into one, both distant, both all-enveloping. As I listened, I forgot where I was. A group of riders was coming up the street which the rows of cars formed. I hardly noticed their approach, so carried away I was by the song and the evening. The soldier softly hummed:

"Someone may be waiting there, loved one. . . ."

But suddenly, out of the group, a familiar figure, a silhouette I knew, swam into my consciousness. There, cantering along on his splendid sorrel, came Villa. He was wearing a brown sweater that revealed every movement of the muscles of his breast and arms. His broad-brimmed hat was pushed back by his thatch of curly hair. I could not analyse any more. As he came towards me, he and his horse seemed to grow and grow until they were too big for my eyes to see them. Again I felt the beating of my heart filling my whole breast, my throat, and throbbing in my temples.

I saw Villa pull up two paces from where I stood. I saw him look at me, throw down his reins, and jump off his horse at one bound.

"He's going to kill me on the spot," I thought to myself, and involuntarily the fingers of my hand behind my back closed on the butt of my pistol.

He reached me in two steps. Then I felt myself lifted a foot off the ground in his arms.

"Roque González Garza," I began, forming the words so clearly that it surprised me. (These three words were floating about in my agitation like three drops of oil on water.)

"Let's not talk about Roque," Villa replied. "Tell me about yourself. Well, well, partner, I knew you wouldn't desert me. You wouldn't do a thing like that, would you?" and he put me down on the ground again.

Slowly I was coming to myself.

"But from now on," he continued, holding me by the lapels of my coat, and fixing his restless eyes on mine, "you're going to stay here with me. I don't want you running round with dirty sons of bitches. When did you get here?"

"About an hour ago, General."

He did not let go of me.

>>>>>>>>>>>>>>>><<<<<<<<<<<<<<<<

"Come on and tell me all about things. You're the first one that's got here since that son of a bitch Ulalio double-crossed me. Oh, the sons of bitches, if I get hold of them, God help them."

With his arm around my shoulders he was gently pushing me towards the steps of his car.

"Come in, come in. You know nobody but men come in here. I want to hear all the details. What do you think of Eugenio Aguirre Benavides? The cock-eyed traitor! And Isabel Robles? But no, he's not to blame, they just got round him some way. Robles is good. If he'd come back, I'd forgive him."

He opened the door of his sitting-room and made me walk in first. I was surprised to find Rodolfo Fierro there, for I thought he was still on the road. Villa exclaimed as he caught sight of him:

"So you're here at last, are you?"

Fierro got up from his chair and replied with an arrogance that showed even through the respect with which he spoke:

"I just got in, General!"

"And a nice story you've got to tell, friend. The more I think about it, the less I understand how you were defeated. . . ."

Fierro prepared to enter upon explanations. "You see, this is what happened: the day after—"

But Villa cut him short. "No, sir. I don't want to hear about your defeats."

And leaving him with the phrase on his lips, he

took me by the arm and led me towards the little corridor that opened into his private office.

We sat down there opposite each other, across a little table fastened to the window-ledge.

Still obsessed by the possible consequences of González Garza's telegram, I began: "You know, Roque—"

But Villa did not let me go on. "Don't talk about Roque, I told you. I don't give a damn about your little fusses. I want to hear about the other thing: why did Ulalio finally decide to play me false? Why did Robles and Aguirre Benavides follow him? You understand?"

"Perfectly, General."

And then I told him everything that had happened, not, however, from the inside, as I knew the facts, but as it would have seemed to a mere spectator. We talked on like this for over an hour. I was on tenterhooks all the time, for he was alert for my every word and gesture, even the most insignificant. Every now and then he would interrupt me:

"Don't tell me that. Is it possible? What a pity I didn't trust you more! We'd have fixed their clock."

The anger he displayed was that they should have taken him in and betrayed him, not because he felt any weaker on account of their defection.

"Those dirty sons of bitches, they'll see who they're up against. Not one of them is going to get away."

Half-way through our talk he ordered his supper
and invited me to join him. With great difficulty I
managed to excuse myself. That night his supper was
more frugal than usual: two glasses of milk and a
piece of baked sweet potato. I talked on while he ate.
Between swallow and swallow the names of my
friends elicited wrathful remarks and judgments:

"I knew that Vasconcelos was nothing but a traitor
with some book-learning. . . .

"General Blanco? That's no general. Nothing but
a show-off full of airs. . . .

"I told you Eugenio was the worst of the lot. He's
the one that spoiled the others. And do you know
what Luisito did, too? I see it, but I can't believe it.
Now you just tell me, in all his miserable existence who
ever treated him the way I did? . . .

"Ulalio is the one I blame least of all. He was no
friend of mine. He told me he'd do it the first chance
he got, and he did. He acted like a man. But those
others, the ones that double-crossed me . . ."

When he had finished eating, he got up and listened
to the remainder of what I was telling him. Then he
walked two or three times up and down the narrow
room and changed the hat he was wearing for another that was hanging there on the hook. As he
reached up, the folds of his sweater revealed the
cartridge-belt full of bullets and the butt of his pistol.

Going over to him, I said: "Well, General . . ."

"Yes, friend," he answered, "you're tired and you

better get some rest. From tonight on you're to stay here with me. Right now I'm going to have them fix up Luisito's room for you because from now on you're to be my secretary. Or don't you want to? Talk to me like a man."

I felt my life hanging once more by a hair. But I had to see the thing through.

"There's just one thing I want to ask of you, General."

"What is it?"

"My family left Mexico City on the last train there was for passengers. I don't know if they got to Chihuahua or not. Maybe they're in El Paso. I should like—if it is possible—you to let me—go and find them. . . ."

Villa bent over me and looked steadily into my eyes; he was holding me by the lapels of my coat.

"You want to desert me, too?"

I seemed to see death in his pupils.

"I, General . . ."

"Don't desert me, friend; don't do it, for, honestly, I'm your friend. You won't desert me, will you?"

"General . . ."

"And go find your family. You have my permission. Do you need money? Do you want a special train?"

I drew a long breath for the first time that evening.

At ten that same night a train left for El Paso. Villa had accompanied me to the Pullman. He came up on the platform and said to the conductor:

"Now, friend, this gentleman here is one of my men. Understand? One of my men. You take good care of him; otherwise, you know me. Remember how I shoot. . . ."

"Oh, General," the conductor answered with a nervous little laugh.

Villa embraced me again before he jumped down.

The train began to speed away through the shadows of the night. Mexico is so big! A thousand miles to the border!

A Note
ON THE TYPE IN
WHICH THIS BOOK IS SET

*This book has been set in a modern
adaptation of a type designed by Wil-
liam Caslon, the first (1692–1766), who,
it is generally conceded, brought the old-style
letter to its highest perfection. An artistic,
easily-read type, Caslon has had two centuries of
ever-increasing popularity in our own country—it
is of interest to note that the first copies of the
Declaration of Independence and the first paper
currency distributed to the citizens of the new-
born nation were printed in this type face.*

SET UP, ELECTROTYPED, PRINTED, AND BOUND
BY VAIL-BALLOU PRESS, INC., BINGHAM-
TON, N. Y. • PAPER MADE BY S. D.
WARREN CO., BOSTON